Footwork

Footwork

Urban Outreach
and Hidden Lives

Tom Hall

PlutoPress
www.plutobooks.com

First published 2017 by Pluto Press
345 Archway Road, London N6 5AA

www.plutobooks.com

British Library Cataloguing in Publication Data
A catalogue record for this book is available from the British Library

ISBN 978 0 7453 3058 7   Hardback
ISBN 978 0 7453 3057 0   Paperback
ISBN 978 1 7837 1764 4   PDF eBook
ISBN 978 1 7837 1766 8   Kindle eBook
ISBN 978 1 7837 1765 1   EPUB eBook

Typeset by Stanford DTP Services, Northampton, England

Simultaneously printed in the United Kingdom and United States of America

For Luke, Lily and Georgie, and Sarah

People cannot simply disappear, abdicate from the soap opera of the city; they must reappear: even the ones who have never been seen before.

Iain Sinclair, City of Disappearances

'Aren't you going to take any notes?' she asked.
I grunted.
'I thought detectives always wrote things down in little note-books.'
'I'll make the gags,' I said.

Raymond Chandler, The Little Sister

Contents

Acknowledgments

All through writing this book I have kept mostly to myself, being lucky in the choice of a very few close friends and colleagues; I owe a particular debt to those who kept their own counsel and left me to it. Robin Smith has been my closest collaborator for some years – and for many more to come, I hope; he has shared in the fieldwork and knows this book as well as anyone (having read none of it); I have borrowed from our many discussions at points, with pleasure. Rob has been particularly good at not asking me how it is going. Sophie Hallett has been, by turns, a student, colleague and confidant and I am the better for it; she will recognise her own contribution – I have borrowed again, with pleasure. Sophie has been very good at asking me how it is going, without making that in any way a difficult question to answer.

I am grateful to all those who work and have worked for Cardiff's City Centre Team, especially its outreach staff, and, among those few, to Jeff, Den, Nicy and Charlie in particular; everyone who works with Cardiff's street homeless deserves a good deal more than my individual thanks. Cardiff's homeless themselves deserve a better deal than any they have been given up till now, and more *recognition* than this book delivers. Thanks also to Cardiff's street cleaners and all on Millicent Street. A final acknowledgment to Steve Hyde, without whose invitation and generosity I would never have come to see Cardiff the way I do now.

Preface

This book draws throughout on observations of 'outreach' work on the streets of Cardiff, most of that work undertaken by employees of Cardiff Council as members of the local authority's City Centre Team. Other street-level operatives figure in the following pages, but it is the work of outreach that holds my essential interest. What I know about outreach, I know directly, having shared the work. I spent the best part of a year embedded in the City Centre Team, and have since continued my close association. All told, the fieldwork basis for the book extends over a period of ten years and covers thousands of miles – almost all of which took me no more than half an hour's walk from Cardiff's central train station.

There are a number of points, signalled in the text, at which I turn from a more general accounting and construal of outreach work and its landscape of practice to what are effectively field reports, extended passages of first-hand description. The latter are intended to evoke the street-level experience of outreach work; some of these passages require further commentary, but most do not.

1

Sleepwalking City

This book is about the city. More than that, or more particularly, it is about city streets and the ways in which those who might come to depend on them are seen by others passing by; not only seen, but sometimes seen to and looked after. This makes it a book about people and what they are prepared to see and do, and the moves they make – again, on the city streets.

The idea that being in the city might be a matter of moves made, suggests a game: turns taken and missed, stratagems and tactics, tricks, forfeits; winners and losers. The comparison would be frivolous were games not a near universal human pastime. Joseph Rykwert takes the dice-and-board game as a guiding analogy in the first few pages of his erudite study *The Seduction of Place: The History and Future of the City*. The point he seeks to make is that cities are not simply given to us in ways we cannot hope to work with(in) and negotiate:

> It seemed to me then – as it still does now … that the city did not grow, as the economists taught, by quasi-natural laws, but was a willed artifact, a human construct in which many conscious and unconscious factors played their part … The principal document and witness to this process was the physical fabric of the city. (2002: 4–5)

We are all of us, Rykwert continues, 'agents as well as patients in the matter of our cities' (2002: 5). Our agency is exercised as improvisation on the rule, after each throw of the dice; we have choices to make, about the sorts of city in which we want to live. The choices Rykwert has in mind are those that have shaped urban planning over the last few hundred years, but the same agency is there all the way down to ground level and can be exercised in the course of something as ordinary as a short walk.[1] There are the rules and conventions with which the material city confronts us – this street, that subway, a bridge, a wall, a doorway – and then there is what we choose to make of these, how we choose to move and where, what we are prepared to do in order then to see what happens next. *Footwork* is a study of just these sorts of moves, rules and gambits, exercised on the city street.

Put concretely, *Footwork* describes the operating practices of a team of 'outreach' workers, charged to look after people found in difficulties on the streets of only one city: Cardiff. Just about all the action in the book comes from Cardiff because that is the city in which I live; I came to Cardiff in 1997 (I was born and grew up in Manchester). This makes it a very local account, and as such it stands for itself. The team I am interested in was established around about the same time that I arrived in Cardiff and continues its work today, so we are inadvertently paired in that way; but I am also close to the team as a result of having purposely shared its work – the various moves that outreach requires – over a number of years, as observer and participant. Which makes this book an ethnography of a certain sort of street work: outreach.

The book has a wider horizon too and I give notice of that in this opening chapter and a good part of the next. To write about a city's streets and what gets done there is to open up the possibility at least that what you have to say might bear on city streets elsewhere and what happens there or might do, and it is absolutely the case that outreach work of something like the sort I will report on here happens in a good few cities around the world. It happens in Manchester, certainly; I've seen it in New York and spent time there with the people whose job it is to do it. But I am reporting only from Cardiff, and as such the book supplies no *evidence;* it does not stand as proof of something else. What it does supply, if not evidence, is an *example.* As anthropologists Lars Højer and Andreas Bandak have it, examples are attentive to 'unruly details' and 'suggestive as much as descriptive'; 'evidence "makes evident" … and can be gathered (the many become one), whereas exemplification multiplies, makes connections and evokes (the one becomes many)' (2015: 8, 12). We shall see.

---

1. Rykwert, it should be noted, is a seasoned city walker, having never learned to drive; perhaps this makes him all the more sensitive to the feel and fabric of the city – underfoot, within reach.

Coming round

Cities grow and change, and sometimes die – or are said to. People do too. People also sleep, which is something the modern city does rather less of, if at all. Almost any city in the twenty-first century might claim to be a *city that never sleeps*, and most would be pleased to do so. For some commentators, these processes of growth and change and death are linked: urban development bereaves us even as it delivers something new. A brand-new building towers where an older one once stood, and mixed in with the thrill of transformation and renewal is the uneasy feeling that a part of the city has been lost.

Some have put it more strongly than that. Louis Chevalier for one, whose angry and partisan account, *The Assassination of Paris*, records a city done to death by indifferent technocrats and greedy developers: skyscrapers, automobiles, chewing gum, 'buildings cheaply thrown up around a supermarket in the middle of a parking lot ... a few stunted trees' (1994: 71; originally 1977); a restless, predatory modernization. Sleep has also had a part to play:

Will Paris always be Paris ...? Without doubt. But these towers suddenly thrusting up on the horizon, all at once, in a few months ... like those monsters in Japanese films who rouse themselves from a millennial sleep, get up on their haunches, and destroy cities ... The towers were there ... everywhere, flaunting their ugly silhouettes, cut off at the top, grotesquely inclined this way and that, like King Kong ... We are only at the beginning, just waking up, and I had, as at any awakening, only a confused, obscure memory of a long and extraordinary illusion. (1994: 3)

Like the monsters recently awakened, Chevalier has been sleeping – has been blind; his eyes closed even when walking the streets:

Perception is itself a matter of habit. Images from the past obscure the eye ... At first we do not see, or we see without registering the image. Then, when it is no longer possible not to see, we arrange things, first instinctively then deliberately, to avoid seeing them as much as possible. We take complicated routes to avoid the monsters ... one can always choose one's subway stop, take another street and even, while in enemy territory, close an eye, open an umbrella … The more present-day Paris annoyed me, the more I turned to the past, played hide-and-seek. (1994: 4)

I will have more to say about hide-and-seek in the city. Chevalier talks of turning to the past, but there are other ways in which to look away, and there is in any case something wholly contemporary about acts of urban unseeing. We all close our eyes to the city some of the time, choosing to ignore a lot of what takes place around us. A sort of blindness might even be necessary to city life, thinning out the massive sensory input available to us at any one time, the artefactual and architectural cacophony of the streets. Urban environments exceed our ability to encompass them, even in a frozen moment – never mind the swinging perspectives brought on by movement, never mind the upheavals of configuration brought on by construction and demolition (Barber, 1995: 29). And in this sense we have no choice at all; the city is too much, and we must shut it out or at any rate manage and prioritise our encounter with it – closing an eye, picking our route, opening an umbrella.

Nor is this just a matter of ourselves and the built environment. We are not alone in the city: there are countless others there too. Some of the ways in which we see and seek out, and also hide from these others, or fail to see them, in the midst of a changing cityscape, is the subject of this book.

Eyes wide shut

The idea of the city as a hard place is an old saw: hard in itself, as a physical site – built to last, like the third little piggy's house – but hard also in the sense that the people living there are said to be distant and unfeeling, with not much time for others they do not already know; they look past you in the street, right through you. To be hard in this way is to belong to the city. The implied contrast is that between an urban way of life and personality and some other existence where something more like kindness and community prevail, most likely rural. But it is not all bad news for the city. If city dwellers are unfriendly, they are also said to be savvy and sharp, go-getting, sophisticated too – although this word can bite back. This distinction between city life and country living reaches back a long way (see Williams, 1973); it is of course ideological and has been variously put to work and imagined – but it is not wholly imaginary, not simply false. As a contrastive device, it has played a particular role in sociological analyses of the modern industrial city and its progeny. It was central to the work of the Chicago school of urban sociology, whose investigations of city life are generally recognised as having established modern urban studies (Hannerz, 1980: 20). For the Chicago sociologists the modern city was 'remaking human nature', establishing new types of personality, modes of thought and a 'city mentality ... clearly differentiated from the rural mind'; the difference was 'not merely one of degree, but of kind' (Wirth, 1984: 219–222; originally 1925). Cities were different sorts of places; city dwellers were different sorts of people.

Central to this analysis was the idea that city life was a matter of living among strangers, and a matter of getting used to this. Strangers in the city were not, as elsewhere, occasional figures not from round here and most likely gone tomorrow. Strangers were locals, the very inhabitants with whom life was going to have to be made from one day to the next; they belonged in the city no less than you did. Strangers *were* the city, and urbanism as a way of life meant managing that extraordinary circumstance somehow. Along something like the same lines, Nigel Thrift has recently argued that the jar and scrape of everyday encounters with others we do not know makes the city essentially anti-social: misanthropy, he suggests, is a 'natural condition of cities, one which cannot be avoided and will not go away' (2005: 140). He describes cities today as threaded through with aversion and ill-will, even hatred: 'cities are full of impulses which are hostile and murderous and which cross the minds and bodies of even the most pacific and well-balanced citizenry' (2005: 140). Is the city really as hard as all that? Here is Jonathan Raban on the well-balanced citizenry of 1970s London:

Coming out of the London Underground at Oxford Circus one afternoon, I saw a man go berserk in the crowd on the stairs. 'You fucking ... fucking bastards!' he shouted, and his words rolled round and round the lavatorial porcelain tube as we ploughed through. He was in a neat city suit, with a neat city paper neatly folded in a pink hand ... What was surprising was that nobody showed surprise: a slight speeding-up in the pace of the crowd, a turned head or two, a quick grimace, but that was all ... Who feels love for his fellow-man at rush hour? Not me. I suspect the best insurance against urban violence is the fact that most of us shrink from contact with strangers. (1988: 12; originally 1974)

A moment of urban frenzy; a decidedly odd thing for a man in a neat city suit to do. And yet the incident is nothing really, not at all newsworthy, just one of those things that happen sometimes in the city, more often than we care to notice.[2]

Most of us are familiar with the sudden flare-up of urban ill-temper, even rage. The impulse is always there, as a possibility, and we are prepared for it. Just another one of those things. Only last week I saw a man assaulted outside a pub, across the road from where I was sitting in my car. It was an explosive escalation of what seemed to have been a petty row, and was all over in seconds. He got up from the ground, his shirt-front spattered with blood, and retreated inside, backing through the pub door, his hands raised. His attacker stayed outside and stalked up and down the pavement, gesturing angrily but with diminishing conviction, running himself down like a clockwork toy. A third man leaning against the wall of the pub watched the whole thing over the top of his pint glass without once moving or giving any sign that he had actually seen anything. I waited for the lights to turn green, and drove on. This was something more than the jar and scrape of city life, but nothing traumatic in any sense that could be said to have widened beyond those directly involved. No one witness to the assault seemed to think it worth doing anything much about, myself included. No one tried to get involved, and no one was visibly upset other than the two protagonists. I did flinch a little, inwardly, at the time, but that was about it. I suppose others – the third man, leaning on the wall – may have done the same.

To flinch is to shy or turn away, also to shrink under pain. The idea that another's pain might be ours as well, or that our sharing of it, imaginatively, might be the way through to fellow-feeling, can be found in Adam Smith's moral philosophy. Smith argues that it is human nature to feel pity or compassion for the misery of others; sympathy: '[t]he greatest

---

2. Raban has noticed, of course, because he is writing a book on city life, and has been carrying the manuscript around with him for eight months – '[i]n orange ring-bound notebooks, growing increasingly pulpy and dog-eared ... locked in my briefcase' (1988 [1974]: 242). But what he has noticed most of all is the general unconcern. It is as if no one has seen anything.

ruffian, the most hardened violator of the laws of society, is not altogether without it' (2002: 11; originally 1759). Yet if we are not without pity this is still some way off from routinely taking a hand in the lives of others – parking the car and getting out and crossing the road to check that someone, a stranger, is going to be OK. Smith's account starts with what we might see, and how that might make us feel: we see a blow fall and we imagine how it might feel to have been hit – perhaps we flinch. But if we (already) shrink from contact with strangers, as Raban has it, what does it matter if we also flinch when we see a stranger hurt? What we see of their injury leads nowhere.[3] Is seeing enough? Not enough for Richard Sennett, who writes:

In the course of the development of modern, urban individualism, the individual fell silent in the city. The street, the café, the department store, the railroad, bus and underground became places of the gaze rather than scenes of discourse. When verbal connections between strangers in the modern city are difficult to sustain, the impulses of sympathy which individuals may feel in the city looking at the scene around them become in turn momentary – a second of response looking at snapshots of life. (2002: 358)

To gaze is to stare, to look vacantly but at the same time fixedly; snapshots are images taken (out) of passing life. But it does not follow that this is

---

3. Smith also notes a general reluctance to yield to sympathy: 'we endeavour, for our own sake, to supress it as much as we can' (2002 [1759]: 54). There are particular occasions on which we might try rather hard not to feel another's pain or discomfort. 'Persons of delicate fibres and a weak constitution of body complain that in looking on the sores and ulcers which are exposed by beggars in the streets, they are apt to feel an itching or uneasy sensation in the correspondent part of their own bodies' (2002 [1759]: 12). Nor are the eyes themselves immune, even as they are doing the looking: 'Men of the most robust make, observe that on looking on sore eyes they often feel a very sensible soreness in their own, which proceeds from the same reason; that organ being in the strongest man more delicate, than any other part of the body is in the weakest.' (2002 [1759]: 12–13). Obviously there is more to this than physical ailment or injury; others' needs don't have to be corporal to be apparent. To put the same point another way, we can say that people come in for all sorts of damage, some of which is inflicted by no one in particular – or no-one else in particular, sometimes appearing self-inflicted – but which wounds just the same, grinding people down; and sometimes we see this on the street – sorrow, distress, confusion – and can be just as sure of it as we are of the physical injury signalled by a bloodied shirt front. And we may flinch, and look away.

how we only ever see, the eye like a camera. There are other ways of looking, not so fixed or photographic. To see in a way that engages others – strangers, and their needs – and the world around us is not so much to gaze at as to enquire and question, to look (out) for and look after. A discursive attention, perhaps. In large part, and in the detail certainly, that is what this book is about. I intend to provide a record of what looking out for others on the city street looks like – how it appeared to me at least, having shared time with a group of people dedicated to just that undertaking.

Strangers, streets and walls

The general problem as some have framed it is that cities bring people together in large numbers but not as one big (happy) family. The effect can be claustrophobic. Living with strangers makes us edgy, but also indifferent; we shrink from contact, and all the while 'the run of daily life ... [feeds] back into the city's fabric as an undertow of spite' (Thrift, 2005: 141). Plaited together, a determined suspicion and unconcern, each of these a refusal properly to *see* another person, supply a necessary technique for managing all that proximity – the push and shove of all those other lives pressed close around us. The classic statement of this urban condition belongs to the German sociologist Georg Simmel, who suggests that 'antipathy which is the latent adumbration of actual antagonism ... brings about the sort of distanciation and deflection without which this type of life could not be carried on at all' (1971: 331; originally 1903).[4] Ill-disposed to others, disinclined to make them our concern, we gaze blankly, or look away. We do not see them and are closed, ourselves, in turn. We may even pick our routes, like Chevalier, arranging things – instinctively, deliberately – so as to avoid encounters with those to whom our sympathy least comfortably extends. Should we come across any one such by chance, we may close an eye – so as not to flinch.

The city street is the archetypal location for such unconcern: the street *is* the place where strangers walk on by. And then what? Where do they

---

4. The Chicago sociologists considered Simmel's essay, *The Metropolis and Mental Life*, to be '[t]he most important single article on the city from the sociological standpoint' (Wirth, 1984: 219; originally 1925).

walk on to, these strangers? Off the edge of the page presumably, because 'the street' as such is an abstraction, is no real street at all; no one ever walked there, or sat importuning passers-by. Actually existing streets, on the other hand, are somewhere in particular. More than that, they are physical settings – as Rykwert insists. The materiality of real streets, their structure and composition, matters for any human encounter we might have on them, be that encounter kind or unkind. Walking on by the needs of others requires a reasonably firm and dependable surface on which to do so. It cannot happen in mid-air. It can go badly wrong in a muddy field. High-quality granite paving on a laying course of minimum compressive strength 30MPa, well maintained and swept clean – all this makes pedestrian indifference that little bit easier, that little bit more smooth.[5] Putting the needs of others behind us is not just a figure of speech: it can be brought off materially, with devastating effect, simply by turning the corner of a building. My point is that the only streets we know are real ones, and real streets are not only physically somewhere, a fragment of geography, but also materially constituted and as such participant in what we might do there. The relationship between the two, between the city street and what we might see and do there, is one of imbrication (Katznelson, 1992: 7).

Given which, if city life is in some ways unseeing we should expect the built environment to confirm this. And in a way it does. To stand on any city street – a real one – is to have one's line of sight and field of vision variously abridged by corners, edges, blocks and towers. Of all the elements of architecture it is one of the more rudimentary, the wall, that most effectively curbs what we see in the city – even as it defines the city street as a space along which we might look. If city life is a life shared with strangers, then perhaps walls are to be expected, appreciated even, as supplying a material analogue to Simmel's necessary distanciation and deflection. Walls curb exposure, and permit difference; they set limits and partition experience. But if walls are all around us, everywhere we

---

5. These specifications can be found in the *Cardiff City Centre Public Realm Manual*, a document approved and adopted by Cardiff Council's Executive in 2009. The manual sets out guidance for all those involved in the 'design, implementation and maintenance' of public space in Cardiff, including developers and 'other interested stakeholders'(Cardiff Council, 2009: 7); it is informed by a range of other strategy documents relating to the role and function of the city centre, including the *City Centre Strategy, 2007–2010* (Cardiff Council, 2007).

look, then this may blunt perception in yet another way: walls may be 'taken for granted, seen but not noticed ... their effects are so strong that they may be sublimated, left beneath conscious acknowledgement ... walls are more powerful than we like to think' (Unwin, 2000: 14). Walls are something we should wake up to, perhaps. Certainly so whenever there is more at issue than the partitioning of difference. Walls secure privilege as well as variation, or can do. That the modern city might be a home to a partitioned inequality was recognised early on, in my home town, by Friedrich Engels:

> The town itself [Manchester] is peculiarly built, so that a person may live in it for years, and go in and out daily without coming into contact with a working-people's quarter or even with workers, that is, so long as he confines himself to his business or to pleasure walks. This arises chiefly from the fact, that by unconscious tacit agreement, as well as with outspoken conscious determination, the working-people's quarters are sharply separated from the sections of the city reserved for the middle class. (1993: 57; originally 1845)

Again the conscious and the unconscious combined, and a screening off of what might otherwise cause a passer-by to flinch:

> ... the finest part of the arrangement is this, that the members of this money aristocracy can take the shortest road through the middle of all the labouring districts to their places of business without ever seeing that they are in the midst of the grimy misery that lurks to the right and the left. For the thoroughfares leading from the Exchange in all directions out of the city are lined, on both sides, with an almost unbroken series of shops ... I have never seen so systematic a shutting out ... so tender a concealment of everything which might affront the eye and the nerves of the bourgeoisie. (1993 [1845]: 58–59)

A retail façade, secured by those with the means to maintain 'a decent and cleanly external appearance' (1993 [1845]: 58); behind which the city is a maze: 'the lanes run now in this direction, now in that, while every two minutes the wanderer gets into a blind alley, or, on turning a corner, finds himself back where he started' (1993 [1845]: 64). Sympathy for strangers seems possible only where like meets like, in the working-class districts where pauper families out on the street appeal to passers-by 'without uttering a word', reckoning on fellow-feeling from those 'who know how it feels to be hungry' (1993 [1845]: 98). The city's homeless 'sleep where they find a place, in passages, arcades, in corners where the police and the owners leave them undisturbed' (1993 [1845]: 44), hoping for indifference sufficient to see them through the night.[6]

Manchester has come a long way since, and slipped back, and come on again; other cities too. Slums have been torn away, and rebuilt; renewal and development schemes have succeeded one another, not always successfully. Of the 20th century's very many great books on the city, probably the best known and arguably the most influential is Jane Jacobs' *The Death and Life of Great American Cities*, published in 1961. New York, and Jacobs' target is urban renewal, the technocrats and developers, the '[t]he pseudoscience of city planning' (1992: 13; originally 1961). As with Chevalier there is the determined suspicion, the accusation, that heedless redevelopment has deadened city life, is killing off the very qualities by which a city might live. For each of these writers, the old and actually existing city, where it remains, is set against (and menaced by) the dreams and visions of urban planners. Jacobs singles out Le Corbusier and his unrealised *Radiant City* design as a primary and malign influence, a model of towering skyscrapers in a park, a dream city 'hailed deliriously by architects, and ... [since] embodied in scores of projects' (1992 [1961]: 23). Attractive, yes; but mechanistic and flashy, and essentially ignorant:

> ... great arterial roads for express one-way traffic ... underground streets for heavy vehicles and deliveries ... pedestrians off the streets and in the parks ... [Le Corbusier's] city was like a wonderful mechanical toy. Furthermore, his conception, as an architectural work, had a dazzling clarity, simplicity and harmony. It was so orderly, so visible, so easy to understand. It said everything in a flash, like a good advertisement. (Jacobs, 1992: 23)

---

6. Engels' proto-ethnography of the 19th-century industrial city is a masterpiece, and the book describes birth not death: a modern, capitalist society, and a city, Manchester, created more or less *de novo* (Joyce, 2003: 9). No assassination, as with Paris; no city done to death (but appalling casualties, terrible losses). And if the beginning of something then perhaps, also, an awakening; but in point of fact not much sleep at all – chronic shortage of sleep and wretched sleeping conditions are a repeated theme.

Or a snapshot, a photograph.

How else might we see the city? At street level, is Jacobs' essential answer, 'adventuring in the real world, ourselves' (1992 [1961]: 13). To do so is to learn to appreciate the ways in which, here and there, not as it ought to be, but as it actually is, the city works already. The street is central to her argument, and to her definition of what a city *is*; so too the figure of the stranger. Cities are full of strangers, and, Jacobs insists, it is streets not walls that will handle this best, if allowed to do so. The true mechanism is shown to be intricate and ordinary, so ordinary in fact that it looks like nothing much at all: everyday attentions shared between strangers – pedestrians, passers-by, residents too – who are prepared to look out for one another; an 'almost unconscious, network of voluntary controls and standards ... enforced by the people themselves' (1992 [1961]: 32) arising from repeated sidewalk encounters which appear lowly and unpurposeful, random even, but 'are the small change from which a city's wealth of public life may grow' (1992 [1961]: 72). Visual perception has a special place in all this, a constant succession of eyes. Busy streets engage the attention and thereby secure a shared awareness of others and what they are up to and how their concerns might mesh or brush against one's own. Jacobs can make no sense of city planners who 'operate on the premise that city people seek the sight of emptiness, obvious order and quiet' (1992 [1961]: 37). There is to be no looking the other way, no blind gaze, and no fencing off of difference. Cities are for strangers, who must see to themselves and look out for one another.

The Death and Life of Great American Cities is concerned with big cities because these are the places Jacobs likes best and cares most about, and within such cities she focuses particularly on what she calls the inner areas, because this is where the most baffling problems appear to lie. Planners did not seem to have the answers. I know the feeling: they didn't seem to have too many answers when I was growing up in Manchester in the 1970s either. But something had started to happen, regardless, around about the time I left in the late 1980s; and was just about getting started in Cardiff around about the time I arrived there in the late 1990s. Which brings me back to these shores and just about into the 21st century. Here is sociologist Fran Tonkiss writing about the sort of thing I have in mind:

> A sign on a disused commercial building in a triangle of back streets
> marks the beginnings of a transformation: ANOTHER PRESTIGIOUS

LUXURY INNER CITY LIFESTYLE DEVELOPMENT. After thirty years the front line of gentrification has reached this pocket of railway arches in inner south-east London ... this is a new sense in which to understand the term 'inner city'. Such an expression has rarely been associated with any concept of lifestyle, much less one that might be considered prestigious ... If a language of urban pathology invented the 'inner city' as a problem, a different sort of language is now seeking to valorise it as an investment prospect ... an older version of the 'inner city' recedes behind the developer's hoarding. (2000: 115–116).

Tonkiss writes as a passer-by. Something is happening, or is about to, and has come to notice; at the same time something else grows fainter and retreats from view. As she suggests, 'in these kinds of transformation, not only buildings but urban perceptions are altered' (2000: 116).

I am establishing themes, to be worked at throughout the rest of this book. What is at stake here? Seeing, undoubtedly – a determined refusal to see, or else the insistence that we must if city streets are to hold strangers together. Certain sorts of care and watchfulness; perception as a matter of habit, or of purposeful enquiry. City visions. Inattention, renewed attention, and what each of these permits. What else? Walls, edges, hoardings, disused buildings; everyday encounters; concealment; hide-and-seek, and rediscovery; complicated routes; surface appearances; streets. Matters of life and death. Sleep, or the lack of it.

Paris, Manchester, New York, London. Next? Cardiff, and its streets and sleepers. Here is a switch, and a sharpening, of focus.

Sleepers

There is an irregular collection of people very close to the centre of this book, whose lived circumstances animate others in various ways and whose use of city space can make them particularly, sometimes painfully, visible even at the same time as that visibility counts for almost nothing (those who set eyes on them don't much care to see them). They are also elusive, practised at skirting the sorts of notice they would rather not attract.

Who are they? Among them are the homeless. Most of them can be called homeless, depending on what the word is taken to mean; some are called street drinkers and street beggars, some are called street prostitutes. They are varied enough in their outlook and character, and as such not so very different from any other collection of people one might choose to nominate and assemble. It would be a mistake to set them apart categorically if doing so were meant to indicate some shared character trait or shortcoming. What they do share is some common portion of a slew of economic and social difficulties, made manifest as personal history and individual circumstance, which has seen them pushed out onto the street. Some are obviously homeless because they live in homeless hostels, which is to say that they have a roof over their heads after all – though they may spend the better part of most days out of doors. Some have homes of their own, or houses, or, more likely, (rented) rooms in houses, though held precariously and quite often on terms that make the street seem a refuge. They do not sleep well (no one in a hostel ever did, to my knowledge), certainly not those who are out of doors at night and up against the hard surfaces of the city, sleeping rough. Here are a few of them:

Gerald sleeps (as I write) against the rear wall of the Glamorgan Building in Cardiff's civic centre. He may not be sleeping at all, may not have slept much all night, but he has made a place for himself there and has occupied it dependably for the last few months, wrapped in a sleeping bag with his minimal possessions arrayed around him. He doesn't move much and doesn't like to be disturbed; he can spend two or three days (and nights) in this same spot without seeming even to stand up. He must sleep some of the time.

The Glamorgan Building, once the county hall of Glamorgan, houses Cardiff University's Schools of *City and Regional Planning* and *Social Sciences*; it is a large, neoclassical, listed (Grade 1) building. I work there, in an office on the first floor with a view out across the city, towards Cardiff Bay. Directly below my window a walkway runs along the side of the building and around a corner to a car park at the back. Here, squeezed between the tarmac apron and the rear wall of the building, under cover of a first-floor balcony and balustrade, are a couple of concrete benches and some bicycle racks; and this is where Gerald has established himself, where he was lying this morning as I passed him on my way into the building. It is a good spot, sheltered from the rain and mostly quiet.

Gerald is one of Cardiff's street homeless and looks the part rather more than some others do: elderly and dishevelled, stooped (when he stands) under the weight of a hopelessly overstuffed duffle bag. He has been on the streets for a number of years, off and on, and has slept all over the city, but seldom in any one place for long. Wherever he goes, he gets moved on. Given which, his occupancy of this little strip of space at the back of the Glamorgan Building is some sort of accomplishment. He has managed to stop somewhere and stay, for three months now, and has yet to be shooed away.

Even so, there is still a problem with him staying where he is – another sort of problem. His physical mobility is poor and failing, and likely to deteriorate all the more quickly the longer he spends cocooned in his sleeping bag. Some days he doesn't get up at all and when he does he struggles, a consequence of which is that he has become more and more isolated and withdrawn. He will not make conversation beyond a word or two, sometimes refusing to speak at all, even to the local authority outreach workers who come out to see him most mornings – pretending to be asleep when it suits him, or quite possibly sleeping. He is unresponsive to any suggestion that he ought to get into a hostel. In what they would argue to be his best interests, those caring for Gerald, or trying to, have seen to it that his current sick note (confirming his frailty and validating his benefit entitlement) runs for only a month at a time. This means that Gerald has to get up and walk across the city centre to his see his GP every few weeks. Gerald would rather he didn't have to go so often. He doesn't like doctors, and doesn't like the benefits people much either; he gets along well enough with Charlie, one of the outreach workers. It is Charlie who has made the arrangement with Gerald's GP to keep his sick note temporary. She hopes to keep him walking that way, and looked over once a month.

'Common sense, isn't it,' says **Paul** tapping his head. 'Don't shit on your own doorstep.' Paul likes things neat and organised, and although he uses some of the same facilities as other rough sleepers in Cardiff, he generally keeps to himself. He is not a drinker, doesn't take drugs, dresses smartly and always hurries along the streets as if he has somewhere to be (which he mostly hasn't).

The same team of welfare professionals that visits Gerald in the early mornings – Cardiff's *City Centre Team* – calls on Paul too, when they can find him; he moves around a bit and every now and then disappears from Cardiff altogether. Paul is in his thirties and has, by his own account, not been settled anywhere very long since he left care in his late teens. He has family locally, he says, but doesn't seem to be much in contact with them or able to stay there. He is almost always cheerful, but insistently so, to the point where it all seems like a bit of an act; there is a stubbornness too that keeps him from accepting offers of help or even acknowledging that he needs any. His longest stay in any one location in Cardiff was in the corner of a church car park off to the side of the city's main pedestrian thoroughfare. His patch there – a square of tarmac beneath a flight of stairs at the back of the building – was characteristically domestic: a bed of wooden pallets with blankets and blue plastic sheeting laid across, or neatly rolled and stored alongside throughout the day; his other, minimal, belongings arrayed on the shelves of a discarded fridge, now a cupboard; two wheelie bins pulled in close as a windbreak when required. Everything just so.

The one time I have seen Paul angry and out of sorts was when his 'room' under the stairs was tidied away. He had returned late one night – later than usual, because there had been something on at the church and he hadn't wanted to disturb anyone, or be disturbed – to find his bed gone, along with all his bedding, the fridge too (he found a bag of his personal belongings in one of the two wheelie bins). The following morning he was sitting on the wall by the entrance to the car park. He was fuming, and prepared to take the story to the local press if the church didn't recompense him in some way; he was going nowhere till he'd seen the vicar. But it all came to nothing (no one turned up, he never went to the papers), and by that evening he had found himself another likely looking corner to bed down in, on the fringe of a stalled building site. The loss of his place by the church still rankled though, and for weeks he would rehearse the injustice to anyone who would listen: 'And I always kept that place clean. Spotless. Not shat it up like others do. Litter in the bin, no mess. Common sense, isn't it. Don't shit on your own doorstep.' But cheery now, like it was basically all OK.

Jackie and **Wayne** are lying down side by side under a blanket with their dog Bruno between them in the covered entrance to the Cardiff International Arena; it is half past two in the morning. Off to one side there are two more figures, curled up in sleeping bags. No one is asleep.

Jackie is seventeen, Wayne in his mid-twenties. They are both well-known on the homeless scene in Cardiff and have been sleeping out in this particular spot for a couple of weeks now. Wayne is a heavy drinker, Jackie is too when she is with him – they are a couple; Jackie has a black eye. The social workers and care professionals who have anything to do with her consider Jackie a priority, especially vulnerable and at risk of exploitation; it is not quite certain that Jackie is selling sex to keep Wayne and herself in drink (she says she isn't), but she has been seen a few too many times in recent weeks in just the places where you would, at just the wrong times. Attempts over the past year to get her into accommodation have come unstuck as often as they have been attempted. Right now, she won't go anywhere without Wayne (and has turned down offers of hostel places twice in the last month on those grounds).

Wayne is bulky, a big man and aggressive with it. He cuts an alarming figure around town, lurching along the pavement swearing at Bruno as the dog strains and growls on a short chain. There are not too many care professionals as worried for Wayne as they are for Jackie.

The two figures off to one side in sleeping bags are a mother and daughter, **Carol** and **Gemma**. Gemma has had nowhere to stay since her boyfriend was placed on remand. Her mum, Carol, is in a (homeless) hostel and cannot take visitors. So the two of them are out together, for tonight. 'You need to see the City Centre Team in the morning,' says Wayne. 'They'll be along about seven.' Four more hours to wait.

Alice is sat up on the steps of a church hall, arms folded in front of her, hands tucked into sleeves. She is wearing a thick duvet jacket, ripped from collar to cuff along one sleeve, with the hood pulled up and cinched tight. All you can see are her eyes. There are carrier bags stuffed with what looks like nothing more than newspaper, either side of her, and she is (presumably) sitting on more of the same. She is wrapped in bedding and blankets from the waist down. She has been in Cardiff for two weeks now, after a few months away. Dennis, Charlie's co-worker, is here following a phone call from a member of the public. Alice will not engage. She waves him off. Dennis says that with people like Alice he feels like he is intruding: 'If she doesn't want to speak to me it's not as if I can make her.' He will contact a mental health social worker when he gets back to the office.

Luke, **Dean** and **Michael** were in Cardiff for six weeks one summer, having been kicked out of a shared house in Merthyr Tydfil. They were related somehow, or claimed to be; cousins perhaps, though it was brothers when they first arrived; all three of them in their teens. They were energetically, if briefly, part of the city's homeless scene, drawing on various local services, particularly the soup runs and outreach services; they all signed up to sell the *Big Issue* and worked at this industriously.[7] It was clear enough from early on that they would take any immediate assistance they could get – clothes, food, sleeping bags, hot drinks (they once made off from the Salvation Army with a dozen donated boxes of cereal) – but wanted no real help beyond that. Nothing that would stop them being homeless for as long as it took them to make whatever decision it was they made to pack it in and leave. Which they did, eventually, owing money to most of those they left behind.

Rose is walking away from a police car, having been told she will be arrested unless she goes home, right away. 'And what would happen then? asks Charlie, reaching into her bag for a handful of condoms. 'If I was arrested? It would depend on the copper,' says Rose. She takes the condoms: 'Thanks. Just the flavoured.' **Katy** comes across to chat, pleased it has now stopped raining as she has nowhere else to go and will be out for the next few hours at least. She has provisionally booked a place at the EOS (the council's 'emergency-overnight-stay' provision), but the doors don't open until 11pm. Charlie would rather Katy had somewhere else to go and asks if she needs help finding a hostel place at least. Katy says no thanks, the EOS isn't so bad, and anyway she might stay out all night, then sleep tomorrow.

Damian arrived in Cardiff homeless and stayed that way for two months, sleeping rough around the city in a dozen different spots, never more than half a mile from Cardiff Central station. He made two close friends early on, for better or worse: Phil and Chrissie. These two, old enough to be his parents, adopted him, after a fashion: they looked out for him, making sure no one took advantage or pushed him around; they introduced him to all the local homeless services. Then one day he left, or disappeared. Nothing was said. He got on a train, or got indoors somewhere (not a hostel, or word would have passed along), or something else happened. No one seemed to know or be prepared to say.

---

7. *The Big Issue* is a UK street newspaper, founded in the early 1990s.

For the time that he was around, the spot in which Damian stayed longest was a swatch of leftover space not much bigger than a room, bounded on two sides by an elevated railway line and the back of an advertising hoarding. The space was a perfect hide even though right beside a main road, wholly obscured from view and accessible only by clambering over a wall and then across a pipe and railings spanning the old dock feeder canal. Nettles, scrub and two large trees had grown untended there, in between which Damian had stamped out a few square yards of bare earth. Looking up you could see nothing but leaves and tree branches and, through these, a patch of sky and the topmost corner of what was at that time one of Cardiff's newest hotels: *The Big Sleep*.

These are (or were) some of Cardiff's homeless and rough sleepers; one way or another they are 'out' and on the street at night.[8] Not so very long ago they could have been expected to have had the city centre more or less to themselves after midnight, once the pubs had closed and people had made their way home. But at least two things have changed – have been changing – over recent years. Cardiff's night-time economy has swollen, as it has in a great many other UK cities. The city centre is now home to 'a complex of themed bar-chains and clubs ... [drawing] up to 70,000 people in a weekend evening' (Lovering, 2006: 183). Nor has this change come about only through unconscious, tacit agreement.

---

8. In directing attention to homeless individuals my aim has been to people this book, early on, with those whose lives and difficulties are at stake throughout, if only just a few of them. I feel they are owed some visibility. But I do not want any brief description of individual character and circumstance to be read as a satisfactory, or even part-way satisfactory, account of the problem. Understanding why some people are homeless is best begun somewhere else. It remains the case that homelessness is something that (only) happens to people, however; and *that* is worth remembering. I have also, at points, obscured things: I have anonymised some of those I am writing about, protecting identities and changing some details – of appearance, sequence of events, particulars. I have done so to afford some privacy to those whose lives are already uncomfortably public. I hope this does not seem inconsistent. I have tried for balance: some visibility, but not too much. Were this book *about* homelessness, or, rather, about *homeless people*, things would be different perhaps. Instead, the homeless are a little off to one side of what I am really about here. Their lived circumstances animate others in various ways, as I have suggested, and it is those others, care and outreach workers moving around the city looking out for people in need, that this book is about if it is about any collection of individuals at all. Accordingly, Charlie *is* Charlie, and Dennis *is* Dennis, because I know them well and have shared their work; and they know me. Visibility – who sees who and on what terms, who sees their (own) name in print – has to be managed.

Cardiff council's strategy for the centre of the city, first published in 1997, identifies the creation of a 24-hour city as one of six development priorities. Meanwhile, a wider, boosterist agenda, shared and promoted by 'networks of investors, entrepreneurs, politicians and planners' (Lovering, 2006: 188), has transformed the city skyline: multiplex cinemas, office buildings, and a number of new hotels and apartment buildings (running the spectrum from student accommodation through to top-end 'prestige living' developments). In consequence of which a great many more people sleep in the middle of Cardiff than used to be the case.

Where does this leave rough sleepers? And how do they sleep? It leaves them with what is left of the old entanglement of homelessness and central space to be observed in towns and cities across the UK. Still there, but no longer because everyone else has gone home. Still there because they have nowhere else to go. And they sleep badly; they are rough sleepers.

Coming round again

If sleep comes in the end, as it must, it is no sure remission on the streets. Rather, it is a hazard, something the homeless must snatch, something they must be careful not to slip too deeply into – you might not wake up again, given the wrong ratio of booze and drugs, or the cold, or anything else that might do for you before the morning. Sleep is not only difficult but dangerous, out of doors in the city, and each of these – difficulty, danger – can have to do with other people. Passers-by may be busily intent on getting somewhere else and, as such, hardly concerned with anyone bedded down in a doorway; but others, similarly indifferent, can be more of a nuisance, idly ranging from one bar or club to the next, shouting and laughing. Still others may be out for mischief, may have something to prove, some supposed grudge or slight to exercise. The point being that other people can keep you up, or wake you, in the street. Noise and inconsideration is one thing, unkindness is another.

Some of those who might wake the homeless or keep them from sleeping do so in an official capacity. Sometimes unintentionally (street cleaners in high-vis jackets, operatives in a genuinely twenty-four-hour enterprise, buzzing around the city streets scraping and sweeping up), but also by design. Security guards patrolling civic and commercial premises – the bus station, university campus, car parks – sometimes make it their business to move rough sleepers on, or wake them early. The rationale for doing so tends to be a little woolly, merging trespass, obstruction and nonspecific 'safety' concerns. Sometimes cleaners and security staff combine their efforts – rousting Wayne and Jackie from the entrance to the Cardiff International Arena on a Saturday morning, for example – with the police called as backup should there be any difficulty.

Others come around in a similarly official capacity, but to help. In Cardiff, the local authority employs a team of care workers whose job it is to look out for the city's homeless and offer to help them. Members of this team – Charlie and Dennis's team, the *City Centre Team* – don't just happen to come across rough sleepers (and sex workers) in the course of other duties, they actively seek them out and are paid to do so. If Damian takes himself off somewhere at night to bed down away from prying eyes and interruption then it is Charlie's job to find him and see that he is OK. Others are engaged in the same sort of hide-and-seek altruism, but as charitable or church volunteers rather than local authority employees. The aim here is not to wake anyone up, any more than the assumption (among experienced workers) is that more than a very few will be sleeping. The aim is to see to those in difficulty, to find ways in which to help. However, helping someone like Jackie in some way that might lead to her not being homeless any more, ever again, may require weeks and months of patient and painstaking work; and in lots of ways homelessness itself, the absence of housing, will be the least of it. There will be financial difficulties, family troubles, health concerns, addictions and suspicions, confusions, wrongs, resentment. In the end, almost any sort of help with any of this might loop back around to sleep. Just where that sleep might happen will be a measure of accomplishment for at least some of those helping Jackie, even at the same time as it may signal nothing so sure as an end to her homelessness.

One more category of caller, one more person coming around: the enumerator. Counting the homeless is hard to do for some of the same reasons that helping them might be, but most major cities in the UK attempt it now and then. Census figures for England and Wales have in the past included a count of 'rough sleepers', incorporating a good few wide awake when counted (you must be 'bedded down' though or just about to, if you are to count at all; if you are up and about, because you can't sleep or don't want to risk it or can't find somewhere, you may not

2

Lost and Found

Things and people can go missing in the city, can go astray or get lost. Finding them again can be hard work and might never happen. On the face of it, the task is hopeless. The city is too big, too intricate and convoluted. There are too many places to hide, and too many corners. Where would you even begin? Yet things (and people) do turn up again, and can be found, if you know where and how to look.

Sometimes the kindness of strangers (in the city, after all!) takes a hand and we 'find' something before we even started looking or knew it was missing. We drop our keys getting off the bus and someone calls us back, or we leave a package at the bar and someone brings it over. If we have already gone, our mislaid items may still be retrieved and set aside for our return. But much more gets lost than gets found again so quickly, if at all; added to which there is the rubbish, the goods got rid of, stuff we don't want and shouldn't care to find again or have brought (back) to our attention. This assortment of litter and effects is not distributed evenly across the city. Things get lost or left in some places rather more than others, and having been left anywhere tend to drift and gather together, given time, in particular locations. The process is partly organic – carrier bags gusted about by passing traffic eventually snag in the branches of trees, joining others already there; every fire-exit doorway has its tide-mark of grit, cigarette ends, bus tickets and whatever else. But it is also systematic. Like most cities, Cardiff benefits from a coordinated infrastructure of waste collection and management that assembles and sorts the stuff that gets left behind on the streets. The local authority provides public bins for the deposit and collection of street rubbish, and a range of services for domestic and commercial waste processing and recycling; it employs a significant workforce of street cleaners whose movements around the city trace out a pattern of practice the rest of us might struggle to see, even as it crosses tracks with our own.

Sometimes it happens the other way around and we are the one who finds the thing someone else has dropped or left behind. Not missing anything of our own, we come across something that nonetheless has the look of being lost, an object that might still matter to someone and for which they could be looking. What next? Should we leave it where it is? If we do, and no one comes to claim it soon, it will not last long. As a minimum, we can pick it up – the bus pass, the child's toy – and set it aside as 'found' and awaiting collection.

Figure 2.1

Or we can hand it in. Cities have extensive facilities for the deposit and collection of lost property, just as they do for rubbish. In central Cardiff there are any number of places you might hand in something you have found, or ask after something you have lost: most public buildings keep some sort of log of lost property and a box (or drawer or shelf) of belongings awaiting collection; most commercial premises do too. Central Square, in the very middle of Cardiff, has one of the more marked concentrations of lost and found facilities. The central train station is here – Cardiff Central – as is the main bus station; there are private coach operators too, and a major taxi rank. Items left or lost at Cardiff

Central are kept at the platform offices or ticket hall to await collection; if unclaimed within a week, they are forwarded to a lost property office in nearby Newport. Belongings left on board Cardiff buses are tagged with the route number and date found, and stored at a Customer Service Office on Wood Street, alongside Central Square. If any single organisation comes close to operating as a clearing house for property lost and found around Cardiff it is the police. Their lost property section, which used to operate from Cardiff Central Police Station but is now based five miles out of town, oversees a packed room of belongings handed in by members of the public; all these to be matched up, where possible, to the thousands of police 'lost' reports filed in Cardiff each year.

Possessions lost or left behind are part of the perceptual small change of city life – the discarded receipt, the carrier bag, the solitary training shoe. Only architects' drawings omit these sorts of detail. Most of us will have lost something in the city ourselves at one time or another, and having done so will have set about getting it back, making calls and leaving messages, supplying details, perhaps retracing steps we took earlier, attending to our surroundings in that particular way that has to do with trying to see something that isn't there – that is missing.

The missing

Something like the same patterns of dispersal, worry and bureaucracy operate for people too. People are not objects or belongings, so the resemblance is only passing. But it is there.

It is almost as easy to get lost or separated from someone in the middle of the city as it is to mislay one's possessions. Puzzlingly easy, when it happens. We pause in the street to say something to whoever it is we are with and, turning their way, we find they are just not there anymore – only they *were* there, just a moment ago. Where are they? People are bigger than most objects we might mislay in the city, which might help; but there are so many others out there too and the urban environment is anyway so perceptually dense that two people can be lost to each other in a moment.[1]

Most of us know this and are prepared for the eventuality. Out in the city with friends we may agree in advance on somewhere to meet

---

1. Cardiff city centre has an estimated annual 'footfall' of over 50 million.

up should anyone get lost. If we have made no such arrangement there will still be places – obvious places – we can head off to, in the hope and expectation that whoever is missing will have had the same idea, or will do eventually. Mobile phones make the whole thing much easier, of course; still, not everyone has a phone (and you may have lost yours).

Objects *per se* are neither lost nor found; it is people who lose them and find them again, a process to which objects themselves are indifferent. People go astray in the same way sometimes, unaware that others are even looking for them until they are 'found' (and scolded, as happens often enough with small children). But, unlike objects, people can also get lost all on their own, without anyone else having missed them. Being lost in this sense – losing one's way – is something a little different, though hardly odd or uncommon. Even so, there is a world of difference between a moment's confusion at a street junction and the more considerable anxiety that comes with not knowing where you are, late at night in some part of town you've never seen before and really don't like the look of. The good news is that we can all do something about it. Objects (once missed) are lost till they are found again; but not people. People can find their own way – home, or anywhere else. Having strayed off course, we can do as we would were we looking for something left behind: retrace our steps, back to where we were when we last knew our whereabouts. Either that or press on, and set about acquainting ourselves with wherever it is we are now.

We may even have a map, though if we do it might not turn out to be as useful as we had at first hoped. Maps present a territory, but typically no clue as to where one might be within it; they are handy if you know where you are, less so if you don't. Regardless, the cityscape itself is crowded with markers and indications: street names, road signs, bus routes and timetables, landmarks. It doesn't take much to string these together and triangulate with our own general sense of direction. Soon enough, often enough, we are back on our way.

And unless we are in some particularly suspect or deserted part of town we can always ask – anyone; passers-by may be able to put us right in a moment. The woman in the news-kiosk will know the way to wherever it is we are trying to find; the drivers at the taxi rank might help, if grudgingly. Other public-service workers perform the same daily duty, whether or not it is any part of their actual job description. Street cleaners, for one, are repeatedly asked for information and directions in the course of their daily patrols, usually by visitors and tourists. These latter are a different sort of lost, if lost is the word at all; they are new in town and have little or no local knowledge to begin with, from which to have strayed. Like most other UK towns and cities, Cardiff makes special provision for visitors. The Cardiff Tourist Information Centre, located in the heart of the city's shopping and pedestrian precinct, offers maps, guides, souvenirs, timetables, lists of local attractions, advice on eating out and getting around; and, behind two desks, uniformed assistants, part of a 'multilingual and knowledgeable team... [who] will help you to make the most of your stay in Cardiff'.[2] Street signs direct you here from various points around the city.

Getting lost just happens to us sometimes, we don't see it coming and suddenly find that we don't know where we are. But it doesn't need to be this way, nor is getting lost only ever a matter of some unintended lapse of those same skills that we then might use to extricate ourselves. Just as they take steps to find themselves, people can get themselves lost in the first place, on purpose; they can go missing. This too takes work. Here is Andrew O'Hagan:

> Whether missed or not, the common condition of all the missing (apart from their being out of sight) is that their documentary lives stop at the point they disappear. This termination, in fact, explains what it means to be a missing person in a country such as Britain. From birth, something like a small maelstrom of official papers swirls around your body, defining your human relations ... your physical progression (medical records) ... your education (report cards, school files) ... your financial status (National Insurance contributions, tax returns, wage slips) ... your domestic routines (phone records, gas bills, newspapers delivered); and hundreds of other extant documents relating to the conduct of your life ... [t]hese official records (to say nothing of private documents, letters and diaries) give a very full account of who you are, and what your movements have been over the course of your life.
>
> Ours is a very written-down sort of life; it can't easily be erased, nor can the binding power of ongoing records be easily snapped. Many of these records follow you wherever you go, and, in the normal run of

---

2.   See www.visitcardiff.com/discover/touristinformationcentres

things, they can cause you to be traced very quickly. A missing person has – for one of a variety of reasons I'm turning over – severed, or been severed from, their written life. They are not cashing cheques in their own name, they are not drawing benefit or earning money through their NI number, they are not paying tax, they are not visiting a doctor or a dentist … You can change your identity, but it is not just a matter of going to another town and calling yourself Jeremy. It is a gigantic undertaking: a trail of subterfuge and avoidance of past documents leads away from the who-you-were to the who-you-are-now. (2004: 142–143)

The missing are not lost, not to themselves; to be missing is something different; unlike getting lost it requires a good deal more than a moment's inattention, at least to hear O'Hagan tell it. Yet it is an everyday occurrence. People go missing all the time – because they want to, or see no other way than to do so, or in consequence of circumstances they cannot control. And having done so, and knowing very well where they are themselves, they are nonetheless lost to others, and are missed. Some of them. In such cases there is no let-up in the paperwork. No sooner is one documentary life given the slip than a second starts up: police reports, briefings, photographs, sightings, case reviews. Another small maelstrom of paperwork, not leading anywhere this time, but circling around the who-you-were and the where-you-were-last-seen. Public attention is sometimes enlisted; the missing may be advertised and in a very few cases the circumstances of their disappearance and the search to find them, become news. Missing ads are a regular item in the back pages of the UK street newspaper *The Big Issue*, posted by the charity *Missing People* (formerly the *National Missing Persons Helpline*). South Wales police receive as many as two thousand reports of missing people every year. Only a handful become major enquiries, though each has the potential to do so, at the outset. The Association of Chief Police Officers (ACPO) defines a missing person as follows: 'Anyone whose whereabouts is unknown, whatever the circumstances of disappearance. They will be considered missing until located and their well-being or otherwise established'.[3]

3. The definition appears on the same page as this stark counsel: 'IF IN DOUBT, THINK MURDER'. (See the *National Policing Improvement Agency Guidance on the Management, Recording and Investigation of Missing Persons 2010*, produced on behalf of ACPO.)

And the search can grow cold, can take years and lead nowhere; in such cases that second documentary life, having first grown fat, thins out again, as a diminished record of continued absence.

Fade away

Not everyone who goes missing is found again. What is more, not everyone who goes missing is even missed. Some absences go unreported; some people disappear without anyone having noticed. These are the unmissed, for whom that second documentary life never begins. Some may be missing from this life altogether, gone for good. Others are missing in the sense of having drifted, or been driven, to the very perimeter of what it means to belong as a member of society; they are missing, then, not in the sense of being looked for but in the sense of being (almost) out of range, of our sympathy and understanding. Here is another way in which to be lost; neither looked for nor unsure of one's location, but past caring.

Among those who might be described this way are the rough-sleeping homeless, particularly the 'entrenched' or 'hard-to-reach' street homeless, as they are sometimes called. More than any other set of individuals in the city, these very few can seem truly lost, in the sense of having lost one's way *in life*. More than that, they sometimes seem to stand for that condition. Cardiff has its share, like any other city; they tend to keep to themselves, but are nonetheless there, never too far away from the middle of things. I have already introduced a few. Gary is another, a familiar figure in the city centre, but profoundly odd and uncommunicative: gaunt, obsessive, unkempt, hurrying about on fugitive errands behind a battered supermarket trolley brimming with lumpy bags and assorted rubbish; he looks like nothing so much as a scarecrow version of a council street cleaner, picking up after the rest of us, heaping together the things that others have dropped or discarded. He 'sleeps' in the bushes by the side of the A470 close to Cardiff Castle where he has assembled an elaborate shelter of scrap and plastic sheeting.

Is Gary past caring? This is the question – the asking of it – that ties him to the city, as removed and unreachable as his life might otherwise appear. He is certainly not going anywhere, or doesn't appear to be; I have never known him leave the same square mile of territory, and if he is lost in some sense of the word – isolated, withdrawn – he is also very much at home on the street, having made this his territory for close to ten years. His relationship to the physical city, its walls, crossings, corners, doorways, is intimate. Sat in the bushes, plastered with street dirt and the residue of exhaust fumes, and with his daily catch of urban detritus assembled around him, he is *of* the city.

Gary is generally unreceptive to any effort made to communicate with him; offers to help, attempts to find out what his problem is, or might be, are typically ignored. Others of the city's homeless are different. Some pester for attention and count on passers-by as a source of occasional income. Four hundred yards along from Gary's encampment in the bushes, the A470 turns right past the main entrance to Cardiff Castle. Here you can sometimes find Yaro, sitting on the pavement, asking for small change. He has a missing foot, and when he begs he usually sits on the ground with the stump of his leg stretched out in front of him. Yaro has not been around as long as Gary, he arrived in Cardiff only two or three years ago; but the scene could be much older and anywhere else. For Peter Ackroyd, London's biographer, the dispossessed 'have always been part of the texture of the city' (2001: 599). But at the same time outside the mainstream of life and missing from view:

> ... the rejected and discarded ... fade into the streets. They fade because nobody sees them. There are certain busy places of London, like the forecourt of Charing Cross Station, where lines of people queue for soup from a Salvation Army mobile canteen; but for the crowds hurrying past them, it is as if they were not there at all ... unacknowledged, unregarded ... these dispossessed people gradually lose all contact with the external world. (2001: 617)[4]

Whatever else they may lose, it seems unlikely that the street homeless 'lose all contact with the external world' in anything other than a literary sense. The external world is something they are hard up against and experience as rather more sharp and unforgiving than do the rest of us.

---

4. The unnoticed and vagrant poor also feature in Ackroyd's fiction, notably his novel *Hawksmoor*. Here a group of street drinkers have found space of their own – 'lost space' in the language of city planning – amidst other cast off bits and pieces: '... a corner of some derelict ground, where unwanted objects from the city had over the years been deposited: broken bottles ... crab grass and different varieties of tall ragweed ... abandoned or burnt-out cars ... rotting mattresses' (1993: 68).

Yet the structure of thought runs very deep: difference accumulating to a tipping point past which one sort of reality slips over into another; and anxious, sometimes intense, feelings about those in the process of crossing over, sometimes visible sometimes not.

Hidden homeless

How else are the homeless lost or missing? Campaigning organisations in the UK sometimes refer to a 'hidden' homeless population omitted from the headline homelessness statistics. These missing thousands are those who have no home of their own to speak of, but do not match the categories of need required to qualify for the main homelessness duty owed by local authorities. They are hidden in the sense that their needs are kept from public attention: 'out of sight in hostels and refuges, bed and breakfasts, squats, unsatisfactory or overcrowded accommodation and on the floors or sofas of friends and families'.[5] A report commissioned by CRISIS, the UK charity for single homeless people, describes this population as 'rendered invisible by their housing situations' (Reeve and Batty, 2011: 7). One could say of some of these hidden homeless that they have been tidied away, like litter: 'an infrastructure of poor-quality and sometimes unprofessional shelters and hostels, usually in the marginal spaces of the city ... [provides] the necessary containers into which homeless people can be swept up' (Cloke et al., 2010: 10). Others have gone to ground on their own initiative and are not to be found. Still others are hidden in open view, as it were, out on the street where nobody sees them.

City streets are one sort of place you might go if you didn't want to be found or wanted people to leave you alone; this might be true of some streets more than others, but in a more general sense it applies to any street in any city. To see another's need is to care to do so, and if the rejected and discarded fade into the city streets, as Ackroyd has it, then this is because such care is absent there; passers-by in the middle of a city are mostly strangers to each other and expect to stay that way. Yet there is a sense in which Cardiff's streets – city streets and busy enough with people going about their own business, largely indifferent to those others

---

5.   See www.crisis.org.uk/pages/about-hidden-homelessness.html [accessed May 2011]; also CRISIS, *Policy Briefing: Introduction to Homelessness & Housing* (2010: 1).

around them – do not lack care. Not the streets themselves. They matter very much and are mostly well looked after, certainly so in the middle of the city where the look of things is nowadays considered essential to the city's success as a retail and tourist destination. Like streets everywhere, they are walked all over, but they are also swept clean and washed down several times a day; if they get knocked about or damaged they are soon repaired, and their layout and appearance is subject to regular appraisals aimed at identifying 'enhancement' opportunities. Several such opportunities can be found in the *Cardiff City Centre Public Realm Manual* (Cardiff Council, 2009).[6] This official publication has little to say about homelessness directly, but a lot to say about clutter and dirt and the ways in which these ought to be handled and, where possible, designed out of the environment. Lost property gets no mention but legibility does: directional fingerposts and tourist information panels are specified as part of an 'overarching way-finding strategy ... with clear linkages to surrounding areas and attractions' (2009: 65). No one need lose their way. Obstructions to pedestrian movement are frowned upon; such '[r]edundant and superfluous items ... create unnecessary clutter in the street and detract from the overall quality of the public realm' and once identified 'should be removed as soon as possible' (2009: 84). Any aspect of design that might trap rubbish or dirt, or that cannot stand up to robust cleaning, is discouraged. The one mention the *Cardiff City Centre Public Realm Manual* does make of homelessness is in relation to the design of street furniture: materials selected for the construction of public seating 'should complement and enhance the character of the street', the seats themselves should be robust, weatherproof and easy to maintain, and the '[p]revention of ... rough sleeping should be integral to the design' (2009: 46). The kindness of strangers, with which I began this chapter, falters here.[7]

---

6. See p. 9, footnote.
7. If a well-cared-for street, kept clean and safe (see Minton, 2009: 44–53), is less than kind to those in need – is cruelly attentive, prickling against the presence of rough sleepers, say – then certain needs may well go missing. In meeting those needs somewhere else, providing care in hostels and daycentres away from the showcased public realm, those voluntary and charitable organisations that make up a large part of the homeless provision in any UK city are perhaps implicated in a process they might otherwise oppose: the withdrawal of rights to the city from those that need it most. Paul Cloke, Jon May and Sarah Johnsen set out this general argument, from a critical distance, in their book *Swept Up Lives? Re-envisioning the Homeless City* (2010, see esp. pp. 1–12). They refer to 'a series

The term 'hidden homelessness' covers more than one way in which we might miss something about what it means to be homeless. The hidden homeless lack entitlement to housing provision and may not 'count' as homeless at all, depending, among other things, on the circumstances in which they left or lost their previous accommodation. They are persons unknown and their numbers are hard to gauge. They may have needs which keep them from accessing even non-statutory provision, or the provision may be full, or they may not know it is there – or, having stayed a night or two, they may have decided to sleep out instead (which would be to make yourself 'intentionally homeless'). They may have non-housing needs similarly missed and unmet, because homeless – which they aren't, officially. The detrimental consequences of hidden homelessness, according to CRISIS, include criminalisation, exploitation, risks to personal safety, health impacts and resort to desperate measures including sex work (Reeve and Batty, 2011: 3–4). At least some of these consequences could be avoided were it not for a baseline scarcity of provision, limited knowledge about entitlement, low expectations among at least some of the hidden homeless and 'inadequate signposting' (Reeve and Batty, 2011: 51); in the absence of which, some people get lost, or stuck, or both.

Litter and missing persons; mislaid possessions; swept-up lives. What I am turning over here are some of the ways in which things and people can get lost in the city, and what happens when they do. There are

---

of attempts by scholars in North America to use homelessness as *the* exemplar of how urban policy from the later twentieth century onwards has willfully marginalized the visible poor' (2010: 3; italics in original). This is the new revanchism; a deliberate hostility taking the place of benign neglect, the homeless driven back by an advancing frontier of gentrification, punitive measures securing 'the requirements of free-flowing commerce and the political and cultural aesthetics of new urban lifestyles' (2010: 5). Kindness has no place in the revanchist thesis as anything much more than a sentimental response, taking some of the sharper edges off the injustices it thereby legitimates. *Swept Up Lives?* is intended as a counter to the revanchist orthodoxy, on at least three scores; the book's authors maintain that revanchist accounts have nothing to say about attempts by the homeless to negotiate and resist regulation, that they generalise too readily and are not sensitive to variations in national and local context, and that the construal of caring and welfare provision as liberal indulgence and legitimation is two-dimensional. Cloke et al. insist on a 'messy middle ground: romanticized, yet often in practice deeply unromantic; easily dismissed as merely upholding the status quo, yet powered by an urge to do something about the injustice of that status quo; a cog in the revanchist engine, yet engineered and operated by people for whom revenge is the last thing on their mind' (2010: 11).

three points I want to distil from the catalogue of circumstances and eventualities I have worked through. The first is that the city presents a particular sort of environment in which to lose things and get lost or go missing; cities afford absence and disposal and cancellation. This goes with the territory; it happens all the time. Secondly, there is a geography of loss in the city. Litter and belongings can be dropped anywhere, but their distribution is not uniform: it is lumpy. Things (and people) that nobody wants or cares to keep, tend to get left in some places in the city rather more than they do in others. Or they make their own way there, wherever it was they first went missing. Up close, this geography is a matter of particular places, of which particular accounts can be given; but the bigger picture is one in which the middle of things in the city – the city centre – seems to exert a more general pull. My third point bears on ways of seeing. However intricate and extensive the urban environment, we are all capable of looking for something we have lost in the city. To do so is to look around – so as to *see*. Ordinarily, not having lost anything or anyone, or at least not aware of having done so, we move around the city *not* seeing. Doing so helps to dampen down some of the general unease and agitation of city life. Cities are sometimes organised – and maintained – so as to keep us from looking too closely.

And then there are the homeless. Whether fading from view on the city streets, or discordantly visible in made-over urban spaces, the homeless experience all sorts of neglect and inattention. They may be unmissed, no longer looked for and long-since given up on; they may not know, themselves, just where they are – if seriously unwell, or dis-orientated. Others may not care to see them and may not much like the look of them when they do. They may be hidden, 'invisible' even, as CRISIS has it; they may have the look of being lost.[8]

---

8. I am thinking about a certain category of homelessness here, not a legislative one exactly. UK legislation defines homelessness in relation to a person's access to secure accommodation and a great many more people experiencing housing difficulties would count as homeless in this essential and important sense than would fit my description of Gary's lived circumstance, for example. Gary corresponds to a cultural type as much as to any bureaucratic one. So too Gerald; so too Wayne with his can of lager and dog (see pp. 16–17). These are the street homeless. They are so simply recognisable as such that it can be hard to get past the type and see the actual person – another way in which the homeless are sometimes hidden. In the language of UK policy the label that comes closest is probably Multiple Exclusion Homelessness (MEH), which refers to those at the sharpest

Cardiff Central

I have already mentioned the particular concentration of services for the collection of lost property in and around Cardiff's Central Square; lots of things get lost or dropped here, so there are services to match, *in situ*. Some of what gets left on Central Square simply isn't wanted and has been discarded rather than misplaced. This is waste, rather than lost property – tickets, receipts, cigarette stubs, chewing gum, newspapers, paper cups and drink cans. Some of it is placed in the bins provided, but quite a lot is thrown away. Early each morning, Central Square gets a special brush-up with a mechanised sweeper, and throughout the rest of the day cleaning crews patrol the area on foot, emptying the bins and sweeping and scraping the pavements. What is being managed here is litter, but also first impressions. Each year, thousands of visitors to the city get their first proper look at Cardiff on arrival in Central Square. Accordingly, those with a stake in its maintenance and development aim for the square to be as safe, clean and welcoming as possible, particularly to newcomers.

Throughout the years I have known it (and still at the time of writing, if only just), Central Square has been a grubby, ordinary sort of place, however; and perhaps, as such, something of a let-down. Stepping out through the doors of the train station ticket hall and into the city what you actually get is a 'rather tired looking and overcrowded' space dominated by the central bus station (Thomas, 2003: 40) and ringed by low-prestige office buildings and a collection of newsagents, sandwich bars and charity shops. The impression is underwhelming: run down

---

end of homelessness, whose accommodation difficulties come mixed up with other severe disadvantages and exclusions:

> People have experienced MEH if they have been '*homeless*' (including experience of temporary/unsuitable accommodation as well as sleeping rough) *and* have also experienced one or more of the following other domains of 'deep social exclusion': '*institutional care*' (prison, local authority care, mental health hospitals or wards); '*substance misuse*' (drug, alcohol, solvent or gas misuse); or participation in 'street culture activities' (begging, street drinking, 'survival' shoplifting or sex work). (Fitzpatrick, et al., 2012: 1; italics in original)

To be this sort of homeless is to lack or have lost quite probably a number of things, more than just a place of one's own. Some might be said to have lost their way, in life – or their self-respect, or their grip on reality, or their looks, or any interest in making any sort of change.

and a little dirty, and that is just the surroundings. Here is Peter Finch, Cardiff poet and literary entrepreneur, on the local occupants:

> On a good day, in steady rain, the mix of destitutes, winos, kids on dope, red-faced vagrants and tattooed, tin-whistled, be-dogged Big Issue sellers could not make a better entrée. Thank you, mate, have a nice day. Right here, where transport, toilet, burger house and porno-rich news-stand meet, Wales raises its flag ... not a glorious place. (2003: 88)

A composite portrait, and not entirely fair – but telling. It is taken from Finch's book *Real Cardiff*, a subversive, insider's guide to the city, full of this sort of 'rueful self-recognition' (Herzfeld, 1997: 4) of grubbiness and shortcomings.

City visitors, city offices

Perhaps Central Square is not Cardiff at its best. But there are good things just around the corner: award-winning hotels and luxury apartments; the Millennium Stadium (a national and international sports venue); the city's 'historic' Victorian and Edwardian shopping arcades; the Cardiff International Arena (an events and exhibition centre); parks and gardens, pedestrianised streets and a so-called café quarter; and the St David's shopping centre, recently extended as part of a massive, retail-led, regeneration programme representing £675m of investment across 967,500 sq ft of land in the centre of the city. Much of the fieldwork on which this book draws was undertaken in the years leading up to, and then during, the great bout of demolition and construction that brought this programme to completion. Now realised, the St David's development – branded St David's 2 – is a consumer spectacle, set in a landscaped public realm – new paving, seating, lighting, public art – 'anchored' by a four-storey department store and topped with 304 luxury apartments: 'high above the lively bustle of daily life in one of Europe's top capital cities'.[9]

9.　This description is taken from the St David's website (www.stdavidscardiff.com), which provides a range of information about the centre and its related projects. Under the heading *Security, First Aid and Cleaning* it has this to say: 'From the minute you walk through

It is easy enough to get lost here too. Maybe not up on the roof of St David's 2, but down below, amidst the reconfigured retail space. And easier still if you are not so new in town. Which might seem odd. Most of the time, not knowing where you are results from having only just arrived. But it can also work the other way around. A newly regenerated cityscape can be most confusing for those already there, who already know – or knew – their way around, for whom the amended layout and surrogate landmarks take some getting used to. New arrivals suffer no such double vision. The city is fresh to them. They may not know their way around, but then they knew that to begin with; they haven't had their knowledge usurped. And help is at hand, at least for visitors.

Cardiff is variously provided to enable new arrivals to sample its attractions. Street signs point the way to different locations, city-centre maps dispensed from vending machines feature retail outlets and sites of historic interest, and during the summer months badged and tabarded guides are on hand to offer assistance and directions to (almost) anyone who looks lost. I have already mentioned the Tourist Information Centre, five minutes' walk from Central Square. The location and premises are prestigious: a grade-II-listed building in the heart of the city's redeveloped public realm. Stone steps and a mobility ramp lead up from the street, through plate-glass frontage into a foyer, beyond which is a brightly lit, open-plan office. Inside, the walls are decked out with Welsh-themed memorabilia and a number of brightly coloured leaflets advertising local attractions, and things to do and places to stay – quality graded from one star ('simple, practical no frills') to five stars ('exceptional, with a degree of luxury').

But not everyone who is new to the city, or who needs help with somewhere to stay in the centre of Cardiff, calls here for the help they need. Some call instead at the office of Cardiff's City Centre Team, or at any rate come to the attention of that team (which distributes its own staff around the city centre, and not only in the summer months). You would not find this office on most maps of Cardiff's city centre, certainly not on any tourist map; not that it is hidden away or at the outskirts of

---

our doors there will be people on hand and a range of services available to you to make sure your day at St. David's is enjoyable and hassle-free. Our cleaners are continuously on-hand to ensure the centre is kept pristine … we have a large team of security guards on patrol, a 24-hour CCTV system and fully trained first-aiders ready to help when needed.'

the city – it is right in the middle of things too, on the second floor of an office building on Central Square, the view from which is not quite that promised prospective residents of the St David's 2 apartments. Of course, views of the city depend to some extent on who is doing the looking, and in this case that would be Steve Hyde, manager of the City Centre Team, looking out and down at the bus station:

> If you think about the city centre – and it is a busy space, Tom – there are some people there who are more or less invisible. You see them all the time but you might not notice them. In some ways it's like they don't belong. But they do. They do belong there. In fact they're there all the time, more than anyone really. It's a bit like they're ghosts. They're there, but you might not see them. Really, though, it's more like everyone else that's a ghost. Everyone else – ordinary people, going to work and shopping and going home again, and tourists, or whatever – they're like a blur really. It's like if you took a film and speeded it up, those are the people that would disappear: they're the ghosts. The ones you're left with, the ones who aren't moving and are there all the time, those are the people we work with. It's like there's two city centres really. Only one of them is hidden away a bit.

A team manager with vision then, not that these aren't also familiar representations of urban life and space. Steve's ghosts are the homeless, and his account of Central Square a match for Ackroyd's Charing Cross.

Marland House

Steve keeps his office window closed, to shut out the city dirt and the noise of the traffic; but his door is usually open, and gives on to a large, open-plan workplace across the floor of which a dozen or so desks are variously organised into twos and threes – little constellations of task and function huddled back-to-back or at right angles – under a suspended ceiling and fluorescent strip lighting. This is the main office of the City Centre Team (CCT), second floor, Marland House, Central Square, Cardiff. A line of windows along the nearside wall gives a widescreen version of the view from Steve's office. Against the far wall there is a row of tables piled with clothes and bags, tins of food and box files, above which, pinned to the wall, are three, large, intricately coloured charts showing the chequered accommodation histories of over forty clients. A door at the rear leads on to a short corridor and two smaller, nondescript meeting rooms. One or two desks are empty, but most are clearly in use, if not presently occupied – loaded with forms and loose-leaf paperwork, computer screens and keyboards, pens, pencils, ornaments, photos, mugs. At work, at several of the desks, are members of the team.

And what does it do exactly, this team? The CCT looks out for vulnerable people in the middle of the city, the sort of people that drift onto Central Square and seem to get stuck there. It does so as a multi-disciplinary team of just over a dozen health, social care and social service professionals. The figure is inexact because that is the way of things with the CCT. Notwithstanding service reorganisations (the repeated need for which seems almost a matter of policy with the local authority), the CCT has a tendency to shift and spread itself about. Workers from related projects in the wider social care field are variously adopted and found space in the office for a few weeks or months to work on some shared initiative. CCT staff in turn are seconded elsewhere, or divide their time between Marland House and a desk in some other location. Grant funding, secured in partnership, brings in a new face for six months, three days a week. Student social workers on placement come and go. And the result is that the team never looks the same from one year to the next and seldom quite the same for two months together. Even so it is still a team and for the purposes of this book its core and mainstay can be described as follows: three social workers of assorted seniority and specialism (including mental health); an NHS nurse funded to work specifically with the homeless; four outreach workers; the manager of the Bus Project (of which more to follow); the co-ordinator of the 'StreetLife' project (of which more to follow) and an associated, part-time case-worker; and two administrative assistants. Among these core staff members are some who have been with the team since it was founded and for more than ten years.

Potential clients of the City Centre Team are those whose behaviour, addictions, health needs, housing needs, financial, family and other cir-cumstances have brought them into some sort of a relationship with the city centre; people who have come unstuck there. This includes street drinkers, beggars, sex workers, heroin addicts and, more than any other group, the homeless; those who might seem adrift in the city were they not so stubbornly fixed in place; those who don't belong on Central Square, but are there all the time.

The essential and most general aims of the City Centre Team are to promote wellbeing and independence and to foster social inclusion; these are its service ideals. To which all that need be added for now is that the gap between service ideals and prevailing circumstances can be a wide one and tends to be so in welfare and public service agencies, what Michael Lipsky (1980) calls street-level bureaucracies. For the moment, however, we are up above street level. And members of the team, ranged across various desks, are hard at work. Doing what, exactly? Their clients are not here right now, and in fact seldom come up to the second floor at all. Not a few are banned from even entering the building. Unlike the Tourist Information Centre, which is *there* for visitors, the CCT office is more a backstage setting, visitors – clients, that is – are not expected. But this does not make it a haven of quiet administration. The telephone sees to that. If the question is what are people doing up here, the answer is that a good part of the time they are talking on the phone – to clients, care workers, third parties, the police. The main office phone rings pretty much nonstop on busy days, and is hardly ever silent for ten minutes together unless someone actually takes it off the hook. Incoming calls are distributed around the room according to specialism and availability. There is a phone on each desk and the sound of the team at work, the soundtrack to any given day, mingled in with the tappity-tap clatter of computer keyboards, is of handsets being lifted and put down again, and of calls in progress: a hubbub of professional concern and flak catching, one (end of a) conversation cutting across the next as you move from one end of the room to the other:

'Let me do some ringing round, and I'll call you back. [...] Not if he's got a dog, no. They won't take dogs –'

'He's not actually in the office this afternoon. [...] No, that's fine. [...] Yes, only there's been a bit of a development since I spoke to you last –'

'I think I know who you mean, but not that name? Does he sometimes go by Ryan? [...] Red hair. As in dyed red? [...] Right. [...] No. [...] Yeah. [...] Are you sure his name's not Ryan? Girlfriend with her arm in a sling? No? [...] I'll pop downstairs now and take a look –'

'Yes, it's here in the office. We found it this morning. [...] Yes, definitely his. [...] Is he sober? [...] Yeah, yeah. [...] Yeah, that's best. [...] Yeah. OK.

He can pick up a food parcel too. [...] Yeah, that's fine. [...] Anytime this
afternoon. [...] OK [...] Yeah. OK. Bye then. Bye –'

'Good morning, Cardiff City Centre Team. [...] Yes, that's ––– [...] Hold on,
hold on Tara. Just slow down and [...] Yes, but he's with someone right now
[...] Slow down a minute. Slow down and just let [...] OK, slow down [...]
I know. [...] I know. [...] And that's fine. We all know that. [...] Let me get a
pen. Wait there for me, my lovely. Wait there –'

Sometimes, and this is not a rare occurrence, more the sort of thing
that happens two or three times a week (perhaps two or three times in
a day if it is turning out to be one of those days), an incoming call or
enquiry trumps all others and everyone breaks off from whatever they
were doing to pool their efforts in conference: 'Hi. Sorry to interrupt,
only the police are on the phone. Donna has OD'd in the bus station
toilets. Does anyone know where they can find Jim O'Connor, only he's
bought from the same dealer this morning?' The police call a lot, and
when they do it usually means work and may mean trouble, certainly
so if there has been an 'incident' and one of the team's clients has done
something the newspapers might get hold of. On such occasions, Steve
will be called on to explain what his team already knew and could or
should have done different. Incidents are a worry to him. 'You always
think, with incidents: *I wonder if it's one of ours?*'

It helps to have a location, a base of operations from which client
cases can be handled, but members of the team are not confined to
the office, and for most of them a day spent up there – for all the work
that might get done and all the calls they might make and handle – is a
day spent 'stuck indoors' or 'catching up'. The real work is somewhere
else, out there on Central Square and around the city centre in those
places where the CCT client group tends to gather together and tuck
itself away (and those settings into which clients have been provisionally corralled – daycentres, night shelters, drop-ins, hostels). Getting out
there means leaving the office behind in more ways than one, but only
ever by the stairs.

Out to work

The only way in and out of the suite of rooms used by Steve and his team
is by a door next to the receptionist's desk. The door opens with a turn

of the handle but locks shut behind you once you step through, and can't be re-opened; to get back in you must either key in a passcode, or press the buzzer and wait for someone to identify you and open up. Stood on the small landing at the top of a stairwell, you have to your left and right two doors, one marked 'Toilets' and the other 'British Transport Police'. Moving downstairs starts you on a zig-zag first towards and then away from a large window and not much of a view: a brickwork and concrete close-up of the multi-storey car park next door. The first floor landing is larger, and likely to be busier. You can hear it coming as you move down – plaintive conversation and irritation, tired chat. Here are the offices of the Legal Services Commission, the local authority Departments of Housing and Homelessness and Advisory Services for Rent, Council Tax and Benefits; street-level bureaucracies every one. In a waiting area off to the right a dozen or so people are sat or slouched along a line of plastic seats bolted to the floor under an electronic display; others stand around, agitated, irritated, bored. To the left, a wall-mounted phone in the lobby of the Housing Advice Unit links directly to the CCT office. Descending again, two more flights of stairs brings you to the ground floor. Turning left here you pass a uniformed security guard cum commissionaire sat at a desk and step through a set of double doors out onto Central Square.

Members of the CCT make this journey every day, shouldering their way in through the doors and up the stairs to the office in the morning and then back down again and out at the end of the day. In between times they make any number of other trips to other parts of the building: down one flight to the Housing Advice Unit to help unravel a complex case; across the landing to confer with the Transport Police; all the way down to the lobby to hear out an irate petitioner refused further admission because drunk. They also leave the building, making their way across the city to attend meetings elsewhere – case conferences, briefings, reviews. But the real work takes place in person, with clients; one-to-one contact with those the team is there to help. This is frontline work and in its own way, for all that it takes place out there in the city and mostly out of doors, it is not always so easy to see.[10]

---

10.   Others have remarked on the unobserved character of social work more generally, describing this as an 'invisible trade' (Pithouse, 1998), in part because social work visits take place in the privacy of people's own homes. This does not hold for the CCT, whose clients are homeless. Encounters between CCT workers and clients are typically more exposed, but can still go unremarked. Two people sat in close conversation on a public bench.

Some of these encounters serve their own purpose: a social worker arranges to meet an elderly client outside the emergency accommodation unit where he spent last night (early morning, hoping to catch him sober), to conduct a needs assessment; the CCT nurse calls on a young couple in a tent by the river to change the dressing on a wound. Others are contributory: workers delivering forms that need signing, or medication that needs taking (and was left at the police station last night). And then there are encounters with no further purpose than that of simply meeting up to see how someone is getting on. Jeff, a CCT outreach worker, leaves the office for lunch at 1pm promising to be back in an hour or so: 'I'm just going to get a sandwich and take a nose down by Penarth Road, where Warren was last night; I promised I'd look in on him.' No more than that, and when he gets there Warren is gone, just a sodden blanket and some empty drinks cans and other litter. Meanwhile Jeff's co-worker Charlie is at her desk, looking out onto Central Square: 'Is that Andy Watkins down there making all that noise? It is, you know. I'm just going to go and have a word, before he gets himself arrested.' All of which has CCT workers up and down the stairs and criss-crossing the city throughout the day (and night, they work out of hours as well as out of doors), looking after, looking out for, accompanying and keeping an eye on things and people. They get about, and expect to; they expect to *have to*, given the nature of the client group.

When Jeff sets off along Penarth Road to see Warren, that is where he (knows he) is going and who he (knows he) is going to meet. Warren is even expecting him – or was supposed to be. But what about Jim O'Connor, homeless like Warren only out there somewhere with a bad batch of heroin and unaware that anyone is even looking for him? He is missing then, not to hand – a known unknown, to borrow a phrase; and needs to be found. The same goes for most CCT clients: they are at large, not reliably anywhere in particular though seldom too far from the middle of things; and they must be found before anything (else) can be done. Any missing thing or person is a known unknown in this sense. But alongside these there are also unknown unknowns: the ones the CCT has not yet met, but which its workers might very well turn up while looking for someone else; people going nowhere in the middle of

---

Who would notice? Perhaps passers-by might take an interest if one party to the conversation was visibly distressed. But they might just as well look the other way.

the city, who seem like they might need help, or are in some other way identifiable as 'one of ours'.

Listing the membership of the CCT earlier, I mentioned four outreach workers. Nicy is another of these – was one of these, when the following took place: an unknown unknown encountered, under the eaves of Marland House in the early morning; not office work at all.

Outreach: Central Square, 7am, heavy rain. Nicy and I are on the Breakfast Run.[11] Nicy parks her car in front of the train station and we take a walk through the ticket hall and back out again. Across the square we can see a group of drinkers sat under the concrete awning at the corner of Marland House and we walk over to say hello. There are three sat down around a couple of bottles of cider and a packet of tobacco, and one standing, wearing a construction worker's high-vis jacket. Standing to one side, hunched up and pinched looking, is a woman dressed for late last night rather than early this morning – a denim jacket and tracksuit top, jeans rolled up to her calves, no socks, and white trainers (bloodied at the heels). The drinkers are keeping dry, but the woman is wet through – she is drinking too, though not cider; she holds a half-empty, half bottle of brandy. The man in the high-vis jacket acts as broker. 'This is the City Centre Team,' he explains. 'They'll look after you.' He turns to Nicy. 'We don't know who she is,' he says. 'She just turned up. She says she's lost, and she's scared of something.'

'What are you scared of,' asks Nicy, turning to the woman.

'I'm scared,' she wails, screwing up her face. She staggers to one side, coming up hard against the wall. 'Don't get the police,' she says. 'I've been walking all night.' She starts to cry.

'I'm not going to phone the police,' says Nicy. 'Listen, my name's Nicy. What's your name?'

'Her name's Cindy,' says the man in the jacket. He only has half a head of hair, the other half is gnarled and taut, scarred; it looks like he's been in a fire. 'This is the City Centre Team,' he says. 'They'll help you. You can trust them. It's not the same as the police.'

'Don't phone the police,' says Cindy, pleading.

Nicy is stood by her now, holding her up by the elbow. 'What's happened Cindy?' she asks. 'You're soaking wet. You're all wet through. Listen, my

---

11. The Breakfast Run is an early morning patrol of the city centre undertaken by the CCT, working together with staff and volunteers from The Wallich, a homelessness charity which runs a number of hostels around the city and a night shelter project. The service was established in 1998 (by The Wallich) and targets rough sleepers, providing information and advice along with hot drinks and something to eat; it operates 365 days a year and stops and sees to anything from one or two to twenty (or more) of Cardiff's street homeless each morning.

name's Nicy and I'm here to help. I can help you if you tell me a little bit about what's wrong.'

'Don't phone the police.'

'I won't phone the police.'

'You don't even know me,' says Cindy, suddenly aggressive. 'You don't know nothing about me.'

'I know, Cindy,' say Nicy. 'And that's OK. I want to help. Why don't you tell me something. We need to get you somewhere warm. If you can tell me something I can help you.'

'Please help me,' says Cindy, her face screwing up. 'Pleeeassssss …' She is sobbing now.

This continues for some time, five or ten minutes, with Cindy pleading, suspicious and insistent by turns. She is barely coherent, with drink and distress. The men ignore her, pouring cider carefully into polystyrene cups on the pavement and rolling cigarettes.

Cindy doesn't trust the police, that much is clear. She says they had her in handcuffs yesterday and holds out her hands and wrists as proof of injury. 'Look at that,' she says. But her wrists are unmarked.

After five more minutes of this the man in the fluorescent jacket wanders off – to work, he says. I leave Nicy to it, not wanting to crowd Cindy, and squat down on the pavement to talk to Rolly, one of the three drinkers. There is no need for Rolly to be out so early as he isn't sleeping rough at the moment; he has been in the night shelter for a couple of weeks now. Even so, he is up and away at first light most mornings to start his drinking. Today he made his way to Central Square under shelter of a blanket, smuggled from his room and since discarded, sopping wet. Rolly likes his cider brown not white, which is what the others are drinking – White Lightning.[12] Another man turns up briefly and sits hunched up with his back to the wall grimacing and telling anyone who asks that his ulcer is playing up.

Nicy breaks off from talking to Cindy, and gestures furtively to me to keep her talking while she makes a couple of calls on her phone – one to the night shelter, the other to Steve. Cindy thinks Nicy may be phoning the police and is getting jittery. Nicy comes off the phone and tries to persuade Cindy to let us drive her to the night shelter, to get dry and have a sit down. She asks Rolly if he might come along, in case Cindy is worried some sort of trick is being pulled on her. Cindy is not buying it. 'You're phoning the police. Don't phone the police!' There is a chorus of reassurance from the drinkers, cut with a little irritation now.

Half an hour on from when we first arrived, Cindy finally agrees to come over to Nicy's car, still parked outside the station: not to go anywhere, just

---

12. A brand of strong white cider, sold in three-litre plastic bottles for under £3; one of a number of cheap, strong ciders popularly associated with underage drinking, anti-social behaviour and homelessness.

to sit down. We walk over together, Nicy, Cindy and me. I leave the two of them to talk. Ten minutes later, Nicy waves at me to get in. We are going to find a toilet because Cindy needs to go. Nicy hands me Cindy's half bottle of brandy and her sodden pack of cigarettes, which she has had off her and which I now pocket. A short drive and we are outside the night shelter, only now Cindy won't get out. Nicy cajoles and coaxes but Cindy, very drunk, is stubborn. She switches between what have become familiar refrains. 'You don't even know me,' she says. 'I'm sorry, I'm soaking wet.' And then, 'Oh my God, I need to wee.'

Nicy gets out and opens the car door for Cindy, but Cindy has taken against the night shelter and won't budge. Nicy reaches inside but then jumps back, her forearm scratched. The situation is frustrating, but getting to be a little funny too: the tables have been turned and Cindy is sort of in control. Back on Central Square we could have (eventually) walked away from her, but not now that she is in the car. We are stuck with her. Nicy holds up her hands, laughing. She starts the car up again and off we go, back to Central Square. 'A nice lie down on the sofa at Marland House,' says Nicy. 'Get you out of those wet clothes.' Cindy has her forehead pressed against the window. 'Oh my God, I need to wee. Oh my God.'

We circle Central Square and turn into the Wood Street car park, where Nicy parks up between a concrete pillar and a rank of cars, manoeuvring backwards and forwards to try and make a little more space on Cindy's side so that we can help her out. Nicy has been on the phone to the office again, who are now expecting us. 'Here we are Cindy,' announces Nicy. 'Let's get to the toilet now, and then that sofa.' Whereupon Cindy catches us both by surprise, swinging her door suddenly open and crashing it into the adjacent car. Nicy winces. The flanking car has a nasty mark down its side. Nicy's patience is being tested, and Cindy is now not sure she wants to be here either and is, again, refusing to budge. We try for about ten minutes, first Nicy then me, standing between the two cars, leaning into the back seat tugging and cajoling: Cindy will not move. She seems, if anything, more drunk than she was an hour ago, and is shivering now. 'No,' she says. 'No.'

Nicy changes tack and gets firm, telling Cindy that this is enough and that she is going to have to help us if she wants us to help her.

'That's enough now Cindy. We need you to come inside. Out you come.'

'No.'

'Yes. Let's go to the toilet – now, Cindy.'

'No.'

'Cindy, listen to me now. You're making this very difficult. You've damaged this car next to us and I haven't got all day. I'm trying to help you. Get out of the car. Come on. Now.'

'I'm sorry.' Cindy screws up her face and looks ready to cry.

'Never mind sorry. Let's get you indoors, somewhere warm.'

'No. You don't even know me. You don't know nothing about me'

'Inside, Cindy.

Silence.

We are at something of an impasse, and it is dawning on Nicy that she may end up doing exactly what Cindy has asked her not to do and what she has as good as promised not to do: phone the police. We can't forcibly remove Cindy from the car. Nicy even tries explaining this to Cindy, but to no avail.

I stay with Cindy while Nicy goes off to Marland House to speak with Steve, and, from there, to call the police for some help in at least getting Cindy from the car to the office.

Suddenly, Cindy gets out, staggers then straightens herself, wriggles her jeans down around her ankles and squats. When she stands again she is unable to get her jeans up, sodden wet as they are. She is wearing no underwear and has already taken off her denim jacket and trainers – these are in the car. So she is now wearing, in total, a tracksuit top (half undone and bikini top under that) and jeans pulled up to her knees. I persuade her to get back into the car. Just where we didn't want her to be five minutes ago. Nicy comes back and we drive to the exit ramp where Steve is waiting with a police officer. Nicy has a further word with Steve who is minded not to have Cindy come up to the office at all. She is too drunk, and now half naked; it is unlikely to work. Steve thinks we won't even get past the com-missionaire. The police can take her into a cell for a while, to sober up, which may be best, but the officer tells us he will have to arrest her. Nicy says we are running out of options really. 'That's why I wanted to get her to the night shelter,' she explains to Steve. 'Get her away from the drinkers. Get a coffee down her. Get a bit of story.'

The police officer wants to know if she is likely to come quietly; he has a van parked round the corner. Nicy walks back to the car to take a look in at Cindy. She is asleep. Can we help lift her, the police officer wants to know. Well, yes, perhaps; it depends. The officer thinks it best to get a colleague along to help out. He will be five minutes, he says, though this turns out to be more like twenty-five, during which time various members of the City Centre Team walk past on their way into work. Two of the social workers stop to see if they can't identify Cindy. No luck. Rosie the nurse gets in beside Cindy and sits her up from her slumped position and checks her breathing. We are just waiting now, for the police.

The police are back, two of them this time. Both officers walk over to the car with Nicy, leaving me with the keys to their van. I open the rear doors and wait. A couple of minutes later they reappear, one either side of Cindy, supporting her by the elbows; she is wrapped in a blanket, looking very bedraggled. With very little protest she (sort of) walks over to the van – half carried, in truth. 'Well done. Big step up now,' says one of the officers. 'We're going to take you down to the station to sleep it off for a couple of hours and then these nice people from the City Centre Team are going to come and take care of you.' And in she goes. The door slams shut and only then, having been almost unresponsive up to that point, does she howl 'No-oooooo'.

No one knows who Cindy is – somebody must, but not on this particular morning, in the middle of the city; she has no account to give of how she came to be here, not one she is prepared to share; she has simply appeared, or rather ended up, come to rest, by the side of Marland House, in the rain; she has made a few friends, though barely that – drinkers (she doesn't really know them, and they don't know her); she is in distress, and wet and cold. And then there is Nicy, here to help though she wasn't looking for Cindy until she found her. Quite possibly Cindy is at the ragged end of a long night out that went a little wrong, no more than that. Nicy suspects there is rather more to it, but never gets close on this occasion. Nor does the City Centre Team see Cindy again – which it surely would if it had turned out that Cindy was in the sort of continuing difficulties that would put her here again, and again – as happens with a shifting handful of others already known to the team. Others the team never sees again include those whose difficulties take some final and decisive turn – Rolly's collapse, one month after the events described, and admission to hospital, followed by surgery and hospice care. In the meantime, and between these two ends of a spectrum of need and attention, there are those whom the City Centre Team and its outreach workers in particular are tasked to locate and reach out to, repeatedly. Given which, a walk through Central Square in the early morning is routine for Nicy and her colleagues. Central Square is always worth a look. You never know what you might find – which, for an outreach worker, is another way of saying that you probably do. Cindy was no surprise.

3

First Aid

Whatever wider arrangements and formal provision exist for the sweeping up, handing in, recording and storage and eventual collection, or disposal, of lost property, there is always a first moment when something (or someone) is found, at which time it may be possible to do something, there and then, to put things right, without any further trouble. Excuse me, did you just drop this? Are you lost? Has anybody seen ...? Immediate assistance, *in situ*, can spare everyone a whole round of administrative process.

Where does this leave outreach work and the sorts of encounter and intervention we see Nicy caught up in at the end of the last chapter? 'What's happened Cindy?' says Nicy. 'You're soaking wet. You're all wet through. Listen, my name's Nicy and I'm here to help.' Yet there is a sense in which she never really gets started. The whole episode ends too soon and badly, or at any rate not as Nicy wants it to end (certainly not as Cindy wants it to end), and the CCT never sees or hears from Cindy again. It is hard to see that anyone has been helped much at all. Nicy and her colleagues would much rather their efforts with people like Cindy, people in difficulties on the city streets, led somewhere. Not that botched and thwarted attempts to make a difference aren't part of the fabric of the work. Even so, the aim is always to try and see to it that people get the help they need. This comes close to being a definition of outreach, certainly one that the CCT would recognise and sanction: helping people who need help (and can't seem to get it themselves) get the help they need. But helping people get help is not quite, not always, the same as simply helping. The sorts of help that some people seem to need go well beyond anything Nicy can offer herself, directly, stood on the pavement outside Marland House at half past seven in the morning. For which there are wider arrangements and configurations of provision, just as for lost property or litter. There is the local hospital and other general practice and specialist health services, the Housing Department, the Community

Addictions Unit (CAU), the local authority social services, the Salvation Army and other providers of housing and social care, JobCentre Plus, the Citizens Advice Bureau. It is an outreach worker's job, having seen the need in the first place, to then make arrangements and put things in train, to fix up assessments and make referrals and appointments, to see to it that people get the help they seem to need. In this sense outreach workers are gatekeepers, guides too, steering uncertain clients towards and then through the rounds of administrative process required to make things better.

But the work is something else as well, or rather something else to begin with. It starts out, and starts again, each morning, as a job that gets done there and then. This chapter is about that first moment when something or someone is found, at which time it may be possible to make things better, if only a little better and temporarily. As such, it develops the description of outreach work begun in the last chapter. First aid is help given to begin with, before anyone else arrives and other – specialist and professional – services are called upon or become available. Assistance then, from those first on the scene. And before that, even – before the offer of assistance – injury.

Somebody in boots

Outreach workers wear boots, mostly – they are certainly supposed to – to protect their feet not only from the mileage they can expect to cover each week but also from the sorts of exposure and injury they are likely to run into given the particular work that they do and where that takes them. In this, they share ground with the city's street cleaners, for whom injuries to hands, feet, shins, knees, backs, shoulders and heads are an occupational hazard, part of the daily toll the job takes. For an outreach worker, however, injuries are not only what they must guard against but also what they are looking out for; outreach workers cast about for those who look like they might be in need or difficulty. Street cleaners don't do this; they are not there to help (others), they are there to sweep up. Even so, their work involves an eye if not for people then for places that seem out of sorts, in poor shape or condition and in need of attention.

Cleaning: Mid-morning, mid-week, central Cardiff; bright and sunny, but cold; November. Terry is pushing his two-bin truck out of Millicent Street, ready to set out on his cleaning rounds. I'm out with him this morning, the same as yesterday except that this time Terry is determined I should get my hands dirty, if only figuratively speaking. I have been issued with a standard high-vis vest and safety gloves. 'He's got to learn,' he tells his supervisor. 'He's got to learn the job for hisself. If he's going to teach the students, he's got to have done it hisself. Hasn't he? Course he does. So I got him the gloves, and now he's doing the work. Learning, see?'

Terry has his own gloves and is otherwise kitted out to keep insulated – from the cold and wet (though there is no rain today) and from all manner of knocks and scrapes. His boots have a grippy sole and steel toecaps; reinforced patches run the length of the front of his work trousers. He spends a good part of the next two hours, as we move around the city centre, talking about injuries he has suffered at work or seen happen, and the risk of injury. 'One time I had a television dropped on me, from up there' he tells me as we sweep up alongside the student accommodation block on Pellett Street. 'A 14-inch television. 14 inches. Smash.' Then there are the routine, if hidden, dangers – more routine than falling televisions – and the awareness of these that marks out what he knows about the city as different from what other people might see and think. He picks up a pile of discarded coat-hangers outside a shop, gleefully demonstrating how the metal hook, torn away from the plastic arms, can be clenched between the middle fingers of a fist, point outwards, and used as a weapon. He feints at me, going for my neck. 'Can't have those lying about. That can kill you. See? Course it can.' We find a discarded base unit for some temporary wire fencing, a concrete slab, which he hefts up onto his cart for removal: 'Saturday night that'll be through a shop window, see.'

With it being November it is not just the litter we are up against but the leaves, in fact we spend most of our time sweeping leaves. These are also 'lethal' according to Terry. By which he means not much more than that they can slip you up. He is anxious to get the busiest pavements clear before someone has a fall and 'puts in a claim'. But he only ever clears the leaves with his brush and shovel, never (as seems obvious and tempting, because so much quicker and less fuss) scooping them up with his hands. He very much wants me to ask him why, and prompts me to do so. So I do. His answer (equally obvious) is that you never know what might be mixed up with the leaves: broken glass, possibly, but also syringes – 'pins'. 'You can't be too careful, Tom, with pins.' Some of the other cleaners are always scooping the leaves up with their hands, says Terry; but he scolds them for this. 'It's not worth it. Not worth the risk. You've got to be careful.'

As a sort of variation on the theme of (the possibility of) physical injury, Terry also keeps on about how members of the public, some of them, can abuse you when you are out picking litter. 'Tell you to get lost and get out of their way. Tell you to fuck off even. That happens, yes. People call you names, see, doing a job like this.' He recounts various incidents. Not that it bothers him, he says. He is thick-skinned about it.

Outreach: Later in the week I am out in the evening with CCT outreach workers Den and Rachel. We are driving through the city's red-light areas, stopping here and there to distribute free condoms, hot drinks and health advice to sex workers – most of them, not all, already known to the team; a few of the women are part of the city's street homeless scene. Most of the women wear boots, though nothing much like the robust hiking boots that Den has on. Even so, it's work wear, and if the boots are there to draw the eye, they also protect and conceal. Bryony, who we see most nights, never works without her boots, and never takes them off when working. 'I'll take my skirt up and my knickers off,' she says, 'and my top and everything. But not my boots. So I can get away.' Bryony's friend Katie agrees. The two of them are at the back of the outreach van, drinking coffee out of polystyrene cups and rifling through the boxes of crisps and condoms on offer, filling their pockets. We are parked on East Moors Road by a warehouse unit, one mile from the city centre. 'And I can move in them too,' says Bryony. 'I'd be flat on my arse in trainers, but I can move in these. You'd never catch me. Murders your feet, mind.' Katie keeps her boots on too, and keeps more in them than just her feet. 'They can nick my bag but they're never getting my boots off me, so everything goes in there.' She shows us the money she has tucked inside, and, in the other boot, her phone. 'Safe down there. See?'

We spend ten minutes together, over coffee. Den is fishing for news and information, as are Bryony and Katie. He wants to know what they've been up to; they want to know who else we've seen tonight and where. There have been developments in the case of a woman assaulted last week, just around the corner from where we are standing, and we all talk about this for a while; Katie thinks she might know the attacker. Bryony asks if she can have a cigarette and if someone will give her a ring tomorrow morning to help her with a letter she has had from the courts. Den takes down her number. I hand out two panic alarms (we have a box of about 40, available to anyone that wants one). Katie sets hers off by accident, then, flustered – panicked – drops it. We scrabble around on the floor trying to fish it out from under the van where it has rolled, all apart from Katie who is moving awkwardly and can't crouch down: she has a large abscess on her thigh, drained now and under wraps but she pulls back the bandage to show us. After five more minutes in conversation we say goodbye; Bryony and Katie are wanting to get back to work. 'Be safe,' says Den. We drive around the corner and park up again to fill in forms recording who we have seen and where, along with other relevant details: Bryony's letter from the courts, Katie's abscess, a list of things they took away with them (hot drinks, food, condoms, panic alarms, also two pairs of gloves from a large bag of woollen goods - hats, scarves, gloves, mittens - donated by local church volunteers). Rachel is our driver tonight and has stayed behind the wheel throughout. She was not supposed to be on duty at all and has come out at short notice after a day spent on a training course. She is dressed more for the office than for outreach, and Den has been teasing her about this, like she is a little too fancy to do the real work. 'Next stop,' he says, 'get out there and do some outreach.' Rachel joins in the joke: 'In these shoes? I don't think so.'

There are all sorts of hints and signals that outreach workers are sensitive to and keep an eye out for as they move around the city; the same is true of street cleaners. Just the way some people look, the way they come across, can tell an outreach worker if not everything they need to know then enough to be going on with. Which is to say that first impressions count, for something, whoever you are and whoever or whatever you might be looking at or out for.

One seeming advantage when looking out for people, rather than litter or leaves, is that people can talk; they can call you over and tell you what's wrong and what they want doing. Anyone in a mess can say so. But not everyone does. Some need persuading to see things quite that way, need persuading that mess, or difficulty, is the right word for whatever it is they are in; some don't know how to ask, or are wary of doing so, or have simply stopped caring one way or the other and don't want to talk to anyone. This is at least one of the reasons why impressions matter in the way that they do, for outreach workers. No one has to say anything, not out loud, not if they don't want to. You can just tell.

But just what it is you can just tell rather depends on the impression given out, or the impression given off; and these two are not the same. Impressions given out are intended, and some such impressions are as good as saying so.[1] Stood by the side of East Moors Road at night, Bryony and Katie are giving out – broadcasting – an impression. They don't have to say anything about what they are up to, because anyone who wants to know can *see*: two young women selling sex, dressed and stood in ways calculated to invite the sorts of attention required,

---

1. Goffman (1990; originally 1959) remarks on the gleaning of clues from conduct and appearance and the promissory character of expressions given and given off, in the introduction to *The Presentation of Self in Everyday Life*. I borrow from him here, and subsequently.

advertising themselves, or a vision or version of themselves. Impressions given off, rather than given out, are not intended. Those giving off such impressions may be aware that they are 'leaking' information in this way, or aware at least of the possibility; and they may do all they can to stop that from happening, to seal the leak. Or the impression given off may be wholly inadvertent, easy enough to see but broadcast unawares. And the two may go together, giving off and giving out.[2]

The impressions to which CCT outreach workers are most keenly attuned are impressions of vulnerability, confusion, illness, injury and damage; especially those given off as opposed to given out. From each of these – impressions given off, impressions given out – they form a judgement as to what it is they are looking at and who needs their help, or might be persuaded that they do. A person's appearance, bearing, dress, behaviour and location are aggregated into a sort of balance sheet and best guess: 'I think we should go over and have a word. Don't you?' Sometimes a single indication is sufficient – soiled trousers or some visible injury (a black eye is a black eye after all, no best guess required). Even so, every indication has its context, its landscape, so to speak. Not everyone with a black eye – not everyone on crutches, or falling over drunk, or walking barefoot in the city centre – is likely to be a person of concern to the CCT outreach team for any more than a passing moment. But if injury or seeming ill-health are not in themselves decisive, they nonetheless count for something. The city's street homeless in particular, almost all of them, look generally knocked about and are as likely as not to carry some visible injury.

Injured and unwell

Very few people sleeping rough in the centre of Cardiff are in rude good health. Most could do with some sort of medical attention, and some need such attention directly. Physical injuries are commonplace, so too illness and infection: coughs, colds, sprains, cuts, tooth decay, runny noses, fat lips, fungal infections, sores, bruising, scalding, rashes, abscesses, fractures, burns, grazes, inflammation. So commonplace are

---

2.   Katie can give off the impression of being someone rather anxious, unhappy and unwell, even as she works hard to give out the impression of being easy and available and up for fun.

these, in fact, that they pass without comment: *everyone* looks a little battered and run down, or feverish. I can't remember the last time I had a black eye, but on any given CCT outreach shift you are as likely to see one as not.

Of the little injuries, the knocks and bangs, many are incidental. If you live and sleep on the streets, you will get worn and scuffed a little. This is the jar and scrape of city life. Not what Nigel Thrift intends, though (see Chapter 1). Strangers may rub us up the wrong way sometimes, but the city can do that too, all on its own. Concrete, steel and glass are sharp and hard materials and make for an unyielding environment. You can get stiff and sore just sitting down for an hour, never mind the trips and falls. Some urban design features even accentuate the potential for discomfort, in an attempt to discourage 'unintended' use and occupancy. Elsewhere, in such of those out-of-the-way corners and patches of neglected ground as remain around the centre of the city, other hazards (barbed wire, rusted cans, broken glass) snag and scratch. Feet come in for a lot of punishment.

Beyond the collateral damage of urban homelessness, the wear and tear and indiscriminate discomfort, there are the injuries actually intended, and inflicted. The prospect of violence is something all rough sleepers live with, around the clock; they *know* violence; the threat of it and the experience and effects of it mark and colour their days, and their bodies. The know it because of where, and who, they are: on the street and in obvious difficulties, with no other means to look after themselves and nowhere else to go. The thing about the street is that people can get to you out there – every rough sleeper knows this; intermittent abuse and intimidation from passers-by is to be expected, particularly late at night. Sleeping on the streets makes you more vulnerable still (which is another reason for not sleeping much at all if you can help it). Those of Cardiff's street homeless who do look to get their heads down for a few hours overnight tend to hide themselves away from the busier streets and the clubs and bars and partygoers. Some find solitary corners, concealed from view; others congregate together, aiming for safety in numbers. Even so, incidents of violence and unpleasantness from members of the public are familiar enough. Everyone knows the risks, and no one sleeps all that soundly.

Yet unpleasantness, and worse, from passers-by is considerably less than the half of it. Most of the routine violence and damage done to the homeless on the streets of Cardiff is done by the homeless themselves. Cardiff's street and homeless 'scene' has a vicious seam running through it that may or may not have all that much to do with a generalised urban misanthropy but certainly owes a good deal to the particular confinement, frustration, aggravation, tedium and incessant petty irritation that come with being down and out in the city. (Confinement may seem like an odd word to use, but it is appropriate: street homelessness is a cramped and claustrophobic experience, limited to a narrow and over-familiar geography of streets and settings and local services from which most of Cardiff's homeless seldom stray. The days are similarly cramped and stale, and the company. Everyone knows everybody else before too long if not already, and anyone wanting to keep to themselves has a job on their hands to do so. Almost all of the work of outreach takes place within ten minutes' walk of the CCT office on Central Square, most of it within five minutes'; this in a city that covers 30 square miles.) To be homeless and on the streets in central Cardiff is to take one's place in a crucible of rumour and circling accusation: insults (real and imagined), betrayals, reprisals, grudges, rivalries, petty quarrels over next to nothing, all of this and more whipped up by the day's contingent dramas – money gone missing, confrontations with authority, the (seeming) caprice of welfare bureaucracies – and, in some cases, a good deal of drink, not to mention the chronic lack of sleep. The result is a daily tally of push and shove, fights and beatings. Most of these are minor scuffles, over in a minute or two and forgotten by the end of the day, everyone friends again, or claiming to be so. Sometimes, however, the violence is shocking, or sustained over days and weeks of bullying and intimidation. The worst, most memorable – harrowing – incidents make up a sort of local lore rehearsed by outreach workers and passed along to new recruits. Tales of the field – grisly, comic, instructive, unlikely – provide a repertoire of pooled experience. They also put individual outreach workers in their place, as a measure of time served.

Still other injuries are self-inflicted, sometimes with intent as part of an unhappy pattern of practice the successive history of which can be traced over wrists and forearms. Yet most of those who hurt themselves do so without having really meant to or thought about it much, having simply lashed out in a moment's anger or frustration.

Outreach: A very wet afternoon, atrocious weather; gusting wind and repeated heavy downpours have all but cleared the streets. I am on my way in to the city centre to join Charlie for the evening's outreach patrol. The rain has been so heavy I have phoned ahead just to see if she isn't going to cancel (at its very worst it has been hard to imagine actually walking around for more than a few minutes in anything other than oilskins). We agree to meet outside Marland House at 5.55pm.

I find Charlie in animated conversation with a client, a number of whom are grouped – sat, hunched, prone, propped – just outside the main entrance to Marland House and along the covered walkway through to the Wood Street car park. Everyone is damp at best, if not sodden, and the pavement and walkway are puddled with water; but the rain has stopped, for the moment.

Charlie catches my eye at once and it is clear from her look that it has been one of those days. The young woman in conversation with Charlie is much the worse for wear and complaining about her hand, which she has up under Charlie's nose. As near as I can make out she has just woken up – she is making a big noise about this in particular – and the others (unspecified) just started in on her, having a go. All of which seems to have led to her injury, her hand bloodied, and swollen across the back and knuckles. Charlie is trying to be sympathetic and offers a trip to the hospital to get the hand looked at; the offer is mostly a gambit, I'd guess, an attempt to call the young woman's bluff (as she doesn't really look like she is going anywhere, or wants to). It's one of those conversations that just goes in a loop: 'I'd only just woke up – they woke me up. Ow, fucking hell, my hand. I was asleep, see, then they just started in on me. And I'd only just woke up. Look at that, look at my hand. I was asleep, wasn't I. I can't feel anything in those fingers. Fuckers. I'd only just woke up and they started in on me ...' Another (older) woman detaches herself from the crowd sheltering in the walkway and joins the conversation. She seems belligerent at first, though soon enough just scolding and even empathetic. The younger woman complains to her: 'Why'd you start in on me? I'd only just woke up. Now look at my fucking hand'. The older woman tells her to come back over to the others:

'We've all done that, haven't we. Punched a wall. She punched a wall, see. That'll be alright, that.'

'No but look at my fucking hand'

'Punched the wall, see. Did she tell you that was how she done it?'

'I was asleep, I was. Why'd they want to fucking start in on me?'

'Do you want to come with us and get it looked at then?' asks Charlie.

'My fucking hand – look at that, look at the knuckles.'

'She punched a wall, see. We've all done that. Silly cow.'

On and on it goes, going nowhere. Set down as dialogue it is almost comic, and scenes like this *are* comic, sometimes (and not only for the observer); but the atmosphere today, this afternoon, is not at all droll. Charlie looks fraught and the knot of clients gathered and milling outside Marland House are giving off all the wrong vibes. There is an edge to it all. Charlie looks keen to get away and soon enough disentangles herself and walks off, signalling with a turn of her head that I should follow along. We walk down to the outreach van, parked in the usual spot by Kentucky Fried Chicken.

Climbing into the front of the van we sit for five minutes while Charlie explains what is going on. It has been a difficult day, all fights and threats and nonsense. The weather has not helped, bunching people together in bits of available shelter, or driving them indoors into day-centres and drop-ins to get on each other's nerves, and everybody's gear getting wet and them getting pissed off about it. There have been arguments and fights and will almost certainly be more. Although the weather hasn't helped, the problems have also had to do with the mix of people 'around' at the moment. Charlie is keen to get some outreach done, but we will have to be careful, she says, as there are a number of individuals 'out' right now who are considered a danger. So rather than walk, we are going to drive about a bit to begin with, and the first port of call will be the Bus Project, or rather the museum steps, because the Bus is cancelled tonight.[3] Charlie wants to get over to there to let anyone waiting know that there will be no drop-in service tonight. The supposedly dangerous individuals are Jason Law (been a pain all day, drunk and looking for a fight), Swansea Nick (same as always), Stuart Payne (who has a grudge against Charlie and has made threats), and a guy whose name no one is too sure of but who used to be around a couple of years ago and had a big 'husky' kind of dog and is back now, without the dog, more than likely wearing a high-vis

---

3. Cardiff bus station is central to the daily lives of a great many of the city's homeless, located as it is on Central Square in amidst so much of everything else that goes on; *the Bus* is no part of the city's transport system, but is, if anything, more central still. The Bus Project, as it is properly known, *is* actually a bus (a double decker) but doesn't cost anything to board and doesn't actually go anywhere, at least not with any passengers. It spends most of every day stationed at a depot on Sloper Road a mile from the city centre along with other out-of-service buses, doing nothing; but in the early evenings it is collected and driven directly to the city centre (without stopping or picking up) and parked up outside the National Museum. Once there, it stands still for a couple of hours, filling with people then emptying out, before being driven off again (empty) to Sloper Road. In the interim, 'passengers' will have been provided with subsidised food and drink, somewhere warm and dry to sit and access to a range of other services as required: advocacy, medical support, needle exchange, chaplaincy and referral to emergency accommodation projects. The Bus is a drop-in facility then, converted to meet the needs of the city's rough sleeping homeless – a basic kitchen and social space downstairs, storage and meeting rooms upstairs; it was established in 2002 with financial support from the Welsh Assembly Government and was managed and staffed by the CCT and Salvation Army together during the time I knew it best.

vest – unstable and paranoid he is, says Charlie, and if he is anywhere to be seen when we drive to the museum steps then we will not even be getting out of the van, if she recognises him, that is (it was easier when he had the dog). Excepting the man without the dog, no one of these characters is necessarily a particular risk, though they are all 'difficult' clients; what has made things dangerous is the close configuration of these few, all out (there somewhere) on this particular day, when so many other tempers are frayed already, when everyone is wet and when it looks like it will pour down with rain in another minute. So, we'll do the (cancelled) Bus Project and then have a look about for an hour or so, on foot if that seems sensible, and then drive over to the soup run. That's the plan.

While Charlie is telling me all this the young woman with the bad hand turns up again and runs through much the same routine as before, through the driver's-side window. Again, Charlie offers to drive her to the hospital and, again, she says no, or, rather, rambles on without seeming to really have heard the question.

First aid is something offered at the scene, of an accident or incident. The settings for outreach work are many and varied and include some rather difficult scenes, some of which pose all manner of risks of further or worsening injury. The number one rule of first aid is to protect yourself (and others) from harm and this is what outreach workers do every time they try to defuse an edgy situation, or pick their way carefully along a glass-strewn corridor in a disused building; it is what Charlie is doing when she retreats back to the van and wonders just how safe it might be to get out again.

CCT outreach workers only ever work in pairs and will cancel scheduled patrols if there is only one worker on duty and available. This is a safety measure too, having someone there to back you up (some of Charlie's uncertainty in the passage above follows from the two of us having bent this rule a little, with me making up the numbers, not strictly speaking an outreach worker at all but someone who has shared and observed the team's work over a number of years). Patrol involves exposure – half of the whole point of outreach patrol is to make yourself available – with which comes risk; the other half is investigation and enquiry – nosing about, looking around. Working in pairs helps with each of these aspects of outreach patrol. A team of two makes things a little safer, and two heads are generally better than one when it comes to looking around. In most cases these two aspects combine. Walking through the city centre at night outreach workers can cover both sides of the street; pausing for a moment, one worker can duck down under some netting, or straddle a low wall, while the other keeps watch. Together at the soup run, one worker can monitor the immediate crowd while the other looks into the distance to see who is or might be coming. Seeing to the needs and vulnerabilities of some clients can mean getting very close to that vulnerability oneself and in a sense sharing it, if only briefly; which an outreach worker can only do in safety if they know someone else is looking out for them. Early in the morning on Central Square, Charlie finds a man lying curled on his side on the concrete floor at the end of an aisle in the bus station; he is fully dressed, it seems, his trainers and the hem of his tracksuit bottoms uncovered, the rest of him draped in a sleeping bag. She moves towards him carefully and asks if he is OK. No response. She asks again, and crouches down next to him. Is he breathing? 'You OK?' asks Charlie. She touches his shoulder. Nothing. She reaches for a bag placed on the floor behind her and extracts a flask of tea and a hot bacon roll wrapped in tin foil. She is down on one knee, keeping a polystyrene cup steady on the ground with the pressure of one finger on the rim; in her other hand is the flask, from which she pours. All her attention is on the man on the ground in front of her – she has eyes only for him; she cannot see anything else crouched down as she is here at the end of the aisle, cannot all that easily back away or wheel around. The man takes a deep breath and stirs. And all the while Jeff is there, a little distance away so as not to cramp Charlie or crowd the man on the floor. Half his attention is on the scene in front of him, the rest is distributed elsewhere, up and down the aisle, alert to possible intrusion. He is there to handle *anything else* while Charlie gives (all) her attention to the man on the floor. He is ready to step closer too, if Charlie needs help. The same, essential vignette is enacted several times each working day and might stand for homeless outreach: three figures, one stood, one crouched, one lying down.

Scenes of difficulty

There is more to say about the scenes at which outreach workers find themselves and to which their work responds. Scenes are settings. The scene of an accident is the physical location and surrounds that position and frame some collision, mishap or injury. Scenes are the places in which action is carried on and in which people play their parts; the word can also refer to the action itself, to some particular episode or complication of events (forming the subject of a narrative). In a still wider sense scene denotes a realm of activity, circumstance, way of life even. This wider sense applies to the work of outreach just as much as the narrower meanings of the word. Charlie and Jeff and the man on the floor, gathered together at the end of an aisle in the bus station on Central Square might constitute a scene, but when Charlie asks him – as she does, moments later – who he is and how he has come to be here this morning and is told that he has been kicked out of the Salvation Army hostel and was staying, until last night, with Andy Watkins and Inky at their new place on Cyfarthfa Street she will have a developing sense that she is dealing with someone not so very new on the 'scene'.

What might that mean? Of course many of those sleeping rough in the middle of Cardiff know one another; they share space as well as circumstances, and they keep each other company sometimes; they share the same local network of provision – again, some of them, sometimes; they see each other every day, at the soup run, at the Bus Project, outside JobCentre Plus, on Central Square. And in sharing all of this they join together in a loose arrangement of familiars. Some stick together around the clock, working (at being homeless) in tandem or larger groups, the same way and for some of the same reasons that outreach workers do. Shifting configurations of friendship, alliance, romantic attachment and also grudge and enmity, pattern the 'scene' and most outreach workers have a confident knowledge of these configurations, of past complications, of established pairings, of recent fallings out and more besides, all of which they bring to any encounter – all of which they employ in seeking out encounters in the first place. Setting out from Marland House to look for a particular client – Malcolm – due to appear in court that day and more than likely needing to be reminded to do so, CCT outreach workers don't cast about aimlessly. They know where Malcolm will have woken up because they saw him bedded down there late last night, they know where he is likely to have spent the early morning because Malcolm has his routines, and they know who he has buddied up with over the last few days – with Wayne and Jackie, both of whom have fallen out with Buster and so won't be anywhere near the station forecourt (where Buster and his crowd have taken to starting their drinking day). Knowing all this, they can place Malcolm with some confidence, because they know where he fits in the wider scene as it is likely arranged this particular morning.

Nor is this just a matter of places and people. The homeless scene has its patterns of practice too, some of which coalesce into scenes within scenes, interior fractions of the whole homeless picture. The 'alkies', the street drinkers, are a definite faction; the 'druggies' too; then there is the younger, rowdier crowd with their dogs, in and out of the hostels; then, over the summer, the encampment of tents and sleeping bags down by the park.

Sometimes all it takes is for a very few individuals to find a corner of the city somewhere, undisturbed for a few days and nights together and there you have it, another 'scene', a little crew of temporary friends making the rounds together, pooling resources, dispersing on various errands then re-assembling back at base: an empty office building on Bridge Street, scheduled for demolition. These shifting collections of three or four or five can be defining for as long as they last. Outreach workers 'discover' the office encampment and take to calling daily, their own practice re-shaped to match the new location and the work occasioned; others call in and pass through as word gets around that Bridge Street is where the action is; the wider homeless scene reorganises and adjusts accordingly, then settles to this new configuration; once-established coalitions shift and regroup. And then, as suddenly as it appeared, Bridge Street is over. One of the regulars gets arrested and taken out of circulation, or someone gets a backdated social security payment and makes themselves scarce; two friends fall out, another moves in, and things just aren't the same.

Knowing who's who out there, for an outreach worker, means knowing Cardiff's street and homeless scene, the smaller component scenes it comprises, the groups and collections, all the way down to the ones and twos. That way you can place a person, make sense of where they are at, what they are up to, where they might be found this morning. And if the smaller scenes come and go then the same holds true for at least some of the individuals that constitute them. People drop in and out of circulation just as the scenes they inhabit wax and then wane; each instability accentuates the other. Some of those that outreach workers take a hand in helping never really become CCT clients at all; they are simply not around, not 'out' or about, not part of any scene, for long enough to start to figure in that way. Others are very well known and have histories as CCT clients that straddle months and years even, and a succession of scenes. Maureen has been known to the team since she first started showing up at the fringe of the homeless scene as a teenager, still in local authority care at that time but frequently absconding and reported as missing. She would sleep out on the steps of the Cardiff International Arena with her then boyfriend Jason. There was a year or more when everyone was terribly worried about Maureen and there were case reviews and numerous attempted social work interventions. Then she got a place of her own and seemed to settle. Then six months later she started showing up in the sort of place and at the sort of time (of night), and with the sort of people – the wrong sort – that had outreach workers wondering if she might be selling sex. Then it seemed she definitely was. Then there were a few months in which she was just everywhere, out of control, her drug use excessive, staying out, sleeping out, overdosing, 'working', robbing punters, starting fights. CCT outreach workers saw her almost every day and spent a lot of time chasing around and mopping up after her. In the end they managed to get her into the night shelter (her flat was long gone) and onto a methadone prescription, then into a hostel. Another period of relative calm. Then she went to prison. Six months later she was back, homeless again. Five years later, at the time of writing, Maureen is living in a shared house ten minutes' walk from Central Square. Not so much of a druggie these days but a heavy drinker, and associated with that crowd, though not closely. She still 'works' sometimes to make a little money if she is short, but she is not really *out* much, not on the scene (plenty of those who are, and are taking up most of the CCT's time these days don't even know who Maureen is). She has some serious health problems that the team continue to help her with – managing appointments, accompanying her to treatment sometimes – even though she is housed and hardly their priority any more (she has a social worker who visits occasionally and a support worker associated with the property in which she lives). Dennis has known her for over ten years, since he first met her at Grassroots, Cardiff's city centre youth project and drop-in.

In the patrol logs used to note the names and number of clients seen in the course of a day's work, workers also record any further particulars relevant to the work they have done or begun. This is what Dennis and Rachel do when they park up around the corner from Bryony and Katie (see pp. 52–3). The log they fill in features two rows of tick-boxes used to record services dispensed (food, hot drink, condoms, panic alarm, information and advice leaflets[4]) and clients' needs or problems (drugs, alcohol, accommodation, health, domestic abuse, assault). Beneath this is a free text space in which to jot down further information. This is where Bryony's letter from the courts gets noted, along with other relevant details gleaned, anything that might go towards a fuller knowledge of a client's circumstances. With Bryony there is always something. Yet, knowing her as they do, and for such a long time – she has not been around as long as Maureen, but has been 'working' for at least three years – the team seldom note all that much anymore. Significant details, novel developments, yes (though even these are familiar enough – the court summons might be recent, but it is hardly unexpected); but nothing much new about Bryony herself. She is so very well known to the team already, what could a short written note really add?

When there really is nothing to note that everyone doesn't already know, rather than leave the space blank (which might look remiss) workers tend to scribble down 'known to team', as a sort of shorthand. 'Known to team' means nothing new, business as usual. Were this someone else though, someone new to the team, the note would be fuller, if only in its statement of just how much there is that isn't yet established. Something like this:

Says her name is Julie (?). Didn't push for surname. Seemed nervous. Definitely young, under 25. Short fair hair, ears pierced, tattoo on side of neck. Dark skirt and boots, denim jacket, white shoulder bag. Living in Splott with boyfriend. Drops her off most evenings – not tonight. Didn't get his name. Will try next time. Both on methadone script (check this?). Originally from Bridgend. Mentioned something about hospital tests coming up but didn't say what for then blanked me. Explained to her about the van and said we'd see her again. Gave her StreetLife number to ring. Said she might call tomorrow.

---

4.   The theme for this chapter is injury (and assistance). I have stepped to one side of that theme in order to work through the idea of street and homeless scenes, but the leaflets routinely distributed to sex workers bring illness and injury back into focus. More than one leaflet contains general information and guidance about sexual health. Others list contact details for different support lines and agencies, including, prominently, the Sexual Assault Referral Centre. There is also a leaflet titled *Ugly Mug Newsletter*, which is used to circulate recent information about attacks on women in the Cardiff area.

As and when Julie is next seen, and the time after that, and the time after that, little pieces of the bigger picture will be gathered up and appended to the record – age, address (plus fragments of her previous accommodation history), boyfriend's name, health problems and hospital appointments, upcoming court appearances, family background, social worker's contact details, the fines she has to pay. More and more added in over the coming weeks and months until knowing Julie (whose name turns out to be Rebecca) reaches some sort of tipping point past which what seems worth writing down begins to diminish. Now less and less. And then, short of anything particularly new and noteworthy, nothing much at all, just a scribbled note that reads 'known to team'. Those known to the team, about whom there is little more to note or say, for now, are important to outreach. They provide a measure of the team's understanding and abilities and a validation of its continuing activity, but also a challenge to its proper remit and purpose.

There is some overlap between the street sex work and homelessness scenes, as might be expected. Most of Cardiff's street sex workers are precariously housed, staying with friends who may or may not have space for too much longer (and may not even be friends by then, if they ever were to begin with) or, if in a place of their own, then not too very far away from losing or leaving it. Some have a talent for this sort of insecurity and manage to keep indoors one way or another without ever really settling anywhere; the most chaotic don't always know, early evening, where they will be sleeping later that same night – if they sleep at all. But they find somewhere. Others don't, and don't expect to; they are sleeping out, very seldom alone, more often part of some little scene that involves a boyfriend.

Then there are the hostels. These are their own scene, and more. When outreach workers hear that a client they haven't seen for a while has 'got in somewhere' they will take this to mean into a hostel rather than anywhere else – a homeless hostel, that is. And they may well leave it at that, pleased enough that what used to be their problem is now (mostly) someone else's, maybe even not so much of a problem anymore. These two possibilities are distinct. For some of those coming in off the streets, hostels provide a way in which to leave homelessness behind. This might seem something to be accomplished at a stroke. One night you are sleeping rough, the next you are in a hostel, no longer homeless. Booking in somewhere certainly gets you a bed indoors, but just as important is a process of estrangement, distancing oneself from the scene (the connections and familiars, the habits, schedules and practices), keeping quiet and staying in until whatever it might have meant to be homeless the way you once were has moved on without you. This movement away from the street by degrees can be confirmed as a sequence of steps from one type of accommodation to the next: a night on the floor in the emergency cold weather shelter, six weeks in a bed at the night shelter, six months in a room of your own in a medium-stay hostel offering key-work support in preparation for 'resettlement', and on to a more or less permanent tenancy in a shared house with continuing support from off-site staff. At the same time there will be others taking these same steps but in the opposite direction, on their way down through a sequence of ever more precarious and undesirable housing options – thrown out of their flat (drugs), evicted from a hostel (non-payment of service charge), banned from the night shelter (fighting), too drunk to make it to the cold weather shelter one night, and then the next, and then definitively 'out', on the street (where CCT outreach then finds them).

The point is that hostels are where the homeless come from just as much as they are somewhere you might go to be something other than homeless. When outreach workers come across someone new, sleeping rough, not known to the team at all or at least not recognised (pending further enquiries, which may reveal they've known them all along), an early question asked is likely to be something along the lines of 'Where were you last night then?' And it will come as no big surprise to be told 'In the night shelter. I was kicked out, wasn't I?' Which is something to be going on with, though not good news necessarily. Those not yet known to the team are, some of them, already very well known to workers in the night shelter and local hostels, and not welcome back.

Outreach: Early January, Breakfast Run. We are a team of four today, two outreach workers and myself accompanied by Dan, a support worker from the Big Issue office who has asked to tag along. We have worked our way around Central Square, Bute Park, Mary Ann Street and the Cardiff International Arena, and are now on Crwys Road with Andy Saville who is complaining, as he always does (between mouthfuls of egg and bacon roll), that nobody helps him. He says he wants to get in to a hostel, but that (unspecified) others have been allowed to 'jump the queue' and get in ahead of him; it is a 'proper' hostel place he wants, he won't consider the night shelter – he has his standards, he tells us. Yesterday he lost his temper and 'kicked off' in the Housing Advice Unit at Marland House, which led to him being forcibly removed and barred. 'How does that help anyone?' he asks. 'All I want is a hostel place. Not in Riverside, mind you. I can't go to Riverside. Too many people know me there, and I've had trouble.' It is always the same with Andy, this mixture of grievance and demand and picky, cryptic hedging. He has been sleeping out in the same spot now for months, no further on.

Acting on a tip-off, we move further away from the city centre than usual, to look for Bobby Renton, who is said to have found a 'skipper' on Pen-y-Waun Lane, a derelict property he has been using to crash overnight (heading back in to the city centre by day to drink and make his usual rounds). We find the place, a ramshackle building tucked away behind residential properties, no doors or windows but the walls are up and the roof is still on, if patchy; the muddy yard outside is littered with debris; to the rear, a rusted yellow bulldozer is parked alongside neat stacks of new concrete blocks. We pick our way across to (what used to be) the front door and shout up the bare stairs inside. Bobby jogs down in shirt sleeves, cheery this morning and oblivious, it seems, to the bitter cold. We had heard he was in there with Beccy Law, who has been sleeping out this week following a fight with her boyfriend – a proper fight, Beccy having lost a tooth. But there is no Beccy. Instead, Bobby introduces us to Tony, whom none of us recognise and is new to the Cardiff scene he tells us (he looks the part though, in his forties probably but seeming older, bearded, a battered hat pulled down over his ears, the backs of his hands scabbed over, unsteady on his feet; he doesn't look like he is new to being homeless). Tony says he would like to get in somewhere, so I ring the night shelter and speak with Robbie. There is a vacancy but Robbie is being cagey:

'What's his name again?'

'Tony Adams'

'Tony Adams? Does he go by any other name?'

'Wait there, I'll check'. Tony shakes his head, puzzled. 'No, just Tony Adams.'

'Does her ever go by Tony Hitchens?'

'I don't think so, no.'

'Describe him again. What colour's his hair?

I describe Tony. There is a pause. 'What's the problem, Robbie?'

'Nothing really. It's just it's been a bit on edge here? And I know a few Tonys, see? Is he ever called Tony Warren?

In the end, stumped, Robbie sighs 'Alright yeah, refer him in. We'll give him a go. He needs to be here at eight, tonight.'

I relay all this to Tony who says yes he'll be there but doesn't know where it is. Bobby says he'll show him later. We wave goodbye and drive back in to the city centre, dropping off some housing benefit forms before returning to the night shelter. (Tony never turns up, and we never see him again.)

Living in a hostel you are a step away from being homeless, in whichever direction. Residents come and go, in from the street and out again, on to somewhere else and back; and where these two flows meet there is a sort of eddy which is the hostel scene itself, and which is not so very distinct from the homeless scene after all. The two overlap, and even reinforce each other. Getting Tony into the night shelter might have been one way for the CCT to conclude its (brief) involvement with him. But no one would have counted on it.[5]

A short stay in a hostel after time spent on the streets can be a welcome respite and change of scene. Sleeping rough can wear you down, and hostels build you up again, or may do; if you keep your head down you can recover yourself, go a bit easier on the drink perhaps, put on some weight. And you may plan to do more than that. But then the rules start to chafe, and there is the service charge to pay, and nothing much to do, and little prospect right now of moving on anywhere else; and then a little drug scene starts up down the hallway, which you would rather steer clear of, or you fall out with someone – or back in with someone else; there is some unpleasantness or other that puts you on edge.[6] And so you slip away one evening (owing money) and don't come back. Until next time.

This is really just another way of recognising a puzzle already encountered. The City Centre Team work with anyone they find on the streets in need or difficulties. This means they work with the homeless as much as anyone else. But not just the homeless. Others too. All sorts. Only, some of those others are homeless after all (because they are in a *homeless* hostel, which ought to make it clear enough, or because they are in the sorts of trouble, and have the sorts of needs, that look like what most people might call homeless, or because they are players in

---

5.   He might have become someone else's problem, might have started to put his problems behind him even, but could just as easily have used the night shelter as a more or less stable base from which to continue being homeless, spending his days drinking with Bobby, circling around the same homeless and welfare services dotted around the city centre, in and out of familiar difficulties, and soon enough as much on the CCT radar as anyone else sleeping rough.

6.   For all the good that they do, hostels can be intimidating places, sometimes violent; some of those who quit them do so because after a few days indoors they start to feel they would be safer sleeping out, less likely to incur injury. Those who stay away from hostels altogether do so for a variety of reasons but seldom fail to mention that they feel safer out of doors.

the sort of homeless-looking scene commuters might hurry past on Cardiff's Central Square). And, then, some of those who were homeless all along, sleeping rough, no bed, no roof – some of these are in the sorts of difficulty that the provision of accommodation is never going to solve, still less if the available provision is a homeless shelter. The problem with homelessness, at least as the CCT encounter it, is that it is nothing so simple as the word might imply. Depending on what you take the word to mean it isn't really homelessness at all. Turned around, the problem is that homelessness is just a word.

Sick again

Injury and assistance are the subject of this chapter. Before pausing to examine Cardiff's homeless 'scene', I had been working through the physical wear and tear that comes with time spent on the streets, the intimidation and aggression to which the homeless are sometimes subject, the violence they inflict on each other and the harm some of them do to themselves. There is more to say. Also injurious if not done simply for injury's sake, is the massive collateral suffering brought on by drink and drug addiction. Not that substance abuse is the preserve of the homeless. Drink and drugs are as much a problem indoors as out, as are all sorts of illness and injury. But brought to the street, quite possibly as precipitating 'causes' of a person's homelessness, these ailments do not go away. Addictions are harder to manage out of doors, where things are that much more desperate and futile. If you are ill on arrival, you can expect to get worse; if you are injured, you risk secondary infection; bandages will get dirty, casts will get wet, medication will get muddled and go missing. There will be no peace, no rest, and never enough sleep. (Nor are chronic ailments best managed on the street: heart conditions, incontinence, asthma, mobility problems, eczema, diabetes.)

Rather than a place of care or recovery, for rough sleepers the street is a place of aggravating circumstance and neglect, including self-neglect, one more variant of self-harm. Taking care of yourself in even those small ways that are such an ordinary part of the domestic routine – brushing teeth and washing hands, cutting nails and changing clothes – is that much more difficult to do, that much more easy to let slip. Some are heroically meticulous about these small chores, taking time and pains to keep hair washed and shoes shined, as a conspicuous display of normality under siege. Others struggle, or care less, too put upon or wrapped up in other concerns and immediate needs. A couple of weeks of this and you really start to look (and smell) homeless, irrespective of your official status and entitlement as such. Eating healthily is nobody's main concern. Nor is this going to be the best time to try and quit smoking – everybody smokes, of course; and everybody takes a good few sugars with their tea. Two sugars is nothing. You can hardly taste two. Three, five, seven even! That's more like it. No one's teeth look anything like the teeth that gleam out from the city's advertising hoardings. Toothache, which could be considered a quarter of human misery back in the days before anaesthetic dentistry (see Gray, 2007: 155) climbs back up that register again, becomes another good reason to get a drink down you first thing.

So homelessness is not good for your health. Sleeping out in the city makes you sick and wears you down and hurts you, or sees you get hurt. And of all the different sorts of damage that homelessness entails, all the unpleasantness it brings on and occasions, it is most often the physical – bodily harm, discomfort and ill health – that first and perceptibly presents itself. Physical injury is a need that can be seen, and needs seeing to, whatever else may be wrong.

All City Centre Team outreach workers are trained in first aid and carry with them a minimum of equipment to deal with injuries (as well as other minor ailments). They are not medical professionals, but they do have a sound and in some respects specialised knowledge of the sorts of damage and treatment that go together with street homelessness. They know an abscess when they see one, and an overdose; they know what to do if someone has a fit or a fall or comes off worse in a fight (they are trained in self-defence and the management of aggressive behaviour).[7] Enquiries about injuries, ill-health or treatment are part of most outreach encounters, if only as a verbal accompaniment to whatever else may be happening or getting done: 'There you go Danny, tea with three sugars. Ouch! What have you done to that finger?' Encountering a potential client for the first time, an obvious opening gambit is to ask after their

---

7. They are more than familiar with (and can roughly diagnose) a range of mental illnesses; they can identify all sorts of drugs and medication, legal and illegal, and predict their likely effects and side-effects in various combinations – anti-psychotics, valium, cocaine, subutex, methadone, temazepam, diazepam, heroin, ketamine, solvents.

health and wellbeing: 'You alright down there? Not too cold?', or 'That's a nasty scrape you've got there my friend. Can you see out of that eye?' Those already known to the team do not escape, not even the ones who are *always* carrying some or other injury: 'Oh dear! What have you done this time?'

Every answer will be a story of sorts, or might become one; and any sort of story, any background information or version of events, is grist to the outreach mill. But all such stories and answers lie the other side of this first line of concerned questioning, and it is a line an outreach worker can only cross if invited. Not everyone wants to say much, if anything at all, about what it is they have done this time, or had done to them. And whatever it is or was, they may not want anything done about it now: no fuss, no bandages, no trip to A&E in the outreach van. Well-meaning outreach enquiries are sometimes met with no more than a shrug, and in such cases workers are in no position to wring out an answer any more than to impose medical treatment. No one has asked them to take an interest in the first place. They can only nag and push; and even then only so far, before they have to let it drop, for today. Tomorrow they can try again. Indeed, workers may find themselves monitoring an illness or injury at a distance, as it were, keeping on at a reluctant client over a period of days and weeks, sometimes longer. As with so much of outreach work, this comes down to striking the right balance; a respectfully insistent asking after someone's wellbeing, not intrusive or patronising, but not prepared to let the matter drop either.

Sometimes waiting is all it takes. Sometimes things get better all on their own – infections clear up, wounds scab over (against the seeming odds, given the lived circumstances of some of the street homeless). And if not, then they get worse; and though no one wants that to happen it may at least force the issue. Past a certain point something will *have* to be done. Workers hope for the best, obviously, but can't be blamed if they also wonder, on occasion, a little guiltily, if it mightn't be just as well if things went the other way this time, precipitating the very intervention they have been working towards from the outset. A hospital admission might make so many things possible: get that leg sorted for one, but also a few days' rest, some proper sleep, some proper food, some time away from the contingencies of the street; appointments could be made, social workers involved, a needs assessment carried out. They might get a client *in* somewhere, at the end of it all.

Outreach: Early morning outreach with Rees from The Wallich. We start out at the night shelter, where we fill the boot of Rees' car with provisions: a Tupperware pot of 25 boiled eggs and the same number of hot bacon sandwiches wrapped in silver foil; two large flasks of hot water, disposable plastic cups and tea bags, instant coffee and sugar. There are three of us on the Breakfast Run this morning: Rees is in charge, and driving; I am standing in for the CCT; and Ruth is here too, a new recruit. Ruth has an administrative job at The Wallich central office, but has spent her first week in post doing the rounds of the various Wallich hostels and projects, as part of her induction; today it is her turn on the Breakfast Run.

We head off into the city. Waiting at the first set of lights, Rees briefs us on who we can expect to find out there and on developments back at the night shelter, where there is a vacancy. This is news, of a sort – the vacancy; sometimes a whole month goes by without any turnover of beds. So we may make a referral this morning, depending on who we see and what they are prepared to put up with (the night shelter is a bit grim, and known to be such).

We trace a more or less familiar circuit, parking the car up at intervals to get out and walk about and poke around; but Rees also gives this morning's route a few early flourishes, taking in one or two more of the out-of-the-way and grubbier locations than is strictly necessary, or at least typical. This is largely for Ruth's benefit, Rees performing the role of outreach worker as custodian of city secrets.

Having trawled the back lanes and impromptu rubbish tips off Tudor Street, we head over to the bus station and spend some time in and around Central Square, before heading across town to Senghenydd Road and the stairs by the Sherman Theatre. There have been reports of rough sleepers bedding down under here, but as yet no sighting by the Breakfast Run. We take our time looking around for corroboration – bottles, cans, blankets, leftovers, syringe caps and 'pins'. The area looks recently cleaned, and it may be that whoever was here, if anyone was here at all, has been moved along. Half an hour later, we arrive at the rear of the Cardiff International Arena (CIA) and step out of the car to continue on foot. Road repairs are underway and most of Mary Ann Street is mud and rubble, cordoned off by traffic cones. We split up. Rees walks around the front of the CIA with Ruth, and I go round the back; they find two sleepers in one doorway and I find none.

We head back across town to the civic centre. The disused toilet block at the rear of the National Museum is a regular stop for the Breakfast Run, and when we arrive Aiden and Paddy S. are already waiting, their sleeping bags and other gear crammed into rucksacks. Aiden takes coffees and rolls for them both, his outstretched hands inflamed and scabby; Paddy wants to know if he can have a travel warrant to go stay with his 'missus' in

Exeter;[8] sipping drinks, the two of them retreat under a nearby tree – it is really beginning to pour now. There is no one else around. The couple that were camping by the side of the toilet block last week have since moved on. Francesca and her lot, over on the Crown Court steps, 'regulars' on the Breakfast Run over the past few months, are staying put and keeping dry under the portico (we no longer 'deliver' to the steps, by agreement, having been asked by the Court not to do so). We take a cursory look around the park and trot back to the car, driving on, damp, to Queen Street and the Hayes and from there along Bute Terrace and back past the CIA and the Big Sleep hotel.

We continue on to City Road where we park up and carry hot drinks and food over to Bobby and John. These two are lying together in the same spot they have occupied for the last three nights: a corner space in the undercroft parking at the rear of an office and retail development. They look even more derelict today than usual. Both are chronic street drinkers, never at their best first thing in the morning. Bobby was hit by a car recently, a deliberate strike, says Rees. His arm was broken but is now out of plaster, though considerably earlier than it should be; his hand is still bandaged, and wrapped in a plastic carrier bag tied off at the wrist, to keep it dry. John has tipped almost a whole bottle of Dettol over his groin in an attempt to keep down a post-operative infection. He was hospitalized recently following a street fight in which he was repeatedly kicked in the testicles. He gives us a gap-toothed grin and reaches up for a mug of sweet tea with a shaking hand. The smell coming off him is strong: stale sweat and booze, disinfectant, urine. Despite the ghastly circumstances, they are both cheery and hatching plans to buy a tent and travel a bit – says Bobby; first things first, though, they are going to have to find something to drink.

Four hundred yards up City Road we make our way along back lanes again, to the Co-op car park, in one corner of which there is a shed once used to store trolleys but since fallen into disrepair and these days home to Colin. Rees is particularly keen for Ruth to meet Colin; not only is his shed fabulously squalid, but Colin is a definite 'character' and believes himself, of late, to be the son of God. Climbing over a low wall at the car park perimeter, we call out to let him know we are coming and he pops up like a jack-in-a-box from out of a tangle of plastic sheeting at the front of the shed, tugs up his trousers with one half a hand (he is missing two fingers) and hurries across the tarmac to meet us. Rees gives us both a 'here we go' look and we ready ourselves for a lively display. Colin confounds expectations. He pockets a roll, with a courteous 'thank you' and rattles on about nothing more than the weather, between sips of sugary tea. The only

---

8. The CCT can sometimes secure warrants for UK bus and rail travel for its clients, though it is cautious about doing so and doesn't generally advertise this facility; Steve signs these off, as team manager.

suggestion he might be unwell is, oddly enough, his seeming sanity. Here he is passing the time of day with us as if we were stood in the supermarket checkout queue, not out in the car park in the half-dark, him in his bare feet, standing in a puddle.

Later that morning I call in at Marland House to drop off a list of those 'seen' on the Breakfast Run (the 'count' is 17). Rosie, the nurse, is at her desk and asks me if I've seen Bobby and John. I tell her about Bobby's broken arm and his being hit by a car. Rosie says this is nonsense. John was hit by a car, but not Bobby. And Bobby's arm is not broken, although he has taken to wearing a grubby foam bandage he picked up somewhere (which Rosie made him take off when she saw him with it yesterday). He does have a nasty injury to his hand though, infected; and Rosie wants him to come in and get some antibiotics from her. Den is there too, preparing to run errands, one of which is to visit an old client in hospital. Mrs M., as she is known to the team, was street homeless and a sometime sex worker when she first came to Cardiff; she has been housed and off the team's books for a couple of years now, but they still keep an eye on her and visit when they can; she has spent the last week in hospital following a major operation. As Den and I leave the office together one of the social workers asks Den to check up on Martin Morgan, also known to the team and still very much *on* the books. Martin phoned the team yesterday from the hospital, following an emergency admission, asking for clothes to be delivered for him (like one or two others, he has a pile of kit stored with the CCT). We take a carrier bag of Martin's stuff with us.

Outside Marland House we are almost immediately accosted by a thin, skimpily dressed woman in her early 30s, brandishing a small bottle of cola and a half bottle of cheap vodka. Her name is Anna Seranno – which we knew already but she is keen to tell us anyway, and everyone passing by: 'My name is Anna Seranno and I am an alcoholic!' She offers this up as barefaced affirmation and challenge, but is met with nothing much more than startled glances and (then) averted eyes – a couple of drinkers sat on the pavement offer encouragement. Clinging on to Den, and seemingly pleased to see him, she insists that he examine her hairline where she has a bloody mark and bruise. She claims that Martin O'Riley did this – hit her with a chair. She's not bothered though, she insists, and is soon enough talking about something else. She tells Den that she has been offered a place in the Salvation Army hostel, starting next week, provided she addresses her drinking: 'I do want that. I want to cut down on the drinking. You know, be a better person. Cos I am an alcoholic. I know that. My name is Anna Seranno and I am an alcoholic.'

We drive to the hospital and to A&E to begin with to track down Martin Morgan. After some initial difficulty with names (Martin has various surnames and aliases, it seems; Den knows most of them) we are directed to a ward where we find his bed empty. He is in theatre, apparently. Den leaves the bag of clothes by his bed. We head off to visit Mrs M. She is pleased to see us, if a little frail and confused. I stay by her bed while Den walks off to have a quiet word with the nurses. He hopes they will agree to keep Mrs M. in long enough for him to stir up some sort of care package.

We never get to see Martin. He is not there the following day; and a couple of phone calls, later in the week, reveal that he has checked out or, rather, disappeared. This is no more than was expected back at Marland House; it was why Martin wanted clean clothes, after all – so he could get away and back to the street.

Nowhere in this account does a worker actually administer medical assistance. Why is that? Not because help isn't needed. John and Bobby need attention certainly, as do various others encountered (not all of whose circumstances are fully transcribed); Aiden has a nasty case of what looks like impetigo; Anna's head is cut and bruised. On another day, with a little more time to spare, and if it wasn't so wet and miserable this morning, Rees might have taken the time to break open the first-aid kit, and would certainly have done so if asked. But no one did. No one asks apart from Anna, and she does not really ask for help; she wants her injuries *seen*, not seen to – she is showing everyone. With John and Bobby it is hard to know where to start, though Rosie is on the case. And then there is Colin.

One way in which to think about any of this would be to go back to the idea of scenes. The point is that nowhere do Rees or Dennis arrive at anything so distinct and stand-alone as the 'scene' of an accident, an occasion and setting at the centre of which something has just happened – gone wrong – and someone has been hurt or cannot go on. Such incidents do occur of course, they litter most days; but the wider work of homeless outreach and the injuries and ailments to which that work is essentially addressed, those that the homeless carry around with them, are seldom so clear cut. Outreach workers do not spend their working days zipping from one incident or accident to another, responding to these as they occur and administering treatment (a remedy, even) there and then, and idling between times; their work is not best understood as responsive in that sense – triggered by incident. Certainly calls do come in to Marland House, most days, in response to which outreach workers may be dispatched here or there, to see if they can't lend a hand. But it does not take a call bringing news of some or other accident to get outreach workers going in the first place. The chances are that they are out already, casting around for difficulties and visible need. Like nurses on a ward, or street cleaners, their work is there already, and needs seeing to, but doesn't have to *happen* before anything gets done. Outreach workers monitor a rolling condition – a realm of activity, circumstance and difficulty, already well underway, a scene in *that* sense; and move accordingly, looking around and reaching out, giving notice. This makes the work an exercise in concern and attention. And if the attention paid seems cursory, then it is also worth recognising what has been accomplished. Ahead of the morning's rush hour, before the day has properly begun, an early-morning patrol has worked its way around the middle of Cardiff looking out for the homeless; a number of the city's most damaged and vulnerable inhabitants have been 'seen', their locations and circumstances noted – no one is in very good shape, but they are all there, alive if not exactly well; hot food and drink have been made available to those who want it; time has been spent – not much, but some – and there have been questions and answers, conversation, a show of concern; attention has been paid and contact established for the day. All of which has to count for something. Not much, perhaps, in the greater scheme of things; and certainly not enough. But a start. The first aid of the day, even if no one has been bandaged up as such.

Roadside repair

Whatever it is that urban outreach might accomplish in particular for an exposed and vulnerable few, acts of care and repair in general and aggregate are surely integral to city life. Cities get knocked about and need care just as much as some people do; nor can they manage very long without such attention. This is perhaps not so readily recognised. But it ought to be. If urban outreach of the sort that Rees practises each morning is a form of care enacted on the street, then it might pay to think for a moment about other forms of care that are similarly street-based but for which the street itself is the object of attention, the thing that needs keeping an eye on and which may be broken and need fixing up.

Nigel Thrift, whose writing on urban misanthropy I have already cited, has good things to say about the city as well as bad, and in the good he has to say he takes his cue from routine activities of care and repair. Such activities, he argues, signal countervailing possibilities for compassion to be set alongside his depiction of ill-feeling as 'a natural condition of cities, one which cannot be avoided and will not go away' (2005: 140); they make the city possible, and constitute an unobtrusive infrastructure of kindness, part of an urban everyday that escapes conscious attention even as it makes up a significant part of our experience of the city:

> various kinds of cleaning, all forms of building maintenance, the constant fight to keep the urban fabric – from pavements and roads to lighting and power – going, emergency call-out to all manner of situations, the repair of all manner of electrical goods, roadside and collision repair of cars, and so on. (Thrift, 2005: 135)

If these activities appear marginal and piecemeal – trifling, in the face of some of the grand, global risks which can be said to menace the contemporary city – then here also lies their strength; they provide an improvisational response to the unforeseen, giving the city a flexible resilience 'when things do not play out exactly as it is intended that they should' (Thrift, 2005: 137). The point is well made – obvious, once made; cities are not just *there*, they must be kept going, kept ticking over. And the work of doing so is all around us.

Roadside repair sees the *physical* makeup of the city – buildings, roads, a broken-down this or that – maintained, and thereby accomplishes 'the systematic replacement of place' (Thrift, 2005: 135); but to this we can add that the city's *social* fabric is similarly maintained by routine and workaday ministrations, and might come undone just as quickly if these myriad services were withdrawn: Rees and his co-workers out on the Breakfast Run perform a daily round of maintenance and supervision, largely unobserved perhaps, but there just the same, keeping things going, making minor adjustments and remedial interventions that are at the same time negligible and sorely needed. Outreach work is roadside repair, of a sort; it is street care.

I do not want to do much more here than signal the comparison as there to be made: repair of the physical fabric of the city and other sorts of care, directed not at the street itself but at those who can be found there, those who have gone public with their hurt and difficulties. This work is most likely negligible in any single instance; but in aggregate it is consequential. And much of it unseen or unremarked – lowly work that goes on all the time and all around us, but which we seldom recognise or think that much about. Outreach workers, for their part, *do* see and think about it. Not only are they practitioners themselves, but they share space and cross tracks with other pedestrian crews and operatives working at street level to keep the city going. First thing in the morning the streets are empty enough for those few who are up and about to notice one another: cleaning crews pushing two-bin trucks along the pavement, stooping and sweeping, covering ground, eyes down, looking for the rubbish and waste, doing the dirty work ahead of the rush hour; outreach workers peering over walls and under bushes, circling the centre, pausing here and there to crouch down and have a word with whoever they have found.[9]

Care avoidance

To have got a client 'in' somewhere – off the streets, that is, and in receipt of care (and supervision) – is to have made some progress. This is certainly so when judged by the more quantitative measures of performance to which the CCT is subject. But why should this be hard to do? If the need is there and everyone wants the same thing – outreach workers, service providers, the homeless – then it ought to be no more than a matter of directing people to whatever services are available locally. Getting 'in somewhere' ought to be no more than a job of matching needs to available means. Yet things do not work out this way at all. Take Martin, rushed to hospital by ambulance having collapsed in the bus station. Two days into his stay, marginally recovered but with some checks still to be run, and with a clean bed and hot food and television in the meantime, and under no notice to quit, he phones through to the CCT to get his clothes sent over and almost as soon as he has these he is off, with nowhere else to go other than back to the city centre. This seems nonsensical. Is he ill? Obviously, yes. But can he not see?

Puzzling as Martin's behaviour might appear, it is nothing new to Dennis. Martin never stays in hospital as long as he is supposed to, and Dennis knew the likely outcome when he delivered the bag of clothes. Martin seldom keeps appointments – those made for him by other

---

9. The parallels are not just descriptive. Outreach workers are moral street sweepers of a sort. There is, as Thrift suggests, there might be (but also in ways he does not much consider) a politics to care and repair.

people, that is; he never makes appointments himself. He routinely fails to turn up to court when required, and can be counted on to miss any compulsory interview at the Housing Department or JobCentre Plus.

Everyone on the City Centre Team knows Martin and the way he is. But knowing Martin is not the only way in which to know this pattern of behaviour. Most of Cardiff's street homeless are a little like that. Some are worse still. John is a serial hospital absconder, with even less regard for his own health and wellbeing than Martin. Anna has lurched from one misfortune or injury to the next for years despite the best and continuing efforts of social and healthcare professionals; she is a prolific interview and appointment defaulter. Colin has never stayed in a hostel bed more than a very few days at most, despite having been offered places in just about all of Cardiff's homeless provision at some time or other – he just ups and leaves. And he will not take his medication. Martin, John, Anna, Colin: one way or another, they are all hard to help. This comes close to being a qualifying condition for the involvement of homeless outreach services. That Martin is in (public) difficulties might be enough to bring him to the attention of an outreach patrol, or ambulance crew; but whatever the difficulties he is in, it is the fact that he is himself difficult that makes him a regular on the Breakfast Run. He is a *typical* client of the City Centre Team, if there is such a thing. The CCT works with a disparate collection of individuals, in different and particular sorts of need and difficulty, but all those they work with share this one characteristic: they do not make good clients.[10]

---

10.   This is a circumstance that does not arise in the maintenance and repair of the city's physical fabric. Not that the repair of objects, a broken-down this or that, is without difficulty. Some damaged objects are easy enough to put right, but others require considerable efforts and expertise. Repair work can be demanding, intricate, awkward; it is work that some of us prefer not to do; it can be dirty work. Some of the most difficult repair work takes place out of doors and *in situ* because it has to; and here the conditions of work are those encountered rather than those ideally suited to the task (see Goffman, 1991 [1961]: 293). Mending a roof in wet weather is hard going; sweeping a windy street is a thankless task (but the street can hardly be brought indoors).

Thinking about repair and why we do it and what it takes to get the work done is therefore suggestive. There are points of convergence and departure; points at which Martin's needs and difficulties can be thought of in terms of what it takes to get on with fixing up a broken-down this or that (or not get on with it). But the crux of the issue is that the repair of objects does not proceed from a reciprocal matching of ready assistance to confessed need. That an object is broken, that it needs repair, that the repair then takes whatever form it takes – all this is a matter for the repairer only. Mending things is a unilateral undertaking. But Martin

Is Martin ill? I have already asked this question, and the answer is yes, of course he is. For one thing he is an alcoholic, and has quit hospital to get back to the drink (and drugs) to which he is addicted. But there are a number of other things wrong with Martin, things that have gone wrong for him, and around him, over a number of years; and these are things – events, circumstances – he has had not only to endure but also to work into some sort of a life. Not a very conventional or pleasant life, viewed from without. Nor a very coherent one. Martin's life is a mess: it appears so to those who see him in the street; it is confirmed as such by anyone who has ever tried to get him to keep an appointment or discuss his finances or plan for the future. He talks about his own life this way too, sometimes with an aggressive sort of relish, but more often bitterly, and sometimes despairingly. He lurches from one crisis to the next, marking time in between drinking and fighting; he is seldom in a fit state to do anything 'about' his situation. Yet it is this same lack of pattern and direction that marks him out as a recognisable 'type'.[11]

---

is a person, not a thing; and he is a person who (sometimes, under some circumstances) doesn't want to be helped, doesn't think he needs helping, and is no help at all to those who nonetheless think that he does. He is contrary.

11.   Martin is one of the 'chaotic' homeless. There are numerous types of homeless person, writes Alexander Masters:

> There are those who were doing all right beforehand, but have suffered a temporary setback ... self confidence is their main problem ... Then there are the ones who suffer from chronic poverty, brought on by illiteracy or social ineptness or what are politely called 'learning disabilities' ... The youngsters who have fallen out with their parents, or have come out of care and don't know what to do next or even how to make their own breakfast: they're a third homeless category ... Ex-convicts and ex-army – take away the format of their lives and all they can do is crumple downwards ... Right at the bottom of this abnormal heap are the people such as Stuart, the 'chaotic' homeless. The chaotic ('kai-yo-ic', as Stuart calls them, drawing out the syllables around his tongue like chewing gum) are beyond repair. (2006: 2)

This is taken from *Stuart: a Life Backwards*, Masters' extraordinary biography of Stuart Shorter, one of the 'chaotic' homeless. I recognise the type, as would Rees and Dennis (as does Stuart himself, as would Martin and many others placed either side of homeless outreach encounters in Cardiff), though I am not so sure that talk of types takes us very far, or even in the right direction. What I am trying to address is the comprehensibility of Martin's flight from hospital and, more widely, the behaviours he shares with a number of others, which mark them out as targets for outreach because they are hard to help and seemingly unwilling or unable to help themselves. Such unwillingness makes sense to CCT outreach at least in the sense that this is what they are looking for and used to working with. Masters' description of the chaotic homeless type continues: 'What unites the chaotic is the confusion of their days. Cause and effect are not connected in the usual way ... they

Making it from one day to the next under such miserably immediate circumstances, requires some adjustment.[12] It is not too hard to see that, even looking in from the outside. Getting by as homeless requires an accumulation of strategies for doing so, of local knowledges and involvements, of site-specific competencies and also an internal recalibration of focus and outlook, squared (up) to life on the streets. To accrue such competencies, resources and outlook is not at all the same as to gather oneself together with a view to getting out, getting help or getting 'in' somewhere.

And this is the 'type' of homeless person Martin is, mostly – if he is any type at all. He is fitted to the contingency and drift of life on the streets; used to being out of doors and looking after his own troubles in his own way, on his own ground; by turns predatory, offhand, mistrustful and evasive in his interactions with others; well enough aware of the low esteem in which he is generally held, and well enough aware too of the power this gives him, to disconcert and unsettle, and of the ways in which that power can be used to momentary advantage, if only to get left alone; prickly about his need; and suspicious of authority, with some good reason – hospitals get to him, as do offices, as do uniforms. If the question is 'What does Martin make of being homeless?', one answer is that he has made a life of sorts. But what does he make of that life, as a matter of concern? Perhaps some lived circumstances can only be adequately described through evaluative description, and I have already used evaluative terms in describing homelessness. Whatever else life on the streets as a rough sleeper is like, it is certainly harsh and meagre, and damaging;[13] whatever else it may be, and whatever sort of life people might make for themselves within it, homelessness is a bad thing (Sayer,

---

are constantly on the brink of raring up or breaking down' (2006: 4). *Beyond repair*, and now *constantly breaking down*.

12.   This could be called a process of accommodation, and it is one of the things that can give outreach an urgency. Work with established clients and the practised homeless proceeds carefully, slowly even, at a pace best suited to the development and consolidation of trust and understanding between worker and client. But if the team comes across or gets to hear about someone new, especially someone young – new to the team, new on the *scene*, unschooled – then they will hurry to sort them out and get them off the street before they get established; before they get used to being homeless, or any good at it.

13.   A report by the UK homelessness charity, CRISIS, claims that homeless people in the UK have a life expectancy about 30 years shorter than the national average (see *The Guardian*, 21 December 2011).

2011: 8). Homelessness is a stigmatised identity, in which circumstance provides proof of failure – failure to cope, to hold down a job, to get on in life. 'Why after all would people stay in a shelter or on the streets unless they couldn't make it in society?' (Rowe, 1999: 42). To be homeless *is* to have failed, and to have done so in the sight of others. As such it is shaming. Is that the way Martin feels about it? The answer is yes, some of the time. There are certainly occasions, low and sober points in his day, when he will say as much. And of course it hurts to do so. Such injuries of the spirit can be added to the bodily harm and physical ill-health that homelessness already brings about. Still, those on the streets don't only suffer such injuries, they manage them, salvaging respect and self-esteem where they are able; they also practise tactics of evasion and defiance and obfuscation; and they seek out different sorts of standing and regard. When not feeling so low (or sober) Martin will tell anyone who wants to listen, not least himself, and with some pride, that he has been on the street for years and doesn't want anything different. 'Everybody knows me,' he shouts, casting his arms wide across the cityscape. This is recognition, of a sort.

Seeing the need

So it is hard to say what Martin makes of being homeless. He makes what he can, makes do and measures up – makes off from the hospital; he makes judgements too and would describe his life as going well or not so well at all, depending on when and how he was asked, and by whom. He has more than one answer to the question, and he knows what he is talking about and might fairly insist that those asking the question do not. At the same time, he has grounds for being not altogether straight with himself, as we all do. Everyone's life is a matter of concern and most of us are capable of appraising how things stand within our own lived circumstance, though this can be hard when things are not going well. If things are particularly tough we may prefer not to let others know or see – until we are ready; we may tell ourselves it's not so bad. And this is a part of what makes Martin hard to help, certainly; what it could cost him to confess his need.

Richard Sennett (2004) has argued that such confessions cost what they do because the needs people have of one another are not so easily expressed in public. The statement 'I need help' is somehow shaming when issued out of doors (not so at home, among friends and family). Sennett links such shame – the stigma of assistance – to fear of exposure, of being seen. Not that visibility need be shaming in itself, any more than dependency; but it can be so, where the person under scrutiny is not ready to be looked at and cannot control the circumstances in which that is happening. This has a bearing on homelessness, as a condition of both need and visibility. Most of the homeless complain at some time or other of the indifference of passers-by who 'look right through' them, as if they were nothing or not even there. But there are also occasions when this plays the other way around and what irritates or demeans is not a seeming invisibility but rather the stares one attracts – people *looking*. Here the register shifts from indifference to its seeming opposite: attention, curiosity. The state Martin and his drinking pals are in sometimes makes it hard *not* to see them. It is hard to look away. Yet to be seen in this way is really only another sort of transparency, another way in which to be looked right through.

In summary then, Cardiff's street homeless present a problem; and the problem can be *seen*, is not hidden away at the margins or concealed behind closed doors. Seeing is easy, perhaps. But *seeing to* is much harder; so too is looking after. Martin's difficulties – their extent, intricacy and imbrication – work against his seeking assistance. He may be needy, but he is also stigmatised, sidelined, hardened and mistrustful, and his immediate needs, the things he has to have – today, right now – consume the better part of his attention and resources, such as these are. In this and other ways he is a difficult person to help; hard to engage, hard to get any sense out of much of the time. He sometimes says he doesn't want help, doesn't need it, and appears to have sabotaged past attempts to 'sort' his situation (he is banned from a number of the local hostels and also from the offices of the Housing Department where he lost his temper once and threatened a member of staff). Passers-by give him a wide berth as he careers along the pavement. Some try not to look, to look through or past him. Others stare, and get short shrift when they do: 'What are you looking at? What? Fucking … yes. Yes, you! Bastards.' (Of course the answer to Martin's question – his challenge – is that passers-by know full well what they are looking at, and Martin knows that they do. They can see him.)

A sticking plaster

Care avoidance and perhaps some degree of institutional disinclination are features of the work of outreach, and in some ways its premise.[14] Outreach is there for Martin, because Martin is out there and not coming in – for treatment, for appointments, from the cold. And if Martin is not coming in then someone will have to go and get him, or look after him where he is; because care is what Martin needs, whether or not he sees that himself.

First aid is a response to harm, to illness or injury; it is addressed to the needs of the moment, as encountered, and is supplied by those who are to hand and able (and willing) to assist in some way. The aims of first aid are to preserve life, prevent further harm and promote recovery. It is *first* aid, carried out before anything else gets done. Sometimes first aid is all that is required – a nick, a slip, a scald, duly cleaned and bandaged; and sometimes it is only just enough to hold things together until some further intervention – more organised, deliberate and expert – can be *arranged*. In this way first aid not only comes first, but is then followed up; something happens next, to make sure the same thing doesn't happen again or get worse. Outreach workers stand on the cusp of this sequence, a little awkwardly.

First aid is *ad hoc* because that is the way with slips and falls; but if outreach work is first aid, of a sort, then the injuries and upsets to which it responds are not only *ad hoc*, but arise in the context of an *ad hoc* sort of life that works against the chances of anything much happening by

---

14. No one particularly wants Martin in their waiting room or appointment diary. For one thing, his difficulties are so many and so knotted together, and for so long now, that setting things right would be a Herculean task. Housing, drinking, health, finances (benefits, fines, debts), court appearances, clean clothes, personal hygiene, that nasty-looking cut on the bridge of his nose. Where would you start? And whose job is this? Or rather, whose job would it be if Martin were amenable and sober, which he isn't. Added to which – to Martin's compound needs and difficulties – there is the fact that he is himself a difficult, disagreeable person. He is hard work, and hard work is not always its own reward: '[c]are providers do not always make a full effort for these people, particularly when they are not motivated or avoid help. What care providers need themselves – the reward that clients follow up instructions, attend appointments, express their gratitude – is not forthcoming' (Schout et al., 2011: 670). Under these conditions care avoidance and institutional disinclination amplify each other. If Martin doesn't like hospitals or JobCentre Plus and doesn't have particularly nice things to say about the people who work there, then the feeling is at least part-way mutual.

arrangement. Martin is not interested in making arrangements; he is not interested in doing much to stop the way his life has been for the last few years from happening again. What is doing him harm out there is what he (sometimes says he) wants. And in the meantime outreach workers feed him hot tea, fetch his clothes, keep an eye on his health, remind him to take his medication, wrap him in blankets; and every now and then, when the moment seems right, they ask him (again) if he wouldn't really like to try coming off the drink and getting in somewhere. If and when he ever says yes, they can make things happen – make arrangements, and quickly. But not really before then, not in a way that would stick. Because although Martin is their concern, his life is his own.

First aid can be urgent and essential – life-saving – and it can be minor and ameliorative, a sticking plaster. As metonym, a sticking plaster can stand for first aid, and bandages are a common enough symbol of wider arrangements for relief and assistance. Bandages are something easily applied and of immediate utility; and there is no necessary shame in it – being bandaged up. Everyone needs a sticking plaster now and then. In this way, first aid gets in ahead of some of the indignities of assistance. Questions of welfare – how one's life is *going* – come freighted with all sorts of difficulty, and can demean. But first aid is something a little different, perhaps. Applying a sticking plaster, no one is being positioned as *needy*; all there is is *a need* – an injury or ailment, the response to which is obvious and uncomplicated.

This can work well for outreach, up to a point. Martin doesn't want to hear (again) about how he needs to get into a hostel and do something about his drinking, but he will take a bacon sandwich and a blanket, and with thanks. Whatever Nicy might want to know about whatever it might be that has brought Cindy to Central Square sopping wet and drunk in the early morning, and whatever she might guess might need to be done about any of that, for now all there is is Cindy and her immediate distress. Temporarily, but repeatedly, this essential scenario – immediate need, practical assistance – excuses outreach workers and those they meet up with from the wider discomforts of assistance as welfare. If CCT workers are held in some regard by Cardiff's homeless – and on the whole they are – then it is because they know their stuff, and they help you out and they don't ask too many questions or stick their noses into your business too much if you don't want them to. Nothing much more than that. Outreach workers rate their own work and worth in a number of ways, and discuss (and argue) among themselves how best to really help their client group – in ways that go beyond whatever it might be they can do for them today. But they all consider it an accomplishment to have finished an evening's outreach patrol and have seen 17 clients, handed out three sleeping bags, a needle exchange pack and sterile wipes, made cup after cup of hot tea and helped patch things up between Wayne and Jackie, for tonight at least.

But framing outreach work as first aid can play badly too, in the sense that no one has any great hopes of sticking plasters. Although they can be of some small use and reassurance, sticking plasters are never going to treat or heal anything but the most minor injury, still less the reasons why the injury happened in the first place. And worse, a sticking plaster can conceal, and postpone proper treatment. Repair work that doesn't get to the root of a problem, that fails to make things much better but allows the rest of us to carry on without really seeing that something ought to be done – we might call this sort of thing a 'sticking plaster' approach. Patching things up – with Wayne and Jackie, or for Bryony and Katie – is absorbing work, but there are days when you don't have to step back too far from an outreach shift to wonder what was the point of it all, really, pleased as you might be with the work itself and your own competency in carrying it out.

Outreach: Back on Central Square, with Charlie and the young woman with the injured hand (see pp. 57–9). There is one piece of work that Charlie hopes to get done before we head off for the museum steps. She is looking through the windscreen of the van across the train station forecourt trying to spot a young man called Ieuan. The team have managed to secure Ieuan a bed for tonight at the night shelter. It has been one of those jobs that has taken some considerable effort and coordination, also persuasion, to bring off – it was Ieuan who needed persuading. And, like all those sort of jobs, it may well now come to nothing because Ieuan will have second thoughts or somehow manage to botch things. His first opportunity to do so is to fail to turn up, as arranged, at or around this time, to meet Charlie. It looks like he might have managed this, only then Charlie spots him on the benches outside the entrance to the train station. Good news. Only not so good because he is not alone. Worse still, he is with Dean, of all people, and Charlie is not going anywhere near Dean tonight if she can help it. So Ieuan will have to wait. We drive off to the museum steps, taking a long loop anti-clockwise in the now sheeting rain.

The rain lets up a bit again as we park up outside the museum. No sign, so far as Charlie can tell, of the man without the dog. So we get out and run up the steps to find two young Polish men, one older woman who has started turning up at the Breakfast Run but who nobody knows much about yet and Robbo, waiting for the Bus. We break the bad news - about the Bus being cancelled. The woman wants a bed tonight. Charlie says she just doesn't know, but to come along to the soup run later when maybe she'll have some idea what's available (it depends what happens with Ieuan).

Back now towards Central Square, though taking a turn down Museum Place, where we spot Gary. He is sitting wrapped in plastic sheeting, alongside his brimming supermarket trolley under the eaves of an empty office building. We don't stop, but Charlie makes a note to check back later.

We park up at Central Square and take a little walk. Soon enough Charlie spots Ieuan. He is leaning unsteadily on the railings outside Marland House, an absurdly big, brimming sports bag slung over his shoulder. There is still a crowd standing and sitting along the covered walkway through to Wood Street; the woman with the injured hand is gone, but not the rest, and others have joined, including Jason Law. Ieuan stands apart from these, though he is close enough to be implicated. He looks sullen and aggrieved. Charlie wants him to come away, but he won't move just yet. He has been picked on or somehow done down by the rest, and much as he doesn't want any more of it he can't quite bring himself to walk off without feeling that he has been shooed away, or bullied. He is also quite drunk and having difficulty standing, never mind walking anywhere. He slurs a few explanations and allegations, which the crowd in the walkway, and Jason in particular, contest or treat with contempt. Then he sort of calls Jason out, hoping maybe that he can do so as a parting shot and just leave. But Jason is there in a moment, right up against us (we have joined Ieuan, in a group of three) and leaning down over Ieuan, head to head, telling him what a cunt he is and to fuck off before he gets a hiding. Charlie starts tugging Ieuan, who won't shift much more than a few yards. Jason is working himself up for a fight. 'You're putting me at risk here,' Charlie tells Ieuan. We get him halfway to the van at which point he decides he doesn't want to come. Jason swaggers back over. Ieuan calls him a bully. Jason hits Ieuan. 'No! Jason, No!' shouts Charlie, pushing herself between the two of them. We start to physically drag Ieuan away. 'You're not the police,' says Ieuan. 'You can't make me.' True enough, and we let him go.

'You fucking ginger cunt. You're a bully. That's all you are.'

'What you fucking say?'

'Ginger cunt.'

Jason twists Ieuan into a headlock and delivers a couple of sharp punches to his head before swinging him round into a staggering fall. There is little we can do really other than physically restrain Jason, which we are unwilling to try just yet. Somehow we get Ieuan back to the van and sit him by the side door, half in, half out. He is crying now. Jason brings the whole show over, raging and posturing, telling us to get rid of Ieuan before he kills him. Ieuan gets thrown around a bit more and ends up on the floor beside the van, me beside him, Jason behind me with Charlie clinging onto his jacket telling him 'Jason, no. Enough. Leave it. Enough'.

We drive directly to the night shelter, where the door is opened by a member of staff, Jean, who says it is the first thing she has heard about any sort of reservation having been made for Ieuan. Charlie and Jean sit in the office talking the situation over. Charlie was unsure, driving over, that the night shelter would take Ieuan anyway, given the state he's in - drunk, that is, and bloodied. But it looks like they will. There is some talk of Jason and the need to keep him away - he was at the night shelter himself last week but not since, and has lost his bed. Charlie sighs. 'I actually took a pay cut to take this job,' she says, not without humour.

We leave Ieuan watching TV, and head back over to Central Square. He spends two nights at the shelter then leaves, telling staff he is going to stay with his Nan.

Perhaps Charlie has done a little good – certainly she tried to do so; there were things she undertook and risked which, it could be claimed, made some sort of a difference. Whatever way the evening might eventually be reckoned – as having counted for something, or as having had little or no real consequence – every one of her colleagues would recognise this as a piece of outreach, typically so. All the nonsense and distress. One of *those* evenings.

This is the second of two chapters to have taken an everyday office of city life as a means by which to introduce the work of outreach – lost property, and now first aid. First aid is a response to physical injury, but I have stretched the term to include other sorts of damage and adversity; such difficulties, in combination, supply the CCT with its operational premise. And the premise is this: something is not quite right out there, in the middle of Cardiff, not at all right for a very few vulnerable people variously put upon – and sometimes set upon – some of them injured and at least a few stubbornly inured to further injury. CCT outreach workers are tasked to do something about that and to be there for those in this sort of difficulty. They are employed to instigate contact and facilitate access to mainstream and specialist services and resources, as required; but they are also, themselves, providers of care and must look out for their clients where they can and where they find them, responding to the needs of the moment. Nicy was *there for* Cindy, and Charlie was *there for* Ieuan, which is what makes me want to call this first aid; it is assistance offered in the first instance and on location. The following chapter begins to ask where this happens – on Central Square certainly, but elsewhere too. Where exactly? Or whereabouts?

4

Round About

Just like everything else, outreach has to happen somewhere; this chapter sets out to say where.

Outreach work with the homeless and other 'vulnerable' individuals in central Cardiff gets done in the city centre, obviously enough and by definition. Similar work could get done elsewhere too (and sometimes does), but there are good reasons why the local authority employs a City Centre Team and not a Suburbs Unit. Much of the work gets done in plain sight and public space, not behind closed doors; home visits are not something an outreach worker can easily arrange with clients with no fixed address. But it is also a hidden practice, riddled in amongst the public realm and city proper, with its own geometry, borders, spatial taboos and favourite routes (Moretti, 1999: 5). Which is to say that there is an urban geography peculiar to the work of outreach. Even so, outreach workers and clients do not own the spaces they share. Settings are borrowed and improvised. 'Step into my office,' says Jeff, gesturing to one of a group of drinkers to join him under a lamppost to examine the crumpled paperwork outcome of a benefits tribunal. 'Anybody home?' shouts Dennis as he picks his way down a muddy slope (a home visit, after all!). Outreach workers are forever clambering over walls, shouldering their way through urban planting and ducking under railings; or, rather, their more memorable and definitive excursions require such efforts. In this sense, of physical transgression, outreach is no great respecter of boundaries – railings, hedges; but (again) it does not take place just where it pleases; it operates under sufferance and subject to assorted surveillance and prohibitions; it is pushed and pulled this way and that by wider considerations and developments. Street carers and those they are there to help come very low in the urban pecking order. For all that it belongs to the middle of things, outreach work is also 'edgework', of a sort; a risky practice, but also aligned to a social and moral perimeter – one that runs, contrarily, through the centre of the city.

Finding the centre

Cities tend to start in the middle and spread outwards, thinning as they go. Most of us know this journey. Leaving the centre, perhaps heading for home, the barrage of advertising and signage falls off; the compacted intricacy of the streets opens out and unravels; the density of traffic eases and inching progress gives way to longer surges of movement; the noise drops a notch or two; a certain tension lets up; the built environment slackens off and crowds the street a little less; the skyline opens out. Headed the other way, the city gathers itself together again and the scale of things shifts upwards until at some point we can say we are more or less back in the middle of things. We recognise the thickening *cityness* of the place, all the familiar stuff of urban phenomenology – lines of taxis, a bunching together of phone boxes, the noise of construction work, cranes on the skyline, discarded flyers and chewing gum underfoot, free papers, tourists and conference attendees lugging baggage (looking lost), developers' hoardings – confirms our suspicions we are there or thereabouts. Stepping out through the doors of Marland House and into Central Square you know immediately that you are in the middle of the city. You couldn't be anywhere else. But how far does it go? At what distance from here does the centre lose its hold? Borders are one of the things that maps are best at showing, but street maps of central Cardiff don't describe the city centre as a particular territory.

One version of Cardiff's city centre, one answer to the question *Where is the city centre?* can be found in the work of outreach I have begun to describe – which is *city centre* outreach, after all. Cardiff's City Centre Team is obviously enough – obvious even to those who know nothing more about it – a team with a patch; these are people with a job to do *in*, a job that has to do *with*, the centre of the city. So do they know where it is? You would hope so. And, yes, they do. Or at least they could all answer the question readily enough. But their answers tend to unravel into rather more involved accounts of where their work takes them and the ways in which that can mostly but not always mean keep close to the middle of things. It's worth noting that the question – my question – is not one that outreach workers ever ask themselves. It is not a question to which they need to know the answer. Their job takes them where it takes them, they go where their clients go, most of the time not very far at all from Central Square. And if it happens on occasion that they need to be somewhere else then the chances are that it has been the mismatch of remote location and familiar client or problem that has brought them there in the first place: a tent pitched in the corner of a suburban park, 'girls' getting in and out of cars at the corner of a residential street, a rolled sleeping bag in a disused allotment shed. I once spent the best part of an hour with Steve and Nicy on the side of a roundabout on the outskirts of Cardiff trying to persuade an uncommunicative client to turn around and head back to the city centre where the team could keep more of an eye on him. The client had other ideas. He was set on walking to Newport, and from there to London. It had taken him a couple of days to get this far, pushing a wonky flat-bed trolley piled high with belongings and bric-a-brac, including two chairs and a chest of drawers. (He made it as far as Bristol, where he was detained under the Mental Health Act.) There are two points to note. First, called on to do so, Nicy and her colleagues work all over the city; if Nicy's job takes her to the suburbs and beyond then that is where it takes her. But the general expectation – this is the second point – is that the centre of the city and (the need for) street-based care will coincide; trips to the edge are uncommon, are outliers. Sat by the roundabout talking with her errant client, Nicy is within her jurisdiction but not on home ground in the way that she is on Central Square.

A straight answer, one that holds good for the most part of this book, is that CCT outreach workers operate in the commercial and administrative heart of the city. They spend time on or nearby the city's busiest streets, close by, outside, and around the back of its main shops and shopping centres, business and commercial offices and civic buildings, and in or on its central parks, squares and public and remaindered spaces – there is much more to say about that last category, remaindered space. Their *patch*, is very roughly triangular, bordered by two railway lines and a river: at the base, the South Wales Main Line service running west to east through the city, from Swansea on to Bristol, Swindon and London; then a curving hypotenuse described by the Valley Line service to Pontypridd, trending upwards, right to left, skirting the city's civic and university buildings; and then, dropping back down on a vertical, the river Taff, flowing south into the centre of the city and out again under Wood Street 100 yards along from Central Square. Not much more than a square mile; two square miles at most.

Figure 4.1

Not much of a triangle but something like that; fuzzy at the edges but more or less the shape of it. Of course, if the map shows anything it shows the territory within which members of the CCT have no need of a map.

It used to be that CCT staff could say they worked in the non-residential areas of the city, and people would understand them to mean the middle, mostly. But that was already changing when the team was first set up in 1998, as it was changing – has changed – in towns and cities across much of the UK. Now large numbers are permanently resident in the centre of the city, many of them in new apartment blocks that have sprung up, a bit like Chevalier's towers: 'thrusting up on the horizon, all at once, in a few months' (1994: 3). Even so, you could say much the same thing today and people would still know what you were on about; the general understanding holds, whatever the demographics: the city centre is public space, no one's turf or home in particular, not in a way that makes it anyone else's business if you want to go there. This is another of those indications that draw together as you make your way in to the middle of a city, a shift towards anonymity, a growing awareness that you will now encounter people on terms a little different from those that hold elsewhere, that different sensibilities and different rules apply – blank looks, civil inattention – that people will (increasingly) mind their own business and not yours.[1] But there is another, and important, category of city-centre resident or local in Cardiff, neither lately ensconced in prestige apartments nor out on the streets (though not too far from being so). Cardiff's city centre is ringed by a collection of homeless hostels and related services (day-centres, drop-ins and advice bureaux), part of that wider urban administration of things and people unwanted or off course; 'necessary containers' (see Cloke, et al., 2010: 10). The pattern is common to most UK cities. These are the sorts of places, the hostels, that people drift in and out of, or end up in – tidied away; a lucky few manage to move on and not slip back. But for so long as they are there they are resident in the centre of the city. Thus, in the immediate vicinity of Central Square, within five minutes' walk of Marland House, there are more than 100 fixed-term and emergency bedspaces for the 'hidden' homeless.

Outreach: Jeff says he'll take me on the 'hostel tour'. This means walking out past the back of Central Station to the Huggard Centre, then next door to Tresillian House and then along to the Salvation Army hostel at the top of Bute Street; the next leg would be to double back to cross the river and turn along the Taff Mead Embankment towards The Wallich night shelter on Clare Street, only we don't make it that far today. Jeff walks this circuit with anyone new. The idea being to cover a little of the local geography and to introduce some of the people and places that matter most to the

---

1. Conventionally, there is an excitement to this, and a sort of security that comes wrapped in the indifference of others. 'Can I help you?' is not a question you hear so much in the city centre (unless you are shopping, and actually inside a shop). Otherwise, no one asks. At least not in the way that they do when what they actually mean is that they're from round here and you're not and you'd better explain yourself. The inadmissibility, or at least the difficulty, of asking after someone in the middle of the city is a daily puzzle for outreach workers, whose job it is to ask again and again of strangers they meet, 'Can I help you?'

team, in this case residents and members of staff at the principal homeless hostels and emergency shelters around the city centre.[2]

Approaching the Huggard Centre, we round a street corner to find a rowdy collection of residents and hangers-on, gathered together by the kerb, everybody shouting and gesturing and swigging in turn from a bottle of cider. This is a regular little drinking school, says Jeff; maybe a little smaller today than usual (there are eight all told, one pudgy young woman and the rest men of indeterminate age), but the same scene every day, with drug dealers coming and going, plying a little trade and chasing debts. All this in a car-parking area alongside a galvanised-steel fence by a patch of wasteland – rubble, grass, weeds, litter – awaiting development, overlooked by a line of terraced houses scheduled for demolition, doors and windows boarded up.

A one-armed man with a thin face and dark, greasy hair peels off from the group and intercepts us. 'Give us a fucking fag,' he instructs Jeff, cheerily. Jeff does so. He knows Danny, has known him for ten years or more. The man is a wreck. One arm is gone and he is limping too. He mentions further hospital treatment. (Jeff tells me later that Danny lost his arm as a result of botched intravenous drug use and bad 'gear' and may yet lose a leg for much the same reason.)

We head inside, leaving Danny to rejoin his drinking partners. Crossing a large canteen area set out with tables and chairs, we make our way into the kitchen to talk with Frank, a member of the Huggard Centre staff. Jeff makes introductions and asks Frank to say a little about the Huggard Centre and its client group and the services available on site. Frank does so, distractedly, passing bowls of soup out through a service hatch. He only breaks off altogether when he gets on to talking about the difficulties they have had over the last couple of months rubbing up against their new neighbours, a vanguard of office workers leading the central business district's push south of the mainline railway. There have been complaints, says Frank. Lots of people who would rather see the Huggard Centre gone, moved elsewhere. But the Huggard – the premises, the services, the client group – was in place before anyone else really wanted to be here, around the back of the station.

---

2.   The Huggard is a daytime drop-in centre with a 20-berth bed unit attached; Tresillian House is a local authority homeless hostel sleeping 25 residents in single rooms and six more on mattresses in an emergency-overnight-stay area (the EOS); the Salvation Army hostel, Tŷ Gobaith, has close to 70 units of accommodation (including 15 rooms adapted for use on the 'Bridge Project' a residential treatment programme for homeless people with substance misuse issues, jointly run by the Salvation Army and the Community Addictions Unit); and the night shelter has 10 beds, 12 at a push, in five shared rooms, allocated on a night-by-night basis. From November to March each year the Huggard also offers Cardiff's 'cold weather provision', 15 to 20 mattress spaces on a cleared floor available on a first-come-first-served basis to any who would otherwise be sleeping out of doors.

'And it's good that we're here really,' says Frank. 'There'd be no point relocating a service like this out somewhere like Ely.[3] No one would go. You'd still have people in the centre – your drinkers, your homeless, by the bus and train station – only there'd be nowhere for them to go. Then you'd really have a problem. Anyway, we were here first, basically.'

We move back to the canteen area and Jeff works the room for ten minutes or so, after which we wave goodbye to Frank and step outside, to be met almost immediately with: 'Give us a cigarette, Jeff.' From this point on Jeff turns down all such requests.

Next is Tresillian House, a local authority homeless hostel. Jeff introduces Roy, the manager, who shows us round: the EOS (six PVC-coated mattresses stacked against one wall; full every night, says Roy); the communal rooms (empty, a TV, mismatched chairs, cigarette burns on every surface); kitchens (locked); laundry (first wash free). You can stay here for £8 a week on top of housing benefit; £25 if you want your meals. There are cameras in every corridor it seems and it is too warm and close for comfort – the heat of institutional buildings. The Salvation Army hostel next door, Tŷ Gobaith, is altogether nicer, brighter, cooler. We get the tour again. Most of the rooms here are pretty good, nothing is quite so battered and institutional as at Tresillian; but there is no doubt that you are in a hostel, no doubt at all about that. There are the same cameras mounted on the ceilings, and the worker showing us around has a jangling bunch of keys and a panic alarm attached to his belt.

Leaving Tŷ Gobaith we encounter Danny again, on Tresillian Way. He is all fired up about some affront or maltreatment he has just suffered, though not too clear on the details. 'Just leave it,' says Jeff. 'Walk away.' But Danny will not. He storms off in no particular direction, raging. Moments later we see him again, on his back in the middle of the road. Has he been hit by a car? A driver has pulled up and got out to help. He is trying to get Danny back on his feet with the help of one of the Huggard crowd. Danny sits up. He has quite a lot of blood running down his face. Jeff and I start over, Jeff wearily. Before we get there Danny is back on his feet – just – wheeling about and shouting. 'Oh, he's arguing,' says Jeff. 'He must be OK.'

Jeff thinks Danny is best left for now; he will see him again later on today and get the full story. Meantime, we head over to Dumball's Road to find a small posse of drinkers – Richie, Raoul (and his dog), Jenna and another man whose name I miss – gathered together on a low bench in a small triangle of dead space by the river bridge. We are met with insistent requests for fags, and with (mock) outrage and disbelief when Jeff turns his pockets out and claims to have none. I am introduced and there is a round of handshakes and fierce stares. Raoul wants Jeff to 'get on the phone to The Wallich' for him. He explains – just about – that he has been evicted,

---

3. A large housing estate on the western edge of the city.

for having a dog. 'They knew I had a dog when they gave me that room,' he says. 'And then they kick me out for having one.' Jeff commiserates and says he'll see what he can do. If he can't do anything, then Raoul will be sleeping out (Jenna too, because she and Raoul are together and she won't have him sleeping out alone, never mind the dog). The other two are 'in somewhere' tonight, or expect to be, one at Tŷ Gobaith, the other at the night shelter. But all that is some way off and rather abstract. There is no real rush, it seems. There is the whole afternoon to get through, sat here across the river from the Millennium Stadium.

Jeff's hostel tour starts to pace out what others have called 'the nodal territory of the homeless city' (Cloke et al., 2010: 62), though Jeff wouldn't call it that. This is another way in which to delineate the team's space of operations; not a perimeter but a constellation of locations and the lines drawn between these – familiar routes.

Leaving Marland House to get down to work, outreach staff sometimes grab a sheaf of leaflets to take with them. There is a rack of these just inside the office door, and little stacks elsewhere around the office, on tables and in desk drawers. Almost all of the (many) health and social care and advisory services that the team has anything to do with have a leaflet or two, setting out what they do and how they can help. The problem is that out walking no one could hope to carry all the leaflets that *could* be carried and do anything much more than struggle along under the weight of paper. The team's answer to this has been to produce its own literature, consolidating the most important and immediately relevant information about local services into a single laminated brochure titled *A Guide to Homeless People in Cardiff.*[4] The *Guide* lists service contact details under the headings *Hostel Accommodation, Housing, Substance Misuse Services* and *Health*. There is also a short note on sleeping rough

---

4. There is a considerable redundancy to getting your message across by leaflet and outreach workers hand out many more copies of the *Guide* (and other leaflets) than they expect to be held on to. For every one that someone keeps and wants, two or three more at least are dropped or thrown away and soon enough pasted into that greasy collage – flyers, promotions, tourist brochures, bus tickets, food wrappers – whose presence underfoot is another sure indication that you are in or approaching the city centre. (Short-lived as any leaflet is once dropped out of doors, indoors some cling on to a curiously extended life, curling at the corners on the bottom rack of a rotary stand or lying dormant at the back of a desk drawer. Dig around in any welfare office and you are likely to find more than one outmoded leaflet describing a service that has long since changed its phone number or address or remit, or is simply no longer around. Nothing left but the leaflet.)

in Cardiff and how to minimise the risks of cold and injury, and across the middle pages a map of the city centre – another version, not quite my rough triangle but close enough – with a scatter of coloured dots marking relevant locations and services: Marland House (Homelessness Office and Out of Hours Homelessness Advice; City Centre Team); the Huggard Centre; Tresillian House; Tŷ Gobaith; Inroads (Drug Advice Centre and needle exchange); Fitzhamon Centre (dry drop-in for anyone whose life has been affected by alcohol); the JobCentre; Grassroots (drop-in for the under-25s); Housing Help Centre; the soup run (free food and hot drinks distributed by local church volunteers every evening outside the Ebenezer Chapel); Big Issue Office; Wallich Nightshelter; TAVS (services for homeless people and those living close to the poverty line, free hot food and clothing). All but one of these is within ten minutes' walk of Central Square.

These are the local stations through which clients of the CCT pass and around which they loop; the sorts of locations at which people in difficulties might present themselves or be handed in. Taken together, they make up a landscape of services (Cloke et al., 2010: 50) that outreach workers hold and work, and walk, in common not only with existing clients but with would-be-clients and soon-to-be-clients and other, allied professionals.

For several years I made my own maps of this territory, marking up photocopied street plans with coloured stickers and felt-tipped pens in an attempt to capture the work of outreach and street care in ever more detail, and over time. The end result – there was no end result, of course, no comprehensive chart – was a series of maps, different versions of the homeless city, showing health and advisory services, hostel accommodation and supported housing, daytime hangouts and places to stash gear (sleeping bags, clothes, shoplifted goods), begging pitches (unsanctioned) and Big Issue pitches (sanctioned), methadone-dispensing chemists, sites for rough sleeping, squatted and derelict premises, and so on; settings for outreach encounters. I also traced out lines of travel, recording the movements of outreach workers between key stations, out on patrol.

Outreach as patrol

As I have said already, clients do not tend to present themselves to the CCT as such, as clients; and they are even less likely to climb the stairs to the second floor of Marland House to do so. Put another way, outreach workers do not get given work, a caseload of clients, so much as they get given the job of finding that work, those clients, for themselves (and for their colleagues). And finding means looking, and looking means moving, which makes outreach an itinerant activity even if the real work might seem to begin only at those points of encounter where a worker stops moving and holds still so as to attend to a person in seeming need – as Nicy does with Cindy, standing together on Central Square in the rain. But to get there, to have encountered Cindy in the first place, Nicy has had to move herself and cast about: not aimlessly, but in the course of a morning's routine patrol of the city centre. In this way, the lines on my map(s) are as important as any points they might appear to connect: they show outreach work in progress (not outreach workers on their way to anywhere in particular, to some location at which outreach work can then begin). Nicy finds Cindy out on patrol and in doing so she does her job.

To patrol is to go about, around, over or along at regular intervals in order to keep watch and to guard or protect something – an area or building; a patrol is a group of people doing just that. And in something like this sense, patrol is what CCT outreach workers do; the word captures the logic of their movements – the lines on my map(s) – and their engagement with the city centre as a territory. Jeff and Nicy may be called on to respond to any number of eventualities in the course of a day's work, may be called out or dispatched to this or that location, may have visits to make and even appointments to keep (very loosely speaking, if clients are involved); but they are most obviously engaged in the work of outreach when they are moving around the city on the lookout, not so much on their way anywhere at all as *out* and on patrol. They do so as and when the opportunity arises, other work commitments permitting: slipping down the stairs and out into Central Square for half an hour 'just to see what's going on', or detouring under the river bridge on their way back from a meeting across town. But they also get around and about, at regular intervals, as part of a scheduled working practice. Two established patrols bookend each working day and provide the frame and mechanism for most outreach encounters. These two patrols are non-negotiable commitments, the only fixed points in the CCT weekly rota other than the Friday morning team meeting, around which all other tasks and duties must be organised. The first of these is the Breakfast Run.

The Breakfast Run (see p. 44n) has been in operation for almost 20 years and the City Centre Team has contributed to its delivery since it was first established, working together with staff and volunteers from The Wallich. Monday to Friday, CCT outreach workers start their working day at 6.45am at the night shelter on Clare Street where they meet up with members of the Rough Sleepers Intervention Team (The Wallich's homeless outreach service – the same service that Rees works for (see pp. 72–4)). Supplies are loaded into someone's car, or the CCT van if it is available, and members of the two teams will brief one another on whatever it is they know and is current – who slept where last night, who has been evicted from which hostel, which little gang has split, acrimoniously, who needs to be kept at arm's length for a day or two, who 'got paid' yesterday and has not been seen since, who is new in town, where exactly the plywood has been prised away from the hoarding put up around the (derelict) Central Hotel and who might be inside. This is 'the latest', as in the last anyone saw or heard; but it is all of it, also, yesterday's news, and as such about to be overhauled. The Breakfast Run leaves Clare Street at 7am and makes its way around the city for the next two hours, sometimes longer, distributing hot food to the bleary-eyed homeless and anyone else who is out and about this early and will settle for tea from a flask and a boiled egg. The route is as much improvised as it is followed. Some sites can be relied upon and are visited more or less every morning – Central Square, for one; others fall in and out of use, are visited every day for weeks or months and then not at all. Changes in the layout and fabric of the city as well as in the configuration of the client group take the Breakfast Run this way then that, and on any given day there is a tension of sorts between reliably showing up at the customary and expected spots at more or less the same time as yesterday, where clients may be waiting, and fulfilling a more exploratory remit. Setting out from Clare Street, whatever 'the latest', no one knows for sure how many clients they will see and where, and in a way that is the point of the exercise, to get out and about and dig around a bit and see who's out there this morning. And that means covering ground. If the CCT has not been across town to the cathedral grounds for a couple of weeks, ever since Billy stopped sleeping there, then maybe this morning would be the time to drive over and take another look. The same investigative urge is given rein every time workers park up the van: they don't stand around waiting for clients to come to them, they have a little scout around, on foot – down that stairwell, over that wall, through those bushes, behind those wheelie bins – just to see who might be there, or what signs there are that someone has been. They are unlikely to catch any of the homeless napping, though some may still be bedded down. Back at the van, drinks are dispensed and food distributed and outreach workers size up needs and priorities and ask around for this morning's news, being careful not to seem overly concerned to be doing so; all this well ahead of office hours, and, for five months of the year, in the dark.

The Breakfast Run gets the day started, underway. All sorts of work may follow, but no further patrol, until the late afternoon. In between are the office hours. (Marland House opens its doors at 8.45am and closes again at 4pm; Cardiff Magistrates' Court opens 15 minutes later at 9am, also closing at 4.30pm; the Job Centre is open 9am to 5pm and the Probation service is the same; the Inroads needle exchange opens at 9.30am and closes at 5pm; the Huggard Centre canteen starts serving food shortly after 9am but stays open late, long after most other services have shut, 8pm. (The night shelter inverts the pattern, closing up for the day at 9.30am and only admitting residents again at 8pm.) Everyone is busy now; the core client group disperses across the city centre and variously regroups, aggregating with others who were 'in' somewhere last night but 'out' now and up to something or other, or nothing much at all, or no good. (Some play this the other way around and use opening hours to get indoors somewhere and away from it all for half the morning or an afternoon, having been out all night, unrested.) The drinking starts as soon as there is drink to be had, and the chasing after little drug deals and debts, and these things take time and application. If someone is in funds – and the trick is to know enough to know who is or might be – then the next few hours can be arranged around the disposal of same. There are plans to hatch, appointments to be made or kept, or missed. In short, the day sets its daily test (the same as the day before), which is no more than to get through from one end to the other. For some of Cardiff's homeless, on some days more than others, there is no wider horizon or prospect.

The CCT office will be busy throughout. Social workers arrive shortly before 9am, and pick up their caseloads, wherever it was these were left off yesterday. Outreach workers arrive a little later, having completed two or three hours work already, depending on wherever it was the Breakfast Run took them and how long it took to get done. On return to the office, outreach workers transcribe a record of those they have seen, noting where and adding in a line of comment or observation, then set about a morning's work: calls to make, referrals to chase up, remedial action prompted by the morning's patrol, meetings to attend (police liaison, safeguarding panels) and training sessions (child protection, drug awareness, self-defence).

Very little of that work, the office work of outreach, figures in these pages; it could be said, therefore, that this book provides only a partial record of what it is to be an outreach worker with the CCT. This would be more of a problem, perhaps, if something of the same discrepancy weren't there in the manner in which outreach workers weigh up their own working days. What counts as work, for Jeff or Dennis, is outreach itself, street work, rather than office duties back at Marland House. Not that office duties aren't important, but the sequence and priority is unquestioned: outreach first and the work it unearths – the problems, the possibilities; and (only) then the follow-up, indoors, upstairs, on the phone. Dress code confirms this. Outreach workers expect to dress for going out and don't change into office wear for those parts of the day they spend sat at a desk. And whatever you might accomplish indoors (and you might accomplish a lot – various food parcels organised, a hostel vacancy secured, a missed Drug Rehabilitation Order appointment rescheduled (and breach avoided), court dates confirmed, an urgent case conference attended) only becomes real once the outcome has been relayed and verified out on the street. If Duffy is in a panic about a letter he has received, care of the Huggard Centre, asking him to confirm his place on a waiting list for council housing, then the issue can be sorted with a phone call and perhaps a quick visit to the Housing Advice Unit; sorted, that is, to the extent that Charlie now understands why the letter was sent and what Duffy needs to do about it. But this counts for nothing until someone actually conveys the news to Duffy, reassures him, and sees to it that he sends a letter in reply, as he has been asked to do. And that means finding Duffy, which means walking down the stairs and out onto Central Square to see if he is in his usual spot by the kiosk. And if he isn't there then he must be somewhere else. But where? Perhaps on Queen Street, ten minutes' walk from Central Square (plus the opportunity to take a look around along the way, and see who else is out there and what they might be up to). An hour later and only then, back in the CCT office, Charlie can sit down at her desk and say 'OK. Sorted'. And then the phone rings.

Outreach: A call comes in to the CCT office from City Centre Management.[5] A car-hire firm out on Ocean Way has a problem. They are scheduled to flush out their fuel storage tanks, something required perhaps once a year, and in order to do this they need to open up an access plate located in a patch of bushes just behind their car park. The difficulty, as reported, is that someone is living there, in the bushes. He's seldom there during the daytime, but there is a large structure of accumulated junk on the spot, inside the bushes – presumably he lives inside this. Can we help? Jeff and Den and I interrupt our debrief of this morning's Breakfast Run and head downstairs. We get into Den's car and drive across town to Ocean way to take a look.

The company manager is outside waiting for us. We pull up in the car park and walk over to the rear wall and the bushes beyond to peer inside. It is hard to see at first, because it is very dark and overgrown; the manager tells us he has been meaning to get the bushes cut back for months. We climb the wall and shoulder our way a yard or two into the foliage, and soon enough we can see the problem: a jumble of litter, leftovers and remnants – bin bags, take-away wrappers, bottles, newspapers, plastic sheeting, three or four umbrellas, lengths of cord, packages of bundled rubbish – loosely assembled, or entangled, into what you might almost call a structure; in the middle, half obscured by a tarpaulin, is a wooden chair and a grim-looking blanket or duvet. We extricate ourselves, not without difficulty. The manager tells us that the bushes are almost always empty during the day, but his staff have seen the guy – youngish, but 'dressed like a tramp, weird-looking' – leaving in the early morning, pushing a supermarket trolley into the city centre. The thing is, says the manager, they feel they have sort of adopted him. There's no ill-will, but health and safety is a worry – 'I don't know if there's drugs in there, or what.' Anyway, now they have to flush out the tanks. The access panel is under the chair. They have tried to find the guy at home, early on, shouting into the bushes to explain the issue to him, but there is never any reply and they can't always be sure that he is actually in there. No one wants to go in and find out. Which is why we are here.

---

5. This is a first mention for City Centre Management (CCM), another local authority team operating in, and with responsibilities for, the middle of Cardiff. Not be confused with the City Centre Team (CCT), the CCM is tasked to work with local traders to improve facilities, promote retail and attract visitors; the team acts as an interface between Cardiff Council and the 'business community', and has a particular (additional) responsibility for the management of the night-time economy – a number of UK cities have something similar.

We are almost certain this is Gary, although we doubt he is sleeping here. He spends most nights just off to one side of Queen Street, and has done so since February. So this is more likely to be a storage site for him, notwithstanding the early-morning sightings; he has at least one other that we know of. We walk over to the office to speak to some of the staff and get a better description - definitely Gary - then step out into the car park again and back over to the bushes. We had better find out what's really in there and what it would take to shift it. Maybe we can find something - discarded correspondence, medication, something - that will positively identify Gary. Maybe there will be some further clue or indication as to who Gary is, where he comes from, what he is up to (we know very little about him, for all that we see him most days). Maybe he is in there right now, keeping quiet and out of sight, behind the tarpaulin. Den leans forward into the bushes, parting the foliage and branches like someone about to start swimming. 'Careful,' he says.

In the very middle of the city, on the busiest streets around Central Square and the Hayes in particular, it can be hard to do the sort of outreach work that the early morning permits at any other time of day, at least until office hours are coming to an end. The middle of the city at noon is not the time and place for outreach. Not that this keeps Charlie or her colleagues indoors. But they make their way out and around the city centre as required, as prompted by the individual tasks they are trying to accomplish and the errands they are running. It is only later, in the mid-afternoon, that the team reassembles at Marland House, the afternoon shift replacing the morning's, in preparation for the second of the two CCT patrols. Those coming off shift brief those coming on, listing jobs and duties still to do or now unnecessary, updating on the day's events and accomplishments (and unravellings). Around 5.30 or 6pm, just as the city centre has begun to thin out a little, evening outreach begins. What follows is two to three hours spent on foot, patrolling around the commercial and civic centre.

Evening outreach is part-way complementary to the Breakfast Run. The Breakfast Run initiates a day in prospect whereas evening outreach draws the same day to a close; evening patrols are largely retrospective, an opportunity to catch up with clients already seen, for whom the day has now played out one way or another. The evening patrol is also an opportunity for workers to spot any new faces, 'arrived' at some point today and with nowhere else to go and now casting about for options. New arrivals might stand out at any time of the day, but they are at their most visible as daytime provision closes up and the street traffic thins out: they are the ones left behind, with no home to go to. Evening outreach shares with the Breakfast Run the possibility that workers will catch clients at a low ebb, and receptive as such, done with – perhaps done in by – the rigours of the day.

Wherever else it goes, the evening patrol usually takes in the front steps of the National Museum, outside which the Bus will be parked, a crowd of drinkers and hardcore homeless, lugging backpacks and blankets, milling around outside, their numbers boosted in good weather by a typically younger crowd of accomplices and hangers-on (there is almost always someone on a mountain bike, often a couple of dogs). This is the same Bus Project encountered in Chapter 2 (see also p. 58n), a reconditioned double-decker modified to accommodate a canteen, drop-in and advisory service, managed by the Salvation Army in association with the City Centre Team. The Bus is an established staging post for clients of the team, an important out-of-hours node in the homeless city, though not fixed permanently – which is the only reason it is here at all, so close to a prime visitor location.[6]

It is in the nature of patrols that they go nowhere, in the sense that they tend to end up back where they started. CCT evening outreach does just that, goes nowhere; it loops through the city centre out as far as the museum and then turns to head back in the general direction of Central Square. So, having left the Bus, outreach workers are into the final hour of evening patrol and headed home – psychologically at least (their spatial practice may be nothing so direct). But they have one more call to make along the way, a timetabled stop they hardly ever miss and to which they will hurry along if they are behind time: the soup run. Every evening at 8pm, opposite the Ebenezer Chapel on Charles Street, a collection of church volunteers arrives by car to unload flasks of hot soup and tea and bags of free food – sandwiches, crisps, biscuits, cake, fruit – to be set out on trestle tables and distributed to all comers. There is usually a crowd of 20 to 30 people waiting, ready to take delivery.

---

6. The Bus is an award-winning outreach project in its own right, but no more than a tolerated presence in the city centre. It is allowed to park up outside the museum and draw a (disreputable) crowd, petrol generator clattering away on the pavement alongside, on the given understanding that it does so only once the museum has closed for the day and that it then drives off again a couple of hours later, and its clients disperse.

For the outreach team, the soup run is something of a liability, and they make it their business to be there when it arrives if only to keep a lid on things. Eight o'clock on Charles Street is a pinch-point in the geography of the day, a short interval, half an hour at most, in which the city centre's most vulnerable and needy inhabitants, along with some of its most difficult and stroppy, congregate, unsupervised, at a single location – out of doors, so not a confined space exactly, but in wet weather no more than 15sq m or so of shelter under a concrete awning. Everyone knows the soup run, and anyone owed money or an apology, or anyone looking to settle a grudge, can pitch up here and expect to make the connection. If things do get heated, or turn nasty, or 'kick off', as they do almost every day somewhere in the city centre for someone known to the CCT, it is as likely to be here as anywhere else. Added to this there is the waiting, which no one seems particularly good at. If the volunteers are even five minutes late the whole scene can turn a little edgy. And when they do arrive, there is the push and shove for what is always taken to be scarce resources even if there is plenty to go around (as there usually is). Everyone wants something, wants their share (and more), wants it now, wants the best of what there is to be had: soup before it goes cold, the pick of the sandwiches, seconds. It can be touch and go at the soup run, and sometimes things 'get silly', as Dennis would say. So the team have made it a part of their evening remit to be there, without ever having really come to terms with the soup runners themselves.

Of course, outreach workers make their own donations of food and drink, and cigarettes (sometimes) and even clothing. So it is not the giving, as such, that troubles them. But they see their own gifts as more carefully managed, thinned out across the city and targeted. In contrast, the soup run is indiscriminate, though no doubt well-intentioned. 'Here we go,' says Jeff as we turn the corner onto Charles Street 'time to play spot the homeless person'. In truth though, the soup run is too good an opportunity to miss. All the usual suspects are there, perhaps only two or three known to be sleeping out right now, but almost all known to the team one way or another, or liable to become known, part of the wider equation of need and public space and difficulty to which CCT outreach is addressed. The soup run is also one of the places where people fetch up, having gone missing or got lost. The young girl over there, sitting on the wall with Bobby and John, is she the same as the one in that photo issued by social services, the runaway? Not just a liability then, but a gift – to an outreach worker; a chance to gather information and follow up on leads, to affirm existing contacts and work the crowd. But short-lived, this opportunity. Twenty minutes after the trestle tables have been set up they are being packed away into car boots again and the soup run is mostly over. The crowd breaks up and spreads away, leaving a widening delta of litter – polystyrene cups and sandwich wrappers – along Charles Street. Outreach workers get moving too, turning off Charles Street and along Cathedral Walk, cutting through the shopping precinct onto the Hayes and from there along Caroline Street back towards Central Square. All done and back at Marland House by 8.30pm, unless something has cropped up and there is a job to do – fetching the van and driving back round to Charles Street to pick up Paddy M. who is in no fit state to make it back to Tresillian House, or a trip out to the hospital and a long wait in accident and emergency with a client who won't stay there on her own – in which case the evening shift will take as long as it takes.

During the year in which I worked most closely with the CCT and was more or less an ancillary member of staff, evening outreach was followed on three or four evenings a week by a third patrol, known as the StreetLife Project. Regrouping at Marland House, outreach workers would stock the boot of a car with a flask of hot water, sachets of instant coffee, hot chocolate and sugar, disposable cups, leaflets, condoms and panic alarms, and then drive around the city's red-light areas, parking up at intervals to make contact with street-based sex workers, some already well known to the team as occasionally homeless and in and out of the local hostels. They would be out until at least 10pm, sometimes well past that, and on a very few occasions into the early hours of the morning. If the week's shift pattern happened to work out that way, Jeff or Dennis could find themselves (yawning) out on the Breakfast Run not much more than six hours after a 'bit of a late one last night on StreetLife'.[7]

---

7. The CCT has stepped back a little since – has had to, following redundancies and re-structuring – allowing StreetLife to establish itself as an independent, grant-funded opera-tion with its own project workers and office space, one of a suite of projects managed by the Cardiff-based charity Safer Wales. But CCT outreach workers still join the StreetLife team on patrol at least once a week, just enough to keep in touch with the women they used to know, and to look out for those they don't yet but are likely to before long.

Heavy scoring

If one of the things that patrol accomplishes is the marking out of a territory and a claim to occupancy then outreach patrol does something like that for the CCT; it measures out a patch of the city that belongs to outreach, to which outreach belongs, a space of operations. To go out on patrol with the team is to be given an answer to the question *Where is the city centre?* (and some sort of answer to the question *What is it?* too). More than this, outreach work *is* this movement – up and down these particular streets, through these spaces, back and forth between these same locations. On my map(s), these daily patrols – outreach as spatial practice – are consolidated and confirmed through heavy scoring of the same circling routes. Inside this perimeter the map is scribbled in and cross-hatched by any number of ventures and errands run, too many to be made out individually – a general rummaging around. Outside, the map is also marked but not nearly so thickly shaded. Single lines of travel record particular journeys. The very few that make it all the way to the edge are, by then, so disentangled from any other as to bring to mind quite clearly the single excursions they represent – Steve and Nicy's journey to intercept their departing client, bent on pushing his trolley to Newport, for example; I can see this on the map and recognise it for what it is. But the real action is in the middle of the page, where things are that much harder to make out.[8]

Why harder to make out? It is not only that the many more excursions congregated here overlap and obscure each other, though there is that too. Rather, they are not produced as lines of practice in quite the same

---

8.   I note here that I don't expect the reader to have a very sure grasp of the configuration of actual streets and landmarks in the centre of Cardiff, a mental map assembled (or on its way to being assembled) from my accounts of outreach practice. That is not what I am trying to put across. Those who already know the city will be able to fit my descriptions to their own place knowledge. Those who don't are at no disadvantage as I see it. What I want to suggest about the work of outreach and, more widely, about being on the streets and looking out for others, does not depend on anyone knowing where the National Museum is exactly or how far it is from the Hayes to Tresillian Way. Being an outreach worker (or an established rough sleeper) in Cardiff *does* rather depend on knowing this sort of thing, or rather it goes together with knowing this sort of thing. Nonetheless, in giving my own account of outreach work I have specified streets and locations and will keep doing so because these are particular places and it would not make the sort of sense I am after here to give an account of outreach as happening abstractly.

way. Only a very few outreach encounters come about as a result of workers having set out with the express purpose of arriving somewhere in order to then 'do' outreach – it doesn't so much matter where, how near or far away. This is what gives Steve and Nicy's outing its distinctive shape. Most outreach encounters look different because they have no real shape at all. They happen along the way, in the course of the routine patrols whose contours they share (and they belong to the swatches of territory so described). Another reason they are hard to see is that my map shows only half the picture. It takes two to intercept, but the lines I have drawn (and this holds good right across the page) trace only the movements of the team, not those of its clients. Even so, the encounters are there, on the map, if you know what you are looking for. They appear not as a crossing of lines – one the outreach worker's and the other a client's – but as moments of pause at which a line of outreach patrol stalls and circles into a little knot before moving on again. This sort of thing happens all the time; it is outreach getting done.

Outreach: Evening patrol with Nicy and Den. At the corner of the Hayes, we meet Nigel – on his way to the soup run, he tells us, though he is a good hour early. Nicy and Den have only so much time for Nigel; they know him, of course – everybody knows Nigel – but he is hard work and not really in the sort of need that the team can do much about: he is a hanger-on, part of the city-centre scene in a way but marginally so – always there, always around but not in with anyone and not 'out' properly speaking (he has his own place, doesn't drink, doesn't beg, borrow or steal, doesn't fight; is just a little odd and solitary – also needy). In a way, Nigel is not 'hard to reach' at all. Reaching out to Nigel is easy. The problem is he won't let go. He will talk forever. Tonight he is lugging around two plastic carrier bags full of something or other and keeps putting these down to rest his hands, at which point we all stop to wait until he is ready to carry on.

'What have you got in the bags, Nigel?'
'Say again?'
'What's in the bags?'
'Oh, nothing much. Just heavy, they are. You're not in a rush are you?'
'Not really, Nigel. No.'

We aren't in a rush, it's true. But we are not getting anywhere standing talking, and Nigel, as is his way, seems immune to any prompt that the conversation might be over or coming to an end. He is also slightly deaf, or claims to be, and it is hard not to suppose that he plays this up sometimes, just to keep you talking while he comes up with something (more) to say:

'So, we're off. Bye then Nigel,' says Nicy cheerily, briskly.

'What did you say?'

'I said bye. We're off. See you later.'

'Not if I see you first! That's what they say isn't it? Did you know that I used to - '

'Well, bye.'

'Say again?'

'Nothing Nigel. It's just we've got to go now. OK?'

'I can't hear sometimes unless you shout,' says Nigel. 'Did I tell you what happened to me on my way in? It was funny really, because - '

'You did Nigel, yes. We'll see you at the soup run OK?' Nicy starts to walk away.

'No, wait. Say again?'

Eventually we do manage to disentangle ourselves, leaving Nigel on a bench with his bags. We cut through to Charles Street and turn left, back up Queen Street towards Bute Park.

Halfway there we come up behind three young people, a girl and two boys in their late teens. They have a certain look about them, and sure enough the girl turns around and recognises Nicy and comes over to say hello. The boys fall in with us too and we are all walking together. 'You OK?' asks Nicy, and the girl's face starts to crumple. We stop. 'Come on, come over here,' says Nicy, and walks the girl - now sobbing - off to one side where they sit down together on a low wall. Den and I keep on ahead with the two boys. Twenty yards on and out of earshot, we slow up and stop to wait. The boys are on their way to the Bus. We thought as much. One of them, 19 years old, is out of prison only yesterday but has not yet been to Housing (where he would be treated as a priority); instead, he plans to sleep out tonight. The other, younger, is known to Den from years back (so too his mum, a CCT client herself).

Nicy and the girl, Susan, catch us up again, all smiles. Susan and the boys set off for the Bus together and we wave goodbye for now, promising to catch up with them again in half an hour or so. We stand in a huddle on Queen Street for five minutes while Nicy fills Den in on the story. Nothing can be done tonight. Something can be done tomorrow. Nicy has some calls to make.

One hour later we are finished at the soup run and headed back to Central Square. We are detained by Nigel, who never made it to the soup run and is sitting more or less where we left him, with his bags. Next to the bench is a seemingly abandoned pushchair. He says that a woman was pushing it only five minutes ago.

'Then it started to rain and she took the baby and ran off over there,' says Nigel.

'Took the baby and just ran off?' asks Nicy.

'Honestly,' says Nigel. 'Just ran off.'

'Which way, Nigel? Where'd she go?' asks Den.

'That way, over there.'

Den walks, then jogs, off in the direction indicated, down the Hayes and around the corner onto Bridge Street. Nicy and I stand with Nigel, who wants to know who was at the soup run and what went on. We are halfway through telling him when Den comes back, with nothing to report – a bit of a puzzle. We break away from Nigel and turn down Caroline Street. Inky is in a doorway, feeding his dog. We say hello, and Nicy pets the dog. A little further on, by the cashpoint, a man sits cross-legged on the pavement asking passers-by for money; a blanket, folded in half and set out in front of him is scattered with coins.

'Any change? Just coppers. Any coppers at all, lads? Spare any change, any coppers?'

He is nondescript, thin, in his thirties maybe. His face and voice are unfamiliar. We slow down. Nicy and Dennis exchange little shrugs and grimaces. Who is he? Nicy inclines her head to Den and he walks over while the two of us hang back.

'Are you OK there mate?' asks Den, crouching down alongside the man.

The man is monosyllabic at first, a little cowed and hostile. 'Just getting some money together,' he says. Doesn't want any trouble.

'Oh, no trouble,' says Nicy, walking over to join Den, now that the conversation has begun. 'We're here to help.' She crouches too.

Den introduces us all by name and offers his hand, which the man shakes. 'Paul, that's me. I'm Paul.'

Den explains a little about the CCT and what they are there to do. He asks if Paul has somewhere to sleep, but this seems a touchy topic – Paul doesn't want to say. Den switches back to pleasantries. Paul says he'd like a drink of water more than anything else right now. Nicy stands up and walks across the road and comes back with a bottle from a corner shop.

'New in town are you, Paul?' asks Nicy.

Paul says no – Cardiff born and bred, but he's been away. Been sleeping rough for years. Not round here though. Den asks if he knows about the soup run and the Bus, the Breakfast Run. Paul says yes he does but he stays away: 'Nah, I stays away. Bullies, they all bullies.'

He doesn't look like an obvious target for bullies (not like Nigel, say). Den gives him a leaflet and tells him to look out for the Breakfast Run tomorrow morning, on Central Square by the train station: 'I'm on tomorrow morning, so it'll be me. I'll look out for you.' Paul shifts his weight to slip the leaflet into the back pocket of his jeans. 'OK, then. Tomorrow,' he says.

Five minutes later we turn the corner onto Central Square and a young man walks over and asks Den for a pen and paper. He says he has a room in Tresillian House and has just turned down the offer of a place (of his own). Too much money and too far away from where he wants to be. He might change his mind though and needs to write down the phone number before it washes off the back of his hand. We wait while he does this and then walk back with him along the side of Marland House to the group of drinkers and others standing where the benches used to be. Big Alan is there, taking charge and ordering others about, as he does. He introduces us to a wobbly, tired-looking man with an American accent.

'These'll help you. Ask them,' says Alan.

The man smells strongly of drink, several days' worth of it, stale, and is having trouble standing. His speech is slurred too, but he seems to be saying something about being on the list for a detox place but fed up of waiting and wanting to know what can be done. Den takes him to one side to see if he can get the story straight, though there will be nothing we can do today and maybe nothing much we can do at all. Meanwhile Alan is talking on and on to anyone who will listen about the ways in which he always helps out on the streets and takes care of people and how he knows everyone and has a kind heart. He starts talking about a young woman in prison who he is looking out for and is going to have bailed to his address, or something like that. It is a name Nicy recognises and she catches my eye to let me know as much. We spend another five minutes listening to Alan (and anyone else who can get a word in), shifting from one foot to the other and nodding until Den is done and joins us again. We walk off and out of earshot and Nicy tells Den about the young woman. There is no way she is having any young woman bailed to Big Alan's address, wherever that might be. Probably it is all nonsense anyway, but she is going to do some digging around tomorrow.

Traced out as a line on a map, Dennis and Nicy's evening patrol winds its way around the city centre gathering up into a knot at each moment of pause and encounter. Put another way, every such moment of pause is marked by a continued moving *around* as outreach workers set about their work. Getting things started with Paul, breaking things off with Nigel, a quiet word with Susan: each of these has its spatial equivalent, its own little choreography. Nothing gets done standing still.

Each of these small scribbles is an intersection, or one half of one (Susan's line of movement can be imagined as tracking across and around the city centre too, making its own fidgety pauses here and there, one of which would be her chat with Nicy). I have used the word intercept, but intersection is a better one in this context. Nicy and Steve might intercept a client on his way out of town, but back in the middle it is *intersections* that matter.[9]

9. To intercept is to catch up with and head off someone or something, having set out to do so; but to intersect is to come across and come together – something less forceful; an intersection is a coming together of itineraries. What matters out on patrol are the looked

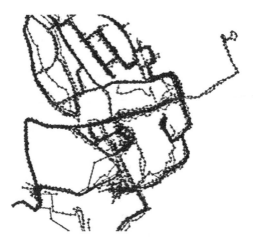

Figure 4.2
(GPS trace of outreach in central Cardiff)

Lines then, lines on the map – my map – do not so much run between moments of encounter as they are productive of those encounters; they are rather more lines of practice than lines of travel, and as such they do not stand still (they shift about, and make their own way). And while it is true to say that evening outreach has its particular shape, an approximate contour heavily scored onto the page as a record of repeated patrol, up close it is just as true to say that no two of the contributing lines are the same. Each one is different. Any single line can be seen to snake and meander either side of any other, hesitating here, turning off there, trembling on the edge of going off somewhere else again before moving back on track, entwined with the rest. This is because Nicy and Dennis are there not to follow a route but to look around; they are in the business of putting themselves about and in the way of others.

As for encounters so too for place. Lines of outreach patrol and those other lines with which they intersect and plait together are not adjuncts to place, strung between fixed locations like tracks running between stations (of the lost). They make the very places they move towards and through and on from.[10] Round the back of Marks and Spencer opposite

for but unforeseen moments at which outreach workers cross tracks with those they are there to help.

10. The three elementary forms of place, according to anthropologist Marc Augé, are 'the line, the intersection of lines and the point of intersection' (1995: 57). A place is, in

the Ebenezer Chapel, about a third of the way down Charles Street –
this doesn't sound much like anywhere in particular, though well enough
specified as a location; it doesn't sound like any sort of *place*. But it *is* –
just that, a place. For half an hour each evening in the centre of Cardiff,
for the shifting collection of people who make their way there, it is the
only place to be: the soup run. It even warrants a dot on the map in
the CCT *Guide* (on my map of Cardiff, marked up to show outreach
patrol, it appears, of course, as a knot of lines). And if lines are practices,
encounters and even places, then the same can be said the other way
round of places, working outwards. These too shift from what they
might first seem to be. To watch the soup run come to a close, the crowd
fragmenting and spreading out along Charles Street, is to see a place
dissolve into the itineraries that first came together to bring it about. And
if the soup run seems too convenient an example, being only a provisional
sort of place to begin with – more an occasion than anything else, and no
part of the built environment – consider Marland House or the Huggard
Centre. The fact is that buildings are fuzzy at the edges too. Certainly
the Huggard Centre is *there* – not only a place but a premises, concretely
established beside Tresillian Way and not about to dissolve in anything
like the way the soup run does, nightly; but it is nothing like a sealed box.
People come and go and linger at the margins, leaning out of windows
talking to friends outside or loafing in the entrance hallway. A sort of
intimacy gradient runs from the seclusion of individual bedrooms out
to the corridors and communal rooms, the busy canteen and reception
area, the main doors and paved porch just beyond; round the corner
there is the access ramp running along the outside of the building, and
adjacent to that a car-parking area, concreted over, with a wonky kerb at
its rim, on and by which a group of drinkers sit and stand, one of them

this sense, not a location to be linked to other such locations by lines of movement, but
instead a gathering together of lines. Tim Ingold, also an anthropologist, has lots to say
about lines of practice and travel, movements through and routes across, and the modern
predisposition to mistake the one for the other; some of which bears on what I have begun
to say about patrol and the city centre: 'we tend to identify traces of the circumambulatory
movements that bring a place into being as boundaries that demarcate the place from its
surrounding space (2011:148; see also 2007). The tendency to (mis)interpret lines as the
limits to life rather than as trajectories of movement is an instance of what Ingold calls
the logic of inversion. Against which, he contends that 'lives are not led inside places but
through, around, to and from them, from and to places elsewhere' (2011: 148). He continues: '[p]laces, then, are like knots' (2011: 149).

Frank, who is looking over (blearily) at someone who has just come into view at the far end of the street, by the row of boarded-up houses: Jeff, possibly; and someone else with him. 'Jeff! Give us a fucking fag.'

The Huggard Centre leaks out into the surrounding streets – most buildings do.[11] Sometimes this happens in such a way as to create a disputable verge; an edge or apron of space along which public and private coincide or might be confused to advantage. The homeless make good use of such spaces where they can, bedding down in locations that are not quite unquestionably anyone's, but not patently everyone's either. Entranceways, stairwells, access ramps, fire exits, forecourts: anything that puts them just about off the street but not so obviously anywhere else as to be trespassing. This is what Gerald has accomplished at the rear of the Glamorgan Building (see pp. 14–15); he has found himself a place that is not so much out of the way – though it is a little bit of that too – as inexact: on the premises but not in the building, round the back but not in the car park (even though the car park is pretty much all there *is* round the back), tucked down by the benches (and edged close enough to benefit indirectly from the shelter and security the building more fully provides those inside). If you were to draft a groundplan of the Glamorgan Building and its environs, marked up to show gradations of territorial differentiation running from private to public, you would have to shade his little strip of space grey. Gary brings off the same trick in setting up his camp, or, rather, assembling it around himself (see pp. 29–30), on an indistinct (and overgrown) ribbon of untended urban planting land between the A470 and Bute Park. On the one side tended lawns and walkways, on the other the tarmac and traffic, and in between the two, Gary, in the bushes.

Cardiff's street cleaners know a disputable verge when they see one – they know all about Gary's encampment – but prefer to keep away; they have enough to do out in the middle of the road, as it were, without straying into some adjacent patch it might not be their job to tidy up. Most can give a very precise account of just where the limits to their duties ought to be drawn; where that road over there stops being an adopted highway and becomes something different, where this pavement

---

11. The tendency with newer buildings seems to be to eliminate such leakage, however. Buildings put up over the last ten years of so in the middle of Cardiff show a preference for sleek and uncompromising exteriors. You are either in these buildings or you are out.

edge here runs into some other territory, itself an edge, the brink of some building or business precinct, responsibility for which lies with someone else or could at any rate be said to: 'Not really my job, that bit under there. Not actually part of the street, see? That's the owner's responsibility that is, the site manager or whoever. They have said it's ours, but it's not, I don't think. Anyway, I don't do under there. Unless I'm told.' Which is the point, after all. So long as no one is making it their job or is even sure just whose job it is, and for so long as no one wants to find out, Gary and the rest can keep to themselves, along the edge of thing, in the middle of the city. Not quite to themselves of course, because these are the same spaces in which the homeless are discovered by those looking out for them. Outreach workers can give just as detailed an account of their spatial practice as any street cleaner, of just where it is that their job takes them. And a lot of the time it takes them to wherever it is that Gary or Gerald have gone to ground – which is the point, after all, or, rather, the edge. Outreach workers operate along and across the same edges at which street cleaners draw a line.

I will draw my own line here, and summarise. In this chapter I have begun to set out a geography of homeless outreach practice, perhaps particular to Cardiff. The work gets done where the need is, but also plaits together with a client group and local scene that assembles, disperses, roves and snags, in and around a city centre. The geography is local and in a sense familiar – the same narrow territory, traversed and reconnoitred. Yet each day begins (again) with an essential uncertainty, the same question: Where is everyone? Outreach workers move around the middle of the city the better to answer this question. Their repeated excursions, pedestrian, exploratory, *are* outreach work.

These excursions, or patrols, move between particular locations, and pockets of likely occupancy, some of which can be mapped – a nodal territory. Such locations matter to outreach workers if not always as places to go then certainly as places to edge up alongside. Every node has its fuzzy rim or apron, at which workers might best discover and sidle up to clients: the museum steps (not the museum); the train station forecourt (not the train station); the kerb by the car park by the Huggard (not the car park, not the Huggard). Some of these spaces are obvious enough, apparent; others are tucked away and belong to a micro-geography of indeterminate, scrubby settings; this geography counts as one of the shared secrets of homelessness – shared by the homeless themselves and those looking out for them. Outreach patrol is misunderstood, however, if it is pieced together as a set of likely (if imprecise) locations and the movements then required to string these together. Out on patrol, workers may very well have some idea of where they are headed next, but they also improvise and readjust, continually, according to this or that trace or intimation; they are typically unhurried; they move along, cut across, double back, in such a way as to give themselves the best chance of *turning up* an encounter with anyone they might already know or ought to get acquainted with – all this quite apart from the business of getting somewhere. Some of their clients will be doing the same, moving about, dawdling, running errands, doubling back, perhaps hoping to bump into someone they think might be out there somewhere – perhaps Jeff, with cigarettes.

5

The Line Inside

The previous chapter asked where the work of outreach gets done, taking this to be a question of urban geography – where in the city, across what kind of territory, within what bounds, in what sort of settings? I have discussed sites and services, routes, locations, intersections, edges, and have circled around the idea of a city centre. Taking outreach to be a spatial practice, I have described workers as making their own particular way around the city centre, in ways that have to do with the work that they are about, and I have suggested that to trace these patrols on paper is to sketch out a map of sorts, if a slightly strange one – unfamiliar, that is, even to those who might think of Cardiff as a place they know their way around. Not that they would be wrong to think so – to think that they know their way around. Mostly we do. We all know the places we spend time in well enough, and move through these in ways that reveal – because they *are* – our relationships with them. To make your way in the city, one way or another, is to live and work there. And we do recognise, though we sometimes need reminding, that there will be other ways through, other lines of practice, different configurations – almost always, and certainly so in any city; we can never know a whole city. This is a part of the challenge and promise of outreach. Every time the team takes someone new out on patrol – a social work trainee on placement, a student doing a research project, a local journalist (usually around Christmas time) – the message is the same: you're going to see a side to the city you may not have realised was there.

But the geography of outreach is twofold. The work itself belongs to the actually existing streets and spaces of the city, whose arrangement shapes the work of outreach, concretely. But even as outreach workers move through an actually existing city – walking, clambering, peering, rummaging around for clients – they inhabit a figurative landscape, a space interior to outreach. The contours of this space are not encountered bodily in quite the same way. But they shape the work of outreach just as surely as does the built environment. I will explain.

Left behind

Perhaps we can return, briefly, to the idea of being lost, discussed in Chapter 2. If we hear it said of someone that they lack direction and have lost their way a little, we are as likely to understand this to be a comment on that person's general life situation and state of mind as on their present ability to locate themselves on a map. Either way, we know we are not being given good news. Being lost is a cause for concern, whether one is off-course in the city or biographically adrift. Possibly there is a sort of freedom that comes with having gone astray, but the prosaic experience is usually discouraging and a source of anxiety. We prefer to know where we are. Anthropologist Edmund Leach suggests this is a universal human need: '[a]ll human beings,' he writes 'have a deep psychological need for the sense of security which comes from knowing where you are'; '[b]ut,' he adds '"knowing where you are" is a matter of recognising social as well as territorial position' (Leach, 1976: 54). And this is my point. Outreach work takes place in the city, but also across a social (and psychological) terrain; its clients are found not only in some or other location – and not just anywhere, it turns out; but as variously positioned in terms of their general circumstances, in terms of how their lives appear to be going. Nor are their lives going just anyhow; there is a patterned distribution here as well.

'Where are we with Tino?' asks Steve at a Friday morning team meeting. 'Not much further along at all,' says Dennis. 'He's still very down. Still drinking. Doesn't want to engage at all. Not in a good place, really. He's been on Crwys Road the last few mornings, in the doorway on the bridge.' No one has to be an outreach worker to understand what is being said here, about where we are with Tino. The language is evaluative. Knowing where you are is one thing, and perhaps it beats being lost; but some places, some positions, are better than others. Knowing where you are – socially, territorially – may not count for much at all if where you are is down and out on Crwys Road. For outreach workers it doesn't. Their job begins, even as they set about approaching clients on their own turf and terms, with the baseline understanding that something is wrong, that there is cause for concern. If Tino could be persuaded just to moderate his drinking that would be a step in the right direction.

That this is such an everyday vocabulary makes it no less effective in shaping an understanding of what it is to be in need and difficulties, to be in a bad place. Commonplace need not mean trivial. Unexamined ideas – ordinary ways of seeing, ways of saying – operate all the more effectively *because* they are unexamined. And there is something powerfully intuitive in the idea that lives are journeys, that troubles are landscaped; so too in a language which tells us that to care for others is to look out for them and feel for them, to have their troubles touch us. The body is the common denominator. We are where we are as embodied persons. We can't move other than as embodied persons; we can't see and sense how things are with the world around us – around what, exactly? – other than through bodily action; nor can we be well if we are not well 'in ourselves', in our own lives, and feel that to be so, bodily. If it makes sense to talk of troubles as landscapes this is only so because landscapes are traversed by a body – which struggles through a difficult patch, gets bogged down or labours uphill. It is the body that matters. Hills are not hard work, in themselves; climbing hills is hard work, and it is the body that climbs. (Going downhill is that much easier – which is sort of the point; downhill is entropic, it is the direction in which things will run if you let them.)

So we can start with the body. Outreach workers start here too, encountering a client for the first time. They see someone slumped or unsteady on their feet, someone injured or dishevelled, someone with the air and appearance of need or damage, and they make their way over. Not a single word spoken, yet: just the look of someone and how they hold themselves. But in another, more general and essential sense, things get started earlier still. Because the body is already available as a basis for making sense of how things are, or might be, with other people long before an outreach worker looks across the street at anyone in particular. With the body things are either up or down, ahead or behind, to one side or the other; added to which the body is where it is, here, and not somewhere else, over there; and this in turn provides a primary basis from which to appreciate distance – things and people not immediately to hand (here) are either near or far away.

Here and there, near and far, up and down, back and front, left and right, constitute the most intimate link between my body and the world. The body thus brings with it a spatial framework organized in terms of these five dyads, the first two of which remain absolute (I cannot be both here and there, things are either near to me, in grasp, or far away), the last three relational. (Tilley, 2004: 10)

This 'spatial framework' provides a basis for encountering the world and making sense of one's place within it;[1] moreover, this is a basis for encountering the world that goes well beyond knowing which way is up. Terms like up and down have a 'fundamental metaphorical significance' and 'common cultural connotations', which are caught up with, and not easily disentangled from, the 'experience of the body and its various states of waking and sleeping, sense or otherwise of well-being' (Tilley, 2004: 5). Here is Edmund Leach again, arguing that codings for the under-standing and arrangement of rank and orientation in human affairs have built into them 'an awareness of the symmetries and asymmetries of the human body' (1976: 53). And here is Alec, sweeping the gutters along Westgate Street, leading to Central Square, nice and slow – 'council pace' – who has worked the bins for 22 years and knows everyone: all the newspaper vendors and security guards and deliverymen, and 'all the dossers, yeah, all the piss-heads and the down and outs'. That is, all those whose lives are scrambled, wrong side up – piss-heads – or who have fallen behind and away from the rest of us somehow, without actually going anywhere.

The terms 'down' and 'out' signal two essential dimensions to the interior geography of outreach, whose figurative connotations run so closely together with bodily experience that it is not always easy or helpful to separate them. Up high in Cardiff means (increasingly) privilege – luxury apartments, elevated status, prospects; down below is the space of pedestrian necessity, the street, and (among others) the homeless. Street level is as low as you can go without digging (without going under); which is to say that every street, no matter where it might lead, is also a sort of dead end. The street is what we hit when we fall or are floored;

---

1. And this holds true whether one is walking past Marks and Spencer in central Cardiff, or encountering ancient stones in prehistoric European landscapes – which is what Christopher Tilley is writing about.

it is where things finish up, get left behind and come to rest. To be in a base condition – to be down, not just on the ground but *down* – is to be depleted, depressed, owing or deficient; it is not a status associated with wellbeing generally. Tilley notes that a 'drooping posture typically goes along with sadness' and that 'consciousness tends to be equated with up and unconsciousness with down (we sleep lying down)' (2004: 5). Or struggle to sleep. Cardiff's street homeless spend a lot of time sitting or lying down. Having done so, some struggle to stand again and remain upright. The longer they are 'out' the harder things go for them. They get ground down. Geoffrey Fletcher's *Down among the Meths Men*, a 1960s study of London's Skid Row, records a world in which '[m]uch attention is paid to the feet … in opposition to the arrangements of the outer world where the head is considered to be of greater importance' (1966: 76).

Outreach work of the sort I am describing is, accordingly, a lowly profession; it so happens that Jeff and Dennis have to descend two flights of stairs to start out on an evening's patrol, but the work involves other sorts of downward movement and would to do so were the CCT office located in a cellar. The pay is modest, the hours are unsocial and the work is physically wearing and goes unremarked by the city at large; it is also dirty work, strongly associated with the grubbier, littered corners of the city centre and with the 'dirt', and smells, of the lower body – of sweaty feet, urine and excrement.

Outreach: Early evening, December. Nicy and I are on patrol together and have made it as far as the top end of the bus station, where the uniformed security staff gather. A quick chat with them is a regular part of evening outreach as they know most of the drinkers and street homeless by sight at least and often have news of whatever has gone on in and around the station since an outreach patrol last passed through. On a bench nearby is Ron Barnard, barely conscious, leaning forward, his hands between his knees in a posture of abjection. The security staff say that they put him – propped him – on the bench an hour ago, having found him on the floor of the gents toilets (he'd had a fall). They have done nothing with him since, and so there he sits, a spent can of lager on the bench beside him.

Nicy goes over to see if she can get anything from him. She has to lean down in order to peer up and sideways at his face. Ron barely responds. Nicy calls Tresillian House, where Ron has a room, to ask if they'll take him back in this state. The answer is yes, and Nicy thinks the only way to do this is to drive him over: he is not up to walking. So we go back across Central Square to the NCP car park to organise Nicy's car (Pete and George are still there, where we left them half an hour earlier, begging for change by the car-park ticket machines). Ron is frequently incontinent and is almost certainly so today, so we arrange blankets and disposable seat-covers for him in the back. We drive around and into the bus station, pulling up in the bay alongside his bench. Together, hands under his armpits, we coax and carry him to the car, his feet lifting up and down, trundling, as if he were a puppet on strings. He is soaked from the waist down. We open the rear door and collapse him in, then I lift and swing his feet in after him, one at a time, by the rank, sopping hems of his jeans.

We drive out of the centre and round to Tresillian House. The journey takes no more than ten minutes, though it seems longer. Nicy winds her window down immediately and I wind mine down soon after: now he is in a warm, enclosed space, the smell coming from Ron is really powerful. Along Clare Street Nicy takes to driving with her head out the window, gagging and laughing at the same time. Ron is asleep in the back, passed out. We arrive at Tresillian House and get the staff to unlock for us, then return to the car and get Ron out – going backwards through the same sequence of moves that it took to get him in there. Ron is no help at all.

Ron's room in Tresillian House smells even stronger than he does, if that were possible. It is awful. Only urine though, and feet and sweat and stale alcohol – no shit, we don't think. Nicy takes a deep breath before we go in, and tries her best to hold it as we carry Ron across to his bed and arrange his covers over him, pulling these up to his chin with pinched thumbs and index fingers. He really needs undressing and a proper sponge down, but the staff are not up for this. Nicy flees the room and is gagging again, this time for real, in the corridor. We wash our hands in the kitchens and make our way back outside to the car.

Dealing with Ron has taken the best part of an hour and we are now behind schedule. Rather than return to Central Square and park Nicy's car there we decide to save time and drive direct to Charles Street and the soup run. First we strip off the soiled (disposable) seat covers and damp blankets and put these in a bin.

Charles Street is, or ought to be, only five minutes away, but the shops are open late tonight in the run-up to Christmas and the traffic in the city centre has coagulated to a near standstill. The journey takes us almost half an hour. We would have been better walking. Finding somewhere to park on Charles Street is slow work too and by the time we are out of the car the soup run is underway: trestle tables have been set up on the pavement alongside the Ebenezer chapel, loaded with boxes of pre-bagged suppers (sandwiches, crisps, chocolate, cake, pieces of fruit) and vacuum flasks of soup and tea and coffee; three volunteers are busy dispensing to a roiling crowd of about two dozen people. There is some of the usual grabbing and shoving and swearing, but some laughter too. The mood seems not so tense. We spot Mark Skinner on the edge of the crowd and he sees us too and comes over to talk, mainly to tell us that he has left the night shelter, for good. The room he was in was terrible, he says: three of them in there and dogs as well, dirty and messy and no one doing anything about it, and people up and talking all through the night. And so he has left. He'd rather be out, and has moved back to his usual spot just around the corner (a fire-exit doorway at the back of one of the shops on Queen Street). He has a sleeping bag (damp) and some cardboard, also, oddly, a portable television, which he took with him from the night shelter and has been storing in a nearby skip. He asks Nicy if she'll mind the television for him until he gets sorted. Nicy says yes, and we walk over together to fish it out. The skip is full of rubble and what looks like kitchen fittings. Mark scrambles up on top, uncovers his television and hands it down to me, muddied and studded with gravel. He can't find the remote, which he thinks must have slipped down the side - he'll root around for it later. We carry the television back to Charles Street and put it on the rear seat of Nicy's car where Ron was sitting an hour ago. Mark takes a new sleeping bag, with thanks. He is off now to get his head down, 'have a quick dig and doze off'. We promise to come and find him in the morning with the Breakfast Run.

It is an outreach worker's occupation to make friends in low places, in unlikely and often unsanitary places. Those not prepared to get down to this level will not cut it in the job for long. Perhaps outreach workers are there to help clear up the mess, to take away the rubbish. Whichever way you look at it, it is dirty work.

Down, and then out. No one wants to be down – in the mouth, at heel – but down and *out* is something else and worse. Mark Skinner is 'out' having quit the night shelter, and for so long as he remains so – out of doors, sleeping rough – he will be a priority for the CCT. Anyone 'out' is a priority. But out means more than out of doors. To be out is to be vulnerable and exposed, and at the same time removed from play, a non-participant (if the stakes of the game are too much for us, we throw in our hand and declare ourselves 'out'). Clients of the team are conspicuously out of all sorts of things: out of pocket, out of work, out of luck, out of order (having lost control, or broken down). They are not much *in* at all, not if in signals social acceptability or the guarantee of success. Getting Mark *in somewhere* means getting him a place (of his own, in a hostel, on a waiting list). For so long as he is out he has nowhere; to be out is to be absent or inexactly located, perhaps lost. Coupled together, out and down signal the end of something: 'down and out' means destitute, derelict – noun and adjective. The team's most totemic clients are down and outs, so called by some of those who see them every day (like Alec, on Westgate Street). Down and out is what and where they are, and it is where outreach workers go to meet them.

The figurative geography of outreach also has a horizontal axis. This is a plane of movement and orientation running front to back, but not disposed to each in the same way or equally. In action we are forward-facing; we see and do things in the world primarily by arranging ourselves so that what we are about is in front of us, to hand and in view. When we move, we move ahead; if we must sometimes retreat then so be it, but in doing so we may feel we have let ourselves and others down. To be forward is to be bold, to be up front is to be honest; we turn our backs on that which does not hold our attention, on those who displease us – unless they cannot be trusted (back and behind are also zones of deceit, where motives are hidden). What might such a spatial framework and its subtexts have to do with outreach work, welfare and homelessness in particular? No one who has spent even half a day at a homeless drop-in centre or hostel talking to members of staff and keyworkers could doubt the connection. Movement and direction provide an essential vocabulary for talking about what has gone wrong for clients and what they need to do to put things right. Service users are stuck or lack orientation; they are 'going nowhere' and face obstacles; they need help moving on and forward from their present difficulties if they are to 'make progress … [and] do better in their day-to-day lives' (Egan, 1994: 49). This is the language of modern welfare. The enemy is passivity, inaction:

> What keeps clients from acting on their own behalf? In physics, the law of inertia states, in part, that a body at rest tends to stay at rest unless something happens to move it along. Many clients are in trouble or stay in trouble because, for whatever reason, they are at rest. (Egan, 1994: 79)

Gerald Egan's acclaimed handbook, *The Skilled Helper*, sets out a problem-management approach to helping clients make changes in their lives and get where it is they want to go – away from the situations and behaviours that make them unhappy but to which they are wedded by inaction.[2] Thus, a scheme in Cardiff offering mentoring and support to

---

2. My own copy of this book was given to me by a keyworker in a short-stay hostel for the single homeless back in the mid-1990s; it was then in its 5th edition, and is now in its 10th.

women at risk of re-offending is called the *Women's Turnaround Project*; its clients, more than a few of them known to the CCT, are assumed to be in the sorts of difficulties they can put behind them given the support and encouragement to look ahead and move off in a new direction. An impact evaluation of the project undertaken by criminologists from the University of Glamorgan refers to the 'positive steps forward' taken by at least some of the those using the service. Clients interviewed for the report use a similar language, talking about the importance of having 'goals to work towards'; they worry too about the possibility that, without the support and direction the project gives them, they may lose ground:

> 'I feel that if I've got no goals to work towards in my life then I probably could get into depression'

> 'I've got nowhere ... I was homeless before I came in see. I reckon I got a feeling I'm going back on drugs. I'm off them now ... even if it's like a B&B or something just so I've got somewhere to go straight away instead of going back onto the street, back into the drugs ...'[3]

Going straight (not back to the street or the drugs) is not easy; unlike letting go and falling behind. Each of these two women sees that. Moving forward is going to be hard for them and they worry they might relapse; and a relapse, like a setback, is only ever a bad thing. Nor is this only a matter of forwards and backwards. You do not have to actually reverse your direction of travel in order to fall behind. All it takes is distraction and a slight shift off-course one way or the other, left or right. It is easy enough to get sidetracked, and the sort of helping that aims to have clients engaged in 'sustained goal accomplishing action' (Egan, 1994: 314) is no more fond of sidetracking and side issues than it is of setbacks. Things off to one or other side of us are peripheral so long as we look ahead; to attend to them directly is to turn off course, lose focus and risk delay. To sidle is to move surreptitiously; to look sideways is to look askance, to regard something or someone in a furtive or suspicious manner –

---

3. See *An Evaluation of the Women's Turnaround Project* (Holloway and Brookman, 2008: 25, 28 and 39). The report adopts 'significant positive steps' and client 'progress' (as recounted by project staff, based on direct observation of changes in behaviour and circumstances) as measures of impact.

sideways is the way that passers-by look at Ron slumped on a bench in the bus station, if they look at all.

Border crossings

Outreach work could hardly be called an up-front and straight-ahead sort of practice, however; it is rather more intricate, more compromised and uncertain. Lots of things get done sideways-on in outreach. Not only the rummaging sorts of movement that characterise outreach patrol – workers zig-zagging this way and that to take a look along the edge and around the back of things – but also the content of outreach encounters, where much that passes between workers and clients does so inexactly and indirectly. Outreach work is an exercise in curiosity and concern and each of these requires tentative movement. Some issues have to be worked at carefully, in a roundabout sort of way. Michael Rowe describes street-based outreach work as Janus-faced: workers befriend and gain the trust of homeless people, offering individual care and attention, but are also expected to manoeuvre their clients off the streets and into accepting treatment in line with 'categorical program requirements' (1999: xiii). The point of balance, or tension, between these two ambitions can be drawn out as a line or edge along and across which outreach work takes place. Rowe's book-length study of encounters between homeless people and outreach workers takes that edge as its organising premise – the book is titled *Crossing the Border*; and he has this to say about homelessness as a category of 'other' out there somewhere, beyond such an edge:

> We cross a foggy border of sleep to find our waking selves. An hour later our working selves greet us at the office. We encounter boundaries of self and other, of task and situation. We create and use borders as starting and stopping points for thought … Homelessness is, in part, a bureaucratic and political category. Its divisions by time served, demographics, disability, or the sheer bad luck of its occupants are abstractions that give order to our thinking and help us allocate scarce resources for unlimited human needs. The otherness of homelessness has its special stigmata, derived from history, from observation of homeless persons, and from our pity, disgust, and fears. We mentally place homeless individuals at our symbolic border and see them as

living apart from us, perhaps because of our uncomfortable feeling of closeness to them. (1999: 156)

For Rowe, the border between ourselves and others makes homelessness what it is.[4]

A border is a limit, and a link. Either way it accrues powers and unease. '[M]argins are dangerous', as Mary Douglas argued 50 years ago; '[i]f they are pulled this way or that the shape of fundamental experience is altered' (1996: 122; originally 1966). They are the edge along which a body, or society, or structure of ideas, is vulnerable; and the points at which such an edge is breached – points of crossing or aperture – are, accordingly, points of acute vulnerability, sometimes hedged about by prohibitions or unusual consideration. Any 'stuff' that might leak across an edge or border, or which gathers at the margins, can arouse strong feelings and may need treating with great care (which need not mean kindness). All of which matters for the work of outreach, which takes place at a social margin and along a moral edge running, perversely, through the middle of the city. It is, again, dirty work.

At, along, but also across; outreach workers are tasked to breach the border that defines the work they do, to extend services and friendships across a divide in their attempts to get clients to 'engage' and get treatment and 'finally, return to society' (Rowe, 1999: 80). Tentative moves are made by both parties, back and forth, each weighing up what can be got from crossing over and what might be risked, lost or left behind in the process. Each side has something to gain, and to lose; each has something to give, though it is only the outreach workers who actually hand anything over – a bacon sandwich, say, or a sleeping bag. These gifts might seem to come for free – and they do, except that they don't. Rowe is particularly strong on this, the transactional nature of outreach work:

---

4. Up and down, back and front and left and right: these are what Tilley refers to as the relational dyads of the body's spatial framework. But two other dyads remain absolute: here and there, and near and far away. As Tilley has it, 'I cannot be both here and there, things are either near to me, in grasp, or far away' (2004: 10). Rowe seems to be suggesting something different. What he calls the otherness of homelessness opens up a gap between homeless persons and ourselves. Homelessness belongs *over there*, some way off from what we are prepared to see and understand. Except that the homeless are also *here*, close at hand and not going anywhere (and we *do* want to look, even as we want to look away). The superimposition of these two – near and far – intensifies our unease: adjacency accentuates otherness.

Homeless persons weigh the offer of housing against the uncertainties that go along with becoming housed persons. They bargain with workers for tangible goods: workers sell treatment and medication to go with these goods. Workers seek to expand their territory, homeless persons to protect theirs. Homeless persons seek a sense of belonging; workers seek to be the experts, friends, and even the heroes who provide it. Workers pursue homeless persons in order to fulfill the requirements of their jobs; homeless individuals who lack the proper disabilities may paste stigmata on themselves in order to qualify. (1999: 81)

The line to be crossed in any welfare encounter is a boundary of inequality (Sennett, 2004: 20); but this does not make the work one-sided. The point is that helping the homeless is a two-way process. Outreach workers need homeless people too. They need to find them, make clients of them, bring them back across. What sort of outreach worker would you be if no one reached back? Meanwhile, homeless clients have themselves to think of: what help they want and when, and how they might get it. This should come as no surprise. All frontiers are zones of trade and negotiation whatever the disparity either side (and regardless of whether the line drawn is supposed to preclude such activity).

Questions of identity are also at issue, at any border. Along the moral edge of outreach, uncertainties of purpose and reach, identity and entitlement, multiply. Is *he* homeless, is *she*? Homeless *enough*, or not really? Or too homeless even, too far gone? Who really needs help, and who wants it? How far should we go with those who say they don't? And who is an outreach worker, anyway, to be asking all these questions? Here to do what exactly, and on whose authority? All of which, and more – difficult questions, uncertainties, encountered along a boundary of belonging and inequality – makes outreach what it is. Rowe's account of outreach work, homeless encounters and border crossings is the best that I know, and I don't seek to improve on its strengths here. It would be hard to do so. But I will return to *Crossing the Border* in later chapters in order to develop different aspects of my own account, some of which lead away from Rowe's preoccupations, or run parallel to these. There is more to say about where outreach work gets done and what it is that outreach workers do.[5]

---

5. There is certainly more to say about borders. Two things need noting – repeating really, as each is implied at various points in this and the preceding chapters. The first of

Time and the street

As anyone knows who has found themselves feeling on edge or unsafe in some part of a city, place can be as much a matter of when as where. Central Square in Cardiff is one sort of place at 10am and quite another at 10pm. So too the front steps of the National Museum or the back of Marks and Spencer, or the alley running between the Tyndall Street Industrial Estate and the railway line. Time matters then, and helps make place. Outreach work takes time to do, and wherever it is they go, outreach workers must pick their moments and settle on the hours that best suit what it is they are up to and hope to accomplish. Consequently, the temporal distribution of homeless outreach is distinctive and says something about what it is that outreach workers are up to. As noted already, a lot of outreach work gets done outside of office hours. Reaching clients who are not at ease with workplace schedules, who have been out all night and whose needs can't wait, means loosening one's grip on nine-to-five administration. Outreach work gets done when it needs doing. Puzzling over how best to help Cindy in the NCP car park, Nicy has been up and at work for a couple of hours; meanwhile, her social work colleagues are on their way in to the office and haven't yet begun their working day (their first appointments still half an hour away). Shift work makes this possible. Outreach begins at 7am, sometimes earlier; workers are still out at 10pm, sometimes later; through the winter

---

these is that the border that Rowe describes, a boundary of inequality and difference, is not something that outreach workers simply encounter and then work their way along and across. Outreach work is there to test and breach the border, to trace its contours and also to redraw these. Which is to say that the work the CCT team gets done in the centre of Cardiff does not simply take place at (and across) a border; rather, it is one of the ways in which the border between the homeless and the rest of us gets pencilled in. Where outreach workers go, what they do, how far they are prepared, or able, to reach *is* where (and the way in which) the line is drawn.

The second point of note has to do with here and there and the distance between the two. I have suggested that the border is a place where these two (must) meet, each defining the other. If so, then to straddle or cross a border is to muddy the distinction between near and far, here and there. But it is likely the border itself does that already, because most borders prove, on inspection, to be something other than a line of the sort specified by Euclid – a breadthless length. Whether material or figurative, borders usually turn out to have a little width and indeterminacy to them. Most borders and frontiers end up being zones, variously marked, either side of their length, by outposts and activities – little forays either side.

months at least, they start and finish in the dark and work by streetlight. Very occasionally, by arrangement, the team works all through the night. Infrequent 'all-nighters' are the most they can manage, and serve as a sort of a scoping exercise, a chance to check up on what is going on at three or four in the morning, just so they know; things are quieter then, but not stopped altogether. They would do more if they could.

Outreach work exceeds office hours then, starts sooner and keeps going later. Another sense in which it gets done out of hours has to do not so much with time of day as timekeeping. Few outreach clients have watches or mind them if they do, and it is very seldom that you see an outreach worker hurrying along to meet a client somewhere by arrangement at some specified time. Workers do sometimes make plans to meet with clients, to fill in a form together, to help with moving belongings from one temporary stop to another; but these meetings are typically inexact, no more than possibilities and understood to be such by both parties. Having seen Paddy M. out on the Breakfast Run and discussed with him the chances of securing a travel warrant to Bristol, Dennis makes plans for the two of them to meet up later. 'Where will you be?' he asks. 'On Queen Street,' says Paddy. 'Begging. Probably. Or with Tony. Or by the CIA.' And that is as good as it gets. Most meetings between outreach workers and clients, if they come to anything at all – and the mildly remarkable thing is that so many of them do – start out as something not much more than that.

Outreach workers have a foot in both camps, of course. They have their own appointments to keep – team meetings, case conferences, task groups – alongside the work that has them cruising Queen Street in the early morning or slipping out of a training session to deal with whatever has just come up for Ryan. And they cross back and forth with clients too, setting off from Central Square with an hour to spare to try and find Wayne Daley, wherever he might be, in order to make sure he gets to court on time, even if that means walking him over there in person.

If outreach hours are not quite office hours in the sense that there are more of them and they are a bit looser, this is not to say that they lack shape. Time spent on the street 'doing outreach' can be scattered across any one working day, as circumstances dictate, but, whatever the spread, it always gathers along the edges, bunched into the two main patrols that outreach workers hardly ever miss: early morning just ahead of the main commuter dash; and then late afternoon and early evening, starting sometime after 5pm and on past the rush hour, all the way up to what used to be last orders.

Times have changed and are changing, however. Cardiff is not quite, not yet, a city that never sleeps, but its night-time economy has boomed over the last decade and more and this has seen High Street and the Hayes and Central Square and its surrounds grow busier, later into the night and early morning. The clock has been pushed back, squeezing the time in which the city centre seems empty or quiet down to only a very few hours. Four o' clock in the morning is probably the cusp of this. The CCT almost certainly gone; the pubs shut and now the clubs as well; straggling parties make their way home; cleaning crews come to the end of their own night shift. The lull in activity lasts an hour or two, not long.

Cleaning: Ronnie comes on shift at 5am and does Mill Lane, Saunders Road and the bus station, also (three times a week) Millennium Walk alongside the stadium. We meet by arrangement at the depot on Millicent Street. Ronnie finishes his tea and we head down the stairs together and out the door. He gets behind one of the motorised sweepers with rotating brushes up front. We set off, cutting through the redeveloped Hayes, Ronnie pausing now and then to stoop and collect a stray can or cup, gathering these in a plastic bag hanging off the handlebars of his sweeper. It is not actually his job to do this; cleaning around the new St. David's development is now privately contracted, no longer a council responsibility – but Ronnie likes to keep things tidy.

Ronnie has been a long time in the job, having started in the early 1970s, never intending to be at it for anything more than six months. Back then the depot would be closed overnight, and the city centre more or less empty. Not anymore. 'Different pattern of life,' says Ronnie. He is thinking of taking early retirement: 'Let a young man have the job. I don't think I could do another winter.'

We cut across St Mary Street, sections of which are scheduled for pedestrianisation, with preparatory work underway – the surface course of the road already skimmed off, and traffic cones set out – and on to Central Square. Ronnie points to some new tarmac underfoot, spotted with flattened blobs of chewing gum. 'We told them not to tarmac,' he says. 'Now look at it. Chewing gum all bedded in and can't be scraped.' Ronnie visits the toilets and then we begin working our way up and down the aisles, Ronnie directing the sweeper and me gathering the odd bits that the machine misses, using a litter-pick grabber. There are cigarette ends (lots of these), paper cups, plastic beakers, empty half-bottles of spirits, cans, flyers, bus tickets, scraps of litter no longer easily identified, and various free newspapers. 'Stapled together now, the newspapers,' says Ronnie. 'Big difference, that makes.' Other things make a difference too. Windy days are a misery. Summer is the dirtiest season: 'More people out on the street, see. More people dropping stuff.' But winter is harder, because cold and wet, even if not so many people – apart from Christmas shopping and the January sales. Weekends are always busy, whatever the weather or season, and last weekend there was a rugby international on in the stadium; it can take several days to bring the city centre back to normal after an international fixture, and Ronnie will be discovering little clots of 'event' rubbish for days to come.

Crossing over the bus lanes to the far side of Central Square we find just that: a scurf of litter like a tidemark, snagged and trodden down along one side of a temporary plastic barricade arranged to cordon fans on their way to the stadium. It is too narrow for the sweeper here so we park it up and set to with the grabber and hands – Ronnie's bare, though he is supposed to wear gloves. Behind us as we work, plywood hoarding marks the perimeter of a demolition site.

We move back to the bus stands to give them a final check over. There is a sleeper at one end, under blankets. He wasn't there an hour ago, and we contour around him (the Breakfast Run will be along within the hour, and they can see to him). A couple of younger men are sitting talking together at the other end of the same aisle, opposite Marland House. Ronnie reaches around one of them to pick up a stray can of lager, only to be told to put it back. Ronnie says sorry, he didn't realise, thought it must be litter at this time in the morning – trying to make a joke of it.

The bus stands are done, and Ronnie is pleased. The motorised sweeper is great at edges and kerbs, cleaning up against things, he says. 'Gives them a real sharp look'. We move along the train station forecourt, where an inlaid metal line in the paving marks the limit of Ronnie's responsibility to clean, though he steps across it to grab a few floating sheets of paper. He does the same five minutes later, by which time we are alongside the NCP car park: the apron of the building is not really our job to do, but Ronnie leans over the low post and chain fence to pick up a few obvious bits of rubbish. There are a number of sagging and split bin bags piled up here too, which he leaves alone for now but will report on return to the depot. We head that way next, back across St. Mary Street. Ronnie looks at the work underway, and the cones. 'You'll like this,' he says, and goes on to tell me how he visited Pompeii on holiday once and was struck, walking round the site, by some big blocks of stone placed across a roadway. He asked the tour-guide what they would have been for and she explained that this was a pedestrian street and the blocks were there to stop traffic – carts and horses, chariots. 'Pedestrian streets. Ha! And we think we're modern,' says Ronnie.

About the time that Ronnie gets back to the depot, CCT outreach workers will be preparing to set out on the Breakfast Run. Why now? Same reason, just about. Because the city is only just getting started and is not yet busy. Outreach workers can get their work done without others getting in the way, and without getting in the way themselves; and before their clients are up and about and who knows where, moved along themselves by the security staff and privately contracted cleaners who patrol and sweep the edges along which various premises – commercial and administrative – meet the street.[6] Something like the same rationale sees the evening patrol set out just as things are starting to slow down, just as people are heading home from work (and a few hours before some of them will head back in). Peaks and troughs of activity and use give each day its temporal contour – rush hours and office hours, home time and night-life – different times of day, in between and either side of which a good part of what counts as proper outreach work ends up getting done. Which is to say that for all its breadth and licence in other respects, outreach patrol is also rather a narrow practice, confined to those hours when there is not much else going on. and the city has time and room to spare.[7] Temporally, it is a niche practice, and crepuscular.

I have already indicated the way in which a spatial vocabulary lends itself to talk about wellbeing, about how it is our lives are going; and also how forward motion can have a particular value in such talk, as something we should look for and work *towards*. We aim to make progress and get

---

6.   Commercial cleaners generally work indoors, employed by the owners of a premises; this helps define their authority. They have somewhere to keep clean, from which they can sweep dirt *out* – and they have somewhere to sweep it out *to* as well: the street. In this sense at least, it is easy enough for cleaners at the CIA to tell a group of drinkers sitting on the steps by the ticket office that the building is about to open and it is time to get up and move along. Local authority street cleaners do not work indoors, and tend to let sleeping 'dossers' lie (edging around them, as Ronnie does in the early morning on Central Square). Their place of work is not a premises, nor privately owned. If someone is (already) sleeping in the street, where would you sweep or shoo them off *to*?

7.   These slow moments on the city clock are not only either side of business and commercial hours, they are also at the fringe of the city's schedule of homeless provision. Those who have managed a night indoors at Tresillian House via emergency-overnight-stay – single mattresses on the floor in a shared room – are ushered back out on the street again in the early morning at around the same time that the Breakfast Run sets out from Clare Street; morning outreach patrol finishes up around the same time the Huggard Centre (and canteen) opens its doors; evening outreach gets underway an hour or so after the Housing Advice Unit has closed and a couple of hours before the nightshelter night shelter opens to admit residents.

on, in life, rather than end up stuck somehow or slipping backwards. The passage of time, our place within it and its place in our lives is caught up in this same pattern of thinking and speaking. The future lies ahead, as a prospect; the past is behind us. If we make progress towards a goal we do so over time, having set out the steps it will take to get us there and formed some idea of when we might expect to accomplish any of these. If we speak of ourselves or others as stuck or going nowhere, we mean this to be a temporal difficulty too, in which time passes but not as the measure of anything more than repetition. For some of the street homeless time can slacken in a sense that goes beyond getting sloppy about appointments. The days blend and seem to lead nowhere, the future gets lost in a circling recurrence of all-too-familiar problems and situations. It can be hard to see your way out of such a muddy timescape; hard for outreach workers too, who must work their way into it somehow if they are to help clients fight free – if only that were what all clients self-evidently and straightforwardly wanted.

Meeting a possible client for the first time, outreach workers straddle the past and future – another edge, between bordering territories. They do so as frontline staff whose encounters with others occur in real time, and so they begin with immediate enquiries: 'Everything OK there? You look a little lost. I'm Nicy. Can I help?' But before very long the talk backs up: 'Where have you come from then? Why don't you tell us what's gone on?' Everyone is who and where they are by way of a past, and outreach workers are always after bits of biography and past history that might help them more fully appreciate their clients' difficulties – without wanting to be seen to pry. This can take time – in the course of which workers and clients build their own history, of repeated contact and growing familiarity – but however long it might take, a Friday-morning team meeting at Marland House will eventually come round at which someone will say: *I think we know where we are with Malcolm now. I think it's time we started to push a little, and see if we can't help him to make some plans. We need to get things moving.* This might seem like the sort of thing someone really ought to have said much sooner. But to think so would be to misunderstand the tact and extended courtship that outreach work can sometimes entail, at least with its essential and defining clients, who won't be rushed into anything and can walk away from the CCT any time they choose to do so – because they know where they are, with the streets, these clients (the street being always *there,* somewhere to keep to or fall back on; perhaps not so enviable but at the very least *known* (see Rowe, 1999: 106), unlike the future).

Time, then, is another aspect of the figurative landscape of homeless outreach. A dimension of lived experience that shapes the work of outreach in ways that are additional to, and overlay, the physical geography of the streets; something you wouldn't find on a map.

And the streets themselves? To say of some outreach clients that they know where they are with the streets is to say something other and more than that they know their way around. The street is a condition as well as a location, also an inclination, a set of skills and routines and dispositions. Outreach work shares in some of this inasmuch as it is definitively street work. There are certain smarts that go together with being good at outreach that are only ever street smarts, and outreach workers are able to get anywhere at all with their most difficult clients on that basis; it being acknowledged that they are not fools, that they know what it is like (to be homeless, among other things) even and especially if the supposed experts don't. On occasion, they trade on this intimacy, sharing jokes at other welfare professionals' expense the better to hit it off with those they are hoping to get through to and help – crouched down beside a sloppily pitched tent in the cold and dark, trying to decipher an obscure and sodden letter from JobCentre Plus, by torchlight.[8]

Just as much as workers' efforts are routinely turned to getting clients in somewhere, so too are those efforts only ever, and essentially, practised out of doors. Outreach work belongs to the street; and all its orientations belong there too, all the ups and downs and rounds and crossings.

Outreach: Early morning mid-October. Breakfast Run with Jeff and Rees, starting out from the night shelter. We turn right off Clare Street to cross the river, then right again around the back of the NCP car park, pulling up on the pavement by the corner of Marland House. I stay put with the flasks

---

8.   Back at the office and at inter-agency meetings – case conferences, care planning and similar – outreach workers lack some of the specialism and accredited expertise that others bring to the table, and may look to colleagues for answers to the questions they have about clients at risk or in need of urgent intervention. Even so, not all answers will suit. What may seem sound enough planning upstairs in Marland House can quickly unravel out of doors on the CIA steps in the rain. This is a lesson well learned – and the team receives repeated instruction. Accordingly, care plan meetings sometimes come full circle, with social work or housing professionals turning back to outreach workers for their view on whether or not proposals, provisionally agreed indoors, are likely to come to anything out on the street.

while Jeff and Rees search Central Square. They come back with a young man who takes a cup of tea and talks briefly, making not very much sense at all, before drifting off into the city. He is new, and we haven't even got a name yet. Too soon to ask, without scaring him off.

We find no one on High Street or in Bute Park (where the summer tent encampment by the College of Music has long since gone), but there are plenty in the civic centre including Mack, Jono, Swansea Nick and others on the steps of the Glamorgan Building. Mack and Jono have moved from their usual spot under the portico of the Crown Court. Perhaps they have been warned off. Either that or they have just shifted along for a change – 'winter quarters,' suggests Jeff, only half in jest. We shout and wave, pointing over to the toilet block at the back of the National Museum where we park up again and wait. Only Mack makes it over. He says the others have been on the gear and the booze and are unlikely to surface – which proves to be the case. Lenny Cooper turns up out of Cathay's Park, takes breakfast and is gone. Mack lingers. He is looking a little better: no shakes this morning. He says this is the result of his having got 'off the white and back on the brown' – cider, that is; a friend of his helped him, another drinker, he doesn't say who. Not his old pal Malcolm Watkins though. Mack has no nice words for Malcom this morning. He has fallen out with him and is not the only one – Swansea Nick and others are after him too. Malcolm's offences are unspecified. He has been spreading rumours, 'stirring things'; he 'needs to grow up'. Mack gets specific: there is a story going around about himself and Emma Riley (Pete Farnwoth's girlfriend). All rubbish, says Mack. In any case, Malcolm is due a kicking and likely to get one, if not from Mack, who admits he is 'not much of a fighter', then from someone else and soon – 'and I hope it's a good one,' says Mack. And where is Malcolm? Nobody knows. He is missing. 'Lying low, if he knows what's good for him,' says Jono, having made his way over at last, trailing a sleeping bag along the ground.

Andy Watkins arrives, with a new friend, or accomplice more like – or victim (Andy is best friends with anyone he thinks might have money to 'lend' him). His pal is a youngish man who tells us he has been staying at a B&B on Newport Road but has left because the place was infested – he shows Jeff his hands, covered in bites; he says he doesn't like Cardiff and is planning to move on to Bristol. Rees keeps him talking, trying to find out a little more about who he is and what he is doing 'out'. Meanwhile Andy has a bone to pick with the team. Once he has got his tea – five sugars – and boiled egg he gets started, working himself into a sort of mock indignation about what he says happened to him yesterday. 'Get this,' he says. Yesterday afternoon he went to an appointment at the Addictions Unit, set up for him by the City Centre Team – no small accomplishment, attending an appointment, for Andy. And do we want to know what the doctors told him? What they said was that he could be sectioned for six months in order to detox and to address his anger management problems. 'Sectioned for six months,' he half-shouts. 'Thanks very much for that City Centre Team. Thanks a lot'. It is an intentionally public performance. He has everyone's attention, and there is laughter as he lards on the details of his consultation. But, as always with Andy, what starts out as pantomime is only ever a wrong word or funny look away from the real thing, from a full-on row and a fight. And he'd like that, or can't seem to help himself. You have to watch your step with Andy. Jeff draws him off to one side, keeping him talking, asking (in jest) if 12 months wouldn't suit him better, playing along, cooling him out. Rees is on the phone to the night shelter to see if there might be space there soon for Andy's new friend. Andy departs, reeling off across the road shouting at some arriving office worker: 'Will you marry me, love?' No, is the swift reply.

We spend the next ten minutes cruising up and down the alley running behind Park Place before moving on to Queen Street – no one there – and the Hayes, ignoring signs prohibiting all but 'authorised traffic' (there are roadworks all over the Hayes, but we weave through). No one on the Hayes either. Next the CIA, where we park the car and set out on foot. Rees goes around one side and Jeff and I go around the other. In the first doorway we come to we find a young couple lying down side by side, the man in a sleeping bag smoking a cigarette, the woman next to him with no bag or covers whatsoever. Around the opposite flank of the building, with Rees, there are five more: Wayne Daley and Jackie Harrison, Hayley and Michael, and Darren. This last one, Darren, was referred to Tresillian House by Nicy on evening outreach a couple of nights ago. It seems he never made it – he claims he couldn't find it – and has been sleeping out instead. A short walk away, at the back of Iceland, there are others: John Heron and Buster. John is not 'homeless' (he has a bedsit room near the prison), though he might as well be; he was a rough sleeper some years back and still looks the part and spends most of his day, and a good part of each night, out and about, walking around Cardiff doing nothing very much in particular. Buster is in somewhere at the moment too, but up early like Paul and hoping for a hot drink and sandwich. Others appear, with orders for drinks and food from those holding their place in the vendors' queue outside the Big Issue office off the side of Charles Street. Jackie walks over from the CIA wearing her sleeping bag like a shawl. We are here for ten minutes serving food and chatting, fielding requests and enquiries, chiselling little bits of information. Jackie wants to take drinks and food back to Wayne but Jeff says no: 'It's not pizza delivery. You have to come over if you want a roll.'

On to Hayes Bridge Road and back past the prison to find Bobby and John in their usual spot – only this morning there is no John. From under a pile of blankets Bobby tells us that he doesn't want any breakfast thank you. We ask about John. John is missing, says Bobby. He doesn't know where. He lost him in town last night. Jeff and Rees exchange an 'Oh yeah?' sort of look. This may be something and it may be nothing, but Bobby and John are seldom separated. Perhaps John *is* just missing, dead drunk in some other corner of the city and soon to reappear. Or it could be something else. It could be, as has happened half a dozen times before, that the two of them have fallen out and fought; and if so, if Bobby has turned on John and beaten him up – it wouldn't happen the other way around, never has. He will need to be found. (Jeff recounts one time when John had had enough of it and went off to Birmingham for four months.)

We are hurrying now, aware that the morning traffic is building. We move up Crwys Road looking for Andy Saville, who is absent from his usual doorway, then on to Colin at the Co-op car park, who is certainly present, but not all there this morning (hopping about from foot to foot talking animated nonsense); then back through the civic centre, past Bute Park and Cardiff Castle and over the river, turning left onto Lower Cathedral Road, and so back to the night shelter to unload the Tupperware boxes and flasks and add up the numbers 'seen'. Kevin Skinner is sat in the front room watching Breakfast TV. Buster rings the doorbell and asks if Kevin and Sean want to pop out for a drink. The three of them leave together, conferring in whispers about some new plan or report. They cross the road to turn right and out of sight down the littered alley that runs behind the properties on Tudor Street.

One more morning spent seeing to those who have passed the night out, and who are, as such, available; reaching out to those prepared to come over and take a bit of help; picking up on news of those gone missing or lying low. The administration of a little roadside kindness, perhaps.

If there is a space interior to outreach, a set of orientations and alignments according to which the work is experienced and understood and in terms of which it can be arranged, then its principal coordinates are those set out in this chapter. The coordinates are figurative and moral, and as such intangible; but they constitute an essential organisation, one which draws the work of outreach together and gives it shape, defining the difficulties it is up against and to which it is addressed.

As I have said already, outreach encounters have to happen somewhere: 'everything is always somewhere, in some place with its thresholds, boundaries, and transitions to other places' (Tilley, 2008: 268). I have also insisted that the only streets we know are real ones. But maybe there is more to it than that. Certainly so if you can be 'on the street' yet at the same time on a building site or under a bush; if you can move up and down an alley without ever leaving the ground; if you can be edged out of the city even as your last remaining hold is on the very middle of things. The material metes and bounds of outreach, traced across a map of the city, are inexact and shifting, but patterned; and I have described these, in the previous chapter, as corroborated and produced in practice. So too, in this chapter, the figurative geography of the work: inexact but inescapably patterned; borne out and traced again in practice. Added to which, these two geographies – the material and the figurative – double up, the one adjacent to or overlaying the other. Sometimes the effect is jarring. The team finds itself dealing with a client slumped down beside the entrance to a busy department store, a parade of bright consumer goods stood blankly to attention in the background. More often location and circumstance merge and borrow, each from the other: an outreach worker turns aside, ducks down, clambers across, in poor light, to find, tucked away and around the back of wherever it might be, on remaindered or derelict ground, a young man in a mess and missing since Tuesday.

6

Leftovers

I have used the preceding chapters to describe the remit and operations of a team of outreach workers. Doing so has meant saying something about the people these workers are employed to look out for and the cityscape through which they move. I have implied that these three – outreach workers, the people they reach out and see to and the landscape of practice across which workers and clients encounter one another – are caught in a patterned entanglement. Outreach workers and the homeless share a vicinity or surrounds, and within that vicinity particular excursions and circuits of activity and availability; they share certain times of the day and night, some rather more than others; their encounters are also shaped by figurative and moral coordinates and orientations, commonly available and mostly unexamined (and none the less powerful for that), which frame what it is to get on in life or to lose one's way, to be down, to reach out – to be an outreach worker. This is to say that outreach workers and their clients are positioned, or at least liable to be so, by the ways in which their encounters with one another are already organised, finding a place prepared for them within existing conformations – of brick, cement, perception and imagination.

In the present chapter I hope to pick up a thread first laid down in Chapter 2 in comments made about things and people somehow lost or left behind. In doing so I aim to further develop my account of outreach and its territory. I am continuing to ask where it is that outreach workers go to do the job set them. Where do homeless outreach encounters happen? To designate outreach and its encounters in this way, as homeless, is not only to signal that those encounters very frequently involve homeless people. More than that, the work of outreach, and the encounters it moves towards, are themselves homeless in that they lack a place.[1] CCT

---

1.   Once again I am following Michael Rowe, who describes meetings between outreach workers and their clients as '[h]omeless encounters … not only because homeless persons are a party to them, but also because they lack a foothold in everyday social interactions' (1999: 1).

outreach gets done away from the office, and mostly out of doors; sharing the streets with passers-by and other users, outreach workers hope to come across clients and then to engage with them, to see how things are and what can be done, but these involvements are public and exposed, or liable to be so. Indoors, trawling the Huggard Centre canteen, or aboard the Bus Project, workers are still not on home ground, nor are their meetings with clients private in anything like the way they could be were Nicy a social worker sitting down with Cindy by appointment in a meeting room set aside for that purpose, or perhaps making a house call – not, in any case, standing on Central Square in the pouring rain, which is where these two do actually encounter one another. True, some outreach clients continue as such long after they have secured accommodation, and outreach workers continue to deal with them, and may call on them – but such calls are infrequent and take place only when there is time to do so, because things at work are in some or other way quiet ('at work' meaning, once again, out of doors and around about the city centre, where homeless outreach is supposed to happen).

Yet outreach workers do make calls and go to see clients without ever entering an operational premises, hostel property or house; and they do so in the course of the same loose and improvised, repeatedly readjusted patrols I have already described, without ever letting those patrols harden into movements of transit between established locations. The settings I have in mind here are material, certainly, and could be found on a map or at least located there; yet they are also unauthorised, part of a sketchy and unofficial city that is liable to shift – pass in and out of existence even – from one day to the next. The chapter title gives the best clue to the sorts of setting I have in mind: leftovers are unwanted, at least for now; they are those things remaindered once current use and appetite have been satisfied; they may be, or become, waste, and as such are liable to make us feel uneasy – if we notice them at all; they are remains. And this is my theme, those remaindered or residual settings towards which the work of outreach is so often directed.

Lost space

In an earlier chapter I quoted Peter Ackroyd on the urban dispossessed, those rejected and discarded who fade into the streets because nobody sees them; he was writing about London in particular and, among others, the lines of people queuing for soup outside Charing Cross Station, ignored by passers-by. He could just as well have been writing about Cardiff, or any other UK city. I also included a passage from Ackroyd's fiction, in which a group of street drinkers are gathered together in a corner of the city that nobody else seems to want or care for, 'derelict ground, where unwanted objects from the city had over the years been deposited ... unrecognisable pieces of metal were strewn over a wide area ... tall ragweed partially obscured the shapes of abandoned or burnt-out cars, while rotting mattresses sank into the soil' (1993: 68). Ackroyd's vagrants, too far gone to know just where they are, seem to have found a place of their own. I suggested that city planners might consider this a 'lost space'.

Writing in the 1980s Roger Trancik proposed lost space as a descriptive and conceptual category that would help in understanding what was wrong with contemporary cities. Lost space, he suggested, appears as a result of urban development that 'treats buildings as isolated objects sited in the landscape, not as part of the larger fabric of streets, squares, and viable open space' (2007: 63; originally 1986), a process exacerbated by the privatisation of public space and by changes in land use as a result of changing economic, industrial and employment patterns. And it looks like this:

Lost space is the leftover unstructured landscape at the base of high-rise towers or the unused sunken plaza away from the flow of pedestrian activity in the city. Lost spaces are the surface parking lots ... the no-man's-lands along the edges of freeways that nobody cares about maintaining, much less using ... abandoned waterfronts, train yards ... vacant blight-clearance sites ... residual areas between districts ... deteriorated parks ... (Trancik, 2007 [1986]: 64)

Such spaces – 'antispaces', Trancik also calls them – fragment the outdoor environment, inserting gaps and fissures into what ought to be a spatially continuous landscape. Attention paid to lost spaces – seeing them for what they are – mimics the problem that such spaces represent. To look at lost space is to look at an isolated element, a patch of remaindered ground. Lost spaces are recognised for what they are once it is seen that they distract from a proper appreciation of the 'larger order of things' (2007 [1986]: 66), of grouping and sequence in what ought to be a unified public realm: a bad thing then; damage done to the urban fabric. But also an opportunity for redevelopment and what Trancik calls 'creative infill' (2007 [1986]: 68). The task is to reclaim lost space through redevelopment, to reintegrate the public environment, to attract people back to the urban core (and so counteract urban sprawl), to make figurative space out of the lost landscape (2007 [1986]: 63).

That was then, the 1980s, and this is now; and in the intervening years a number of cities have done something not so very far away from what Trancik was proposing. There is less lost space around than there used to be – arguably; there has been creative infill. But less does not mean none at all. Outreach work in Cardiff would be a very different practice if it did. Although there has been something of a squeeze on lost space in Cardiff in recent years, lost spaces can still be found and are still the setting for a great many of the encounters between CCT outreach workers and their clients. Taken together, these spaces make up the most significant part of the physical geography of outreach work (and confirm its figurative contours also). The most experienced CCT outreach workers are aficionados of underused and leftover locations, gaps in the spatial continuity of the city. Knowing where these spaces are, and how to find them, is something every outreach worker has to learn. The learning is physical – you have to put yourself about a bit; but it also involves a subtle readjustment of focus. Lost space can be hard to see at first. Most obviously so when it is tucked away somewhere, out of sight and off to the side of things, as it often is. The possibility that it could be any kind of place at all – anywhere you might recognise as such – is sometimes obscured, even when you have fought your way through to it. You climb a wall and edge along some bushes to find what? Nothing. A patch of muddy ground you didn't know was there before and a discarded blanket. *Is this it?* you want to ask. *Are we there yet?*

There is nothing here so ripe as Ackroyd's imagined dereliction – which is a point worth getting straight. In actually existing cities lost space tends to the mundane, even the bits that are hidden away – and certainly the bits that aren't, of which there are more than enough in just about any city centre. Cardiff certainly has its share – unconcealed, unremarkable; anyone prepared to walk around Cardiff's city centre for half an hour would be sure to see all sorts of lost space (no need to pry, to clamber over or edge along anything at all). But would they know they had done so? Would they actually see anything at all? If lost space is often rather ordinary, it does not follow that it is always apparent. Being ordinary can turn out to be another way in which to go undetected. Some sorts of space – lost, ordinary, unremarkable – hide in plain sight. Even when you look right at them there is not a lot to see: a wedge of cross-hatched tarmac on the first floor of a multi-storey car park, a little too tapered to work as a viable bay; the triangular void beneath the bottom flight of a fire-exit stairwell. Who really notices these sorts of space at all, or needs to? Outreach workers do. These are just the sorts of space they go out of their way to take a look at, and look around. Their work puts them in the way of such spaces, of necessity.

Spaces of necessity

Seeing like an outreach worker involves, among other things, a sort of inversion: gaps in the city picture warrant close examination;[2] empty buildings appear as the sort of place you might go to find people; dead ends lead somewhere, or look like they might. At the same time, the city's majority layout and set-piece locations lose interest and perceptual content, becoming indistinct; they matter less than they do for others.

What I have called gaps in the city picture, what Trancik calls lost space or antispace, can also be called nonplace. Writing about outreach work and homelessness in New York, Anne Lovell describes (mental health) outreach programmes as 'interstitial organizations' (1997: 357) whose constituted practices do not quite fit established models and whose physical space of operations is similarly inexact and precarious. Outreach workers must take work where they can find it (in New York

---

2.   Orthodox visual theory makes its own claims for creative infill in explaining how it is that breaks in a visual field – blind spots – do not disrupt our sensory experience and can be hard to 'see' sometimes. Gaps in vision are not experienced as such. A related phenomenon is the difficulty we can have 'seeing' change. If our attention is elsewhere, or briefly distracted, we can fail to notice quite significant changes in whatever it was we were looking at. Vision, it seems, depends on the exercise of attention, such that perfectly visible objects and alterations to a picture or scene can be missed if they fall 'outside the scope of attention' (Noë, 2004: 52). Louis Chevalier's (1994) failure to see the towers – the monsters – suddenly thrusting up on the Paris skyline (see Chapter 1) could be taken as a working example, writ large, of what others have called 'inattentional blindness' (Mack and Rock, 1998); he writes: 'at first we do not see, or we see without registering the image' (1994: 4). Chevalier puts his not seeing down to perception being a matter of habit, but this may fall short as a proper explanation of what it is we are doing when we see, and the way in which this then explains how and what we don't see.

and Cardiff both); or, rather, they must take themselves to where their work can be found:

> 'places in-between' ... anonymous spaces without history or collective identity that Marc Augé (1992) calls 'nonplaces' or *non-lieux*: empty lots between residential buildings, the neutral grounds of wide streets, abandoned tunnels, subway stations, parks, the no-man's-land under bridges or highway abutments. Homeless persons and other street people appropriate these spaces for themselves, if only temporarily, as dwelling places or for other everyday uses. (1997: 357)

Whether or not these are exactly the sorts of setting that Augé intends by the term nonplace,[3] they would be familiar enough to CCT outreach workers in Cardiff, and we could call some of them lost or leftover. Lovell's depiction of outreach as interstitial work, practised in places in-between, consolidates Rowe's (1999) portrayal of homeless encounters as lacking a foothold in the ordinary business of city life.

Lovell's is not a detailed account of outreach practice *per se*, or where that work will take you. Her interest is in narrative, specifically the stories that homeless persons tell about who they are and where they have been. But her passing description is astute:

> As potential clients hesitate to contact them, the services go 'in vivo' seeking homeless persons out in the spaces of their everyday lives. Thus outreach workers cruise city parks and transportation terminals, comb drop-in centres, and occupy empty storefronts. Mobile psychiatric emergency teams roam shantytowns and the less visible recesses of the urban infrastructures ... A continuity is perpetuated between the movement of homeless persons in and out of anonymous urban spaces and the mobility of mental health service workers. Each accelerates the other. (1997: 357)

The vernacular is New York but each of these sites has its Cardiff equivalent more or less: city parks, transportation terminals (the bus

---

3. I suspect they are not. Motorways, supermarkets, airports: these are the 'real non-places of supermodernity' according to Augé (2008: 77). Any concealment or anonymity they might seem to offer is guaranteed by contractual relations and identity checks, not neglect. (They are also, typically, very *clean* places, where anything dropped or left behind is briskly removed.)

and train stations), drop-in centres (the Huggard canteen, one among half a dozen such that CCT outreach workers might themselves drop in at), empty storefronts (fewer of these in the middle of the city, but certainly one or two), empty lots between residential buildings, neutral grounds, roadside verges, the no-man's-land under bridges. Lost space is everywhere, and everywhere more or less the same. To know these places and why they matter, to see the city that way, is already to understand something about outreach work and how it gets done. These are the sorts of places you need to go to if you want to find someone, as an outreach worker. Moreover, these are the sorts of places you need to learn how to find. The thing about lost space is that it is always being found: turned up and uncovered by workers and clients alike, nosing around the city for somewhere to go and get things done without too much notice being taken by anyone else.

Outreach: Early morning, August. We are halfway through the Breakfast Run and still keeping an eye out for Tony who was involved in some sort of set-to in the night shelter kitchen yesterday and has not been seen since he came back from the hospital (a plate was smashed and Tony's head was cut, requiring 14 stitches; his bed was empty last night). We have done the station and Central Square, picking up conflicting accounts of the kitchen fracas but no certain news of Tony's whereabouts. We have seen Buster on a bench in the park and then looked for and failed to find Don, who Buster told us was sleeping under the footbridge; also, in the civic centre, Andy Saville, Len Goodyear, Mark, Paul Short and Lizzie, and a young man who says his name is Aaron who we haven't seen before. Paul and Lizzie are sleeping in a shed close to the College of Music. Pete Farnworth – aka Razzer – has been following us round on his bike, miffed that his 'usual' egg roll (he doesn't like bacon) has not been prepared for him. We have done the lanes, looking for Brian Tucker who we know to be sleeping there but isn't today, it seems; and then the CIA and the back of Iceland where we turn up Inky (plus dog), Mandy B. and her new boyfriend, Andrew Hayes, a young couple who don't want to talk today and nobody seems to know, and Sara and Robbo, drunk already.

We do not go to the cage today; Ian and Ryan have been evicted, if the word applies, and the cage has been cleaned out and locked up.[4] It

---

4. I have suggested that lost space is unremarkable, and most of it is, certainly so in Cardiff. But not quite all of it. If you wanted to, it would be easy enough to top the derelict space of Ackroyd's fiction with one or two actually existing sites in the middle of the city, known to outreach workers and their clients over the years. At the peak of its most squalid and disreputable occupancy, the cage, a railway arch beneath the elevated train line from Cardiff Queen Street to Cardiff Bay, would be one such.

is hard to imagine just what the clean-up operation must have involved or how long it must have taken. Where would you even begin? Instead, we turn onto John Street and stop by the Johnston's building, former home of the Welsh National Opera (WNO), but empty since the WNO relocated, and boarded up for now to prevent unauthorised entry. Warning signs read *Keep Out, Hazardous Building*. Black on yellow with a large exclamation mark for good measure. An invitation, surely?

Alongside the building, what used to be a car park or storage yard stands empty, well on its way to becoming derelict space; weeds are thriving unchecked along the far edge, ready to make their move across the tarmac. It is a big space, mostly empty (a few littered objects have already come to rest: a tyre, a scaffold pole, a pair of trousers) and open to the sky, but also sort of private thanks to the post-and-chain fencing across the entrance and the row of large advertising hoardings along two sides, facing out onto Callaghan Square, which shield the whole site from passing view. The yard is home to a new encampment, discovered by Den only yesterday afternoon. In the near corner, to our left as we enter, are Phil and Chrissie. They are lying next to one another on a double mattress, under a grubby blanket and a single sleeping bag laid crossways. Chrissie is barely awake and looking weak and old; Phil is asleep (he has been ill, Den tells me). Various bags and belongings are lined up either side of their bed creating a sort of room. At the rear of the yard, away from Phil and Chrissie, a small hideout has been rigged up. Lines of cord strung between the overhanging branch of a tree and the rear-side support struts of the advertising hoardings have been draped with blankets creating a screen and a sheltered space behind it. We walk over and 'knock', shouting hellos. Peering through, we see a number of people inside, some standing or sitting, smoking, others still 'in bed' under covers. It is a young crowd. John and Len are there, along with Paddy M. and Daniel McBride (who Den knows well and thinks is too young to be out, and 'only playing' at being homeless anyway – so he tells me, later on). I unpack rolls and eggs and start taking orders for coffee while Den has a word with Paddy M about his DTTO (Drug Treatment and Testing Order) appointment later this morning, which Paddy *must not miss*. Daniel is being a pain and acting up, testing the boundaries with Den. Apparently Carrie Evans is somewhere back there, though we neither see nor hear her. Len takes an extra coffee and roll for her (or two for himself, if she isn't there at all). We leave tea and boiled eggs on either side of Phil and Chrissie, neither of whom is saying much, though Phil grunts a thank you – he wasn't asleep after all, or has woken.

Street cleaners in Cardiff stop short of spaces like this, because they are off the street and private; private, that is, in the nominal sense of – probably, surely – belonging to someone, despite appearances (because appearances, the actual experience of standing in the space and looking around you, would seem to suggest the opposite, that the space has been forgotten or abandoned and belongs to no one). But outreach workers don't. Outreach workers switch back and forth, along the street then off to one side into other sorts of space, not so obviously public – not so obviously any sort of space at all, or anyone's. Private property? Strictly speaking, no. Private property is off-limits, other than by invitation. But it is appearance and use that matters here, not legal possession. Outreach workers are especially interested in spaces that just might not be private and will test and stretch that definition, nosing, clambering, shouldering their way off the street, just as those they are looking for (may) have nosed and clambered ahead of them, testing and stretching that same definition in search of somewhere to rest up and hide out. I have already described outreach patrol as a combination of routine and improvisation, and in the latter mode, testing and investigating, it is a tentative movement.

Working their way into somewhere new, only recently turned up, outreach workers have two reasons to tread carefully. The space may be private, and private property is out of bounds; outreach workers have no real authority to breach restricted or privately owned space in the city centre and would much prefer not to draw attention to their activities or to rub anyone up the wrong way by getting 'caught' where they shouldn't be. It would be embarrassing too, to be found out and shooed off by a security guard; a blow to outreach esteem and a source of jokes and teasing subsequently. But they are good judges, mostly, of where they can or can't go, or can get away with going; and if outreach workers are picking their way, however hesitantly, into some space or corner they have not been before or any time recently, the chances are that ownership is (already) moot. Why else would they be there? Stepping over the loops of post-and-chain fencing and into the space alongside the Johnston's building, Dennis is a little cautious, of course, having been here only once before. But he expects to go unchallenged (it looks that way), and hopefully unremarked if he can just steal along, briskly now, behind the advertising hoardings and out of sight of the street. But no sooner has he done so than he must start again. If outreach workers have an eye for spaces that have slipped out of use and gone unnoticed, this is only because the city's homeless do too, looking for somewhere to go and be left alone with whatever it is they need or feel they have to do. And here they are: tucked up in bed in the near corner of the yard, gathered together by the tree at the far end. What used to be the WNO's is Phil and Chrissie's now, or on its way to becoming so (and John's and Len's and Paddy M's, and maybe Daniel's; Carrie's too, if she is in there somewhere behind the draped blankets). So Dennis must watch his step a second time. Straddling the post-and-chain fence he was a sort of trespasser; twenty yards further on he has become a sort of visitor, and there are rules for visitors. No one can be much of a visitor uninvited. Dennis and his colleagues trespass readily enough, if warily, where a seeming lack of attention suggests they might get away with it. But where the smallest sign suggests ownership in use (if not in law) they are conspicuously attentive and considerate.

There is something intensely private about the small corners of the cityscape in which outreach workers sometimes find those they hope to help and work with. But this is a privacy of setting (and a quality of encounter) that has little to do with what private might mean displayed on a signpost or noticeboard, prohibiting unauthorised entry. 'Private property' denotes privilege and exclusivity; the privacy that outreach workers look to uncover – and intrude on, as visitors – has to do with privation and the sort of seclusion it leads to and sometimes requires; the need to find a little room somewhere. The possibility of doing so in the yard alongside the Johnston's building arises *because* the claims of private property have retreated. What used to be somewhere in particular has lost its look of being anywhere, any sort of place at all. There has been a *loosening* of a once-established use and function,[5] sufficient to allow a petty reappropriation – important, for Phil and Chrissie, but petty in the sense of being ever so precarious; this is a cloistered space, but only so long as no one else much minds or sticks their nose in or has anything to say about it. And someone almost always does, before too long. Three

---

5. Karen A. Frank and Quentin Stevens describe loose space as a space in which people are able to recognise the possibilities for unintended activity, 'opportunities for exploration and discovery, for the unexpected, the unregulated, the spontaneous and the risky' (2007: 3). Thus defined, loose space might seem better suited to something more recreational and miscellaneous than what Cardiff's homeless are mostly after. Alongside the Johnston's Building Phil and Chrissie have found somewhere to lie down on a grubby mattress and do drugs, nothing much more than that. But if loose space is open (to possibility), that doesn't mean it has to be public; it can also be lost and leftover: '... without any assigned function ... having no intended use and often lacking conventionally appealing features ... allowing the insertion of activities in search of a home' (2007: 7–8).

days on from Dennis's visit, the hideout at the rear of the yard is empty; John has left for Swansea and Len is in the night shelter, Paddy M. has moved somewhere quieter – the Crown Court steps – having fallen out with Carrie (who has since disappeared), and Daniel has taken up the offer of a place on the floor in his brother's flat in Grangetown. One week later Phil and Chrissie are gone too: there has been some new activity in the yard; a large skip has been delivered and a work crew has been in and out of the building a couple of times; the place has come to notice, again.

Looking out for others

Phil and Chrissie were a fixed point around which CCT outreach moved for well over a year. Not fixed in space (they moved around a lot), but always there, out together, sleeping rough in the city centre for almost 18 months with hardly a break. You could expect to see them most days. In itself this was, and is, uncommon. Every morning, outreach patrol finds someone sleeping rough, every day of the year (the numbers fluctuate, mostly somewhere between five and 25); but there is a high turnover. Half of those seen one morning will not be there the next week; no two mornings are quite identical in terms of who the team uncover where – or hardly ever. Evening patrols are the same, never quite the same from one day to the next. New faces appear and are added to the roll call of current clients or possibles; old faces – familiar, forgotten – reappear just as suddenly. At the same time there is at least some stability. Along with the churning movement of those counted as 'out' on any given patrol, bedding down for the night as outreach workers head home, or huddled up against the morning cold as the next shift makes its way around with breakfast, there are clients you can count on, 'regulars' who *are* there from one day to the next in more or less the same spot. But not for a year and a half. A few weeks together, a couple of months perhaps, before something gives or moves or is made to happen.

Here is the outreach log for one Tuesday morning's patrol in mid-January:

Name	Location	Notes
No Name	Bus station	About 30 years old, in sleeping bag by kiosk
Bernard	Bus station	Seemed confused, didn't want breakfast
Tony Harris	Car park ramp	Been inside last nine months, back now

Name	Location	Notes
Donna	Car park ramp	Tony's girlfriend
Gavin E	Bute Park	Wants travel warrant for Leeds, to see family
Lotta Brookes	Bute Park	One eye swollen, is using again
No Name	Bute Park	Stayed in bag, didn't want breakfast
No Name	Bute Park	Stayed in bag, possibly Liam Sadler
Jason	CIA	Looking for hostel place
Lisa	CIA	Jason's girlfriend, looking for hostel place
No Name	CIA	All tucked up, not stirring
No Name	CIA	All tucked up, not stirring
No Name	CIA	Same
No Name	CIA	Same
Razzer	Iceland	
No Name	Big Issue Office	With Razzer, was in EOS last night possibly (check?)
Andy Saville	Crwys Road	In a good mood for once
Bobby R	Toilet block	
John Royal	Toilet block	Referred to night shelter

The Breakfast Run has moved through Central Square, as it almost always does, and has found Bernard, as expected (he has been there most mornings for a couple of weeks); someone else as well, unrecognised and unidentified for now. Just around the corner, on the car-park exit ramp (frequently used of late, but empty for the last few days since Paul Short moved into the night shelter), Tony and Donna have settled in; Tony has been away but it is no real surprise to find him back again now that he is 'out'. Bute Park is quiet but just at the perimeter, in the porch entrance to the College of Music, Gavin (who has been in this spot for over a week) has been joined by a younger crowd, including Lotta (known to the team as an occasional sex worker). Half an hour's trawl through the civic centre, along the lanes off Park Place and onto Queen Street and the Hayes turns up nothing, but the CIA is busy: six sleepers, none actually asleep though four are tucked in under blankets and not getting up (grunts of 'no thanks' and 'not today'); Jason and Lisa are up and about hopping from foot to foot to keep warm, wanting to get in somewhere together tonight if possible – but only if they can share a room. Handing out food and hot tea outside Iceland, Razzer turns up on his bike, having passed the night who knows where (he isn't saying). Round the corner just off Charles Street we meet a friend of his, waiting for the Big Issue Office to open. Another half hour trawling streets and one of the city's multi-storey car parks (scheduled for demolition but still in use, if a little neglected of late). Then out to Crwys Road, where we know we will find Andy Saville. And then back to the night shelter, cutting through the civic centre once more to check the toilet block, where we find Bobby and John, having missed them first time.

And here is another Breakfast Run, another Tuesday, one week on:

Name	Location	Notes
Bernard	Bus station	
Gavin E	Bute Park	Says he will be gone tomorrow
Jon Finch	Museum steps	Supposed to be in EOS last night (check?)
Pat Connerton	Queen Street	Drunk
Ben Ribble	CIA/Iceland	
Mark Cooper	CIA/Iceland	Wants to register for the Big Issue
Ian Cooper	CIA/Iceland	Wants to register for the Big Issue
Ricardo	CIA/Iceland	Agitated
Ronnie Hughes	CIA	Didn't come over to Iceland
No Name	CIA	Didn't come over
Lizzie P.	CIA	Didn't come over
No name	CIA	Probably Richard Spears
Liam Sadler + 2	CIA	All in doorway 7
Andy Saville	Crwys Road	
Bobby R.	Miskin Street	Garden shed, off the lane behind Ruthin Gardens
Beccy	Miskin Street	Garden shed, with Bobby

The Run has started out on Central Square, where Bernard is still based – propped upright, half asleep on the 'perch rail' seating in the bus station this morning. He has been in the bus station for three weeks now and has become a particular concern. He has no shoes. The only word he has ever spoken to any of the outreach workers is 'tea'. Steve, the CCT manager, has called a multi-agency meeting to try to initiate a formal (mental health) assessment and intervention. On to Bute Park, which is still quiet, with only Gavin in his usual spot (Lotta OD'd over the weekend and has not been seen since she left hospital). The civic centre is quiet too, out of favour for a month or more now; Jon Finch is the only one there, on the museum steps. And then we see no one, and no sign of anyone, until we spot Pat Connerton weaving his way up Queen Street, too drunk to give any account of where he spent the night. The CIA is busy though, reliably so. Ben and the Cooper brothers have been there for two weeks now, off and on, sometimes sleeping in the NCP car park next door. Ricardo is new at the CIA this morning though well known to the team. He was evicted from the EOS yesterday and is out of sorts and angry this morning – but mostly incoherent as his English is poor at the best of times. There are eleven in all, distributed around the edge of the building, including Liam Sadler with two unidentified hangers-on (Jason and Lisa are gone, having taken up Jason's mum's offer of a room in her house in Newport). No sign of Pete Farnworth (Razzer) this morning, though he must be somewhere. And then on to Andy Saville who has re-established himself on Crwys Road over the last couple of weeks after several months in Andy Watkins' disreputable flat on Salisbury Road. Bobby R. and Beccy are in a bad way (as usual) in the shambolic remains of a shed in the overgrown garden of an empty property just off Miskin Street. This is a new location, tracked down this morning following a tip-off.

In the space of a week some things have changed and some have stayed the same, and no two days in between have been identical. Bernard and Andy Saville are more or less established in locations that have become routine stops; Gavin too, though he is likely to leave any day now as he never stays in Cardiff for too long. Others have already moved on or away, or have been missed this morning but will be back again tomorrow – one day's absence (or presence) being proof of nothing much at all. The Cooper brothers are becoming central players in a small scene, a younger crowd getting together in the vicinity of the CIA most nights but not quite reliably so. Not a priority for the team in the way that Bobby and Beccy are (if these two stay put long enough the team will have another go at getting Bobby into rehab; he sometimes says he wants it, but then he says something else, and then he moves on and disappears for a week or so until the team finds him again and has to start over).

The locations at which outreach workers pause to nose around and perhaps pour out a coffee and get a little work done (if it turns out there *is* someone there under the pile of blankets beside the bins behind the supermarket) have something of the same 'now you see them, now you don't' sort of quality that the homeless do. True, there are a handful of locations likely to figure in almost any outreach patrol, whatever the time of year and whatever else may be going on or have happened over the last couple of days to stir things up. Central Square and Bute Park are always worth a look; most mornings there will be someone in a sleeping bag on the Crown Court steps or the museum steps; the toilet block behind the museum can also be relied on. These few locations stay more or less the same. But the rest slip in and out of view, depending on use and occupancy. Just as homeless clients recorded as 'seen' one day may be gone from the outreach log the next, so too sites and locations appear and then disappear from the written record. Alongside the half dozen or so locations that outreach workers on the Breakfast Run may have it in mind to visit as they leave the nightshelter on any given morning (three or four places they almost always go, and three or four they will visit today in particular because of who they expect to find there) there are many, many others that will be no part of that morning's patrol. These are dormant locations, not in use of late so far as anyone knows and not mentioned in this week's – this month's, last month's, last year's – log of outreach encounters. Not that outreach workers would need to consult the logs to be reminded of where these locations are exactly and who was in them last time they were occupied. You can't walk down the street with a CCT outreach worker, at least not in central Cardiff, without getting some account of who used to sleep where, just off to the side behind this or that building: 'We never go there now, it's boarded up. But that was where Phil and Chrissie were, for months, last winter. Remember that?'

Some of these locations don't only pass in and out of use, they also pass in and out of existence. Empty ground gets built over, disused toilet blocks demolished; the muddy slope by the river under the road bridge, littered with cans and food wrappers and old blankets, gets cleaned up one day and then dug up the next, then tarmacked and then connected to the other sections of the cycle path it has now become part of. But set against the sorts of reclamation that sees lost space gone for good are processes of unintended creation. Just as some spaces disappear, others come into existence, sometimes suddenly: yesterday there was nothing there, but this morning there is a brand new set of exterior stairs in galvanised steel running up the side of a building and a sleeping bag laid out neatly below the bottom flight. And sometimes slowly: a corner or square of space becoming that little bit more lost or leftover as the days and weeks pass by, as happened with the yard by the Johnston's building after the WNO had left and before Phil and Chrissie moved in. What was once nothing, to an outreach worker or a rough sleeper, becomes something of use and interest, somewhere to go.

And what about Phil and Chrissie? They don't appear in either of the outreach logs above, though they were both 'out' at the time, so far as anyone knew. Having been well established at the same spot on Central Square since November, tucked up together under a heap of blankets alongside an empty office block, they had moved on and not yet settled anywhere else (this was six months before they made their way to the Johnston's building). No one on the CCT was too worried, just yet. Outreach workers were seeing Phil most evenings at the soup run. And just seeing – not *seeing to*, or doing much – is a part of what outreach work is there to accomplish. Phil and Chrissie were probably OK; peripheral vision confirmed as much.

Niche settings

In early February Phil and Chrissie reappeared, taking possession of a fire-exit doorway along the side of the CIA, one of several such, variously occupied by what had become a little scene associated with a string of encampments around the building's perimeter.

Outreach: We have been out for an hour in the early morning, and are now taking a turn around the Cardiff International Arena (CIA). This is a regular point of call for the Breakfast Run, as reliably occupied as Central Square. It is the design of building as much as anything else that makes this so; roughly circular in shape, the CIA has one main entrance and a number of fire exits, the latter spaced at intervals around its circumference, each one set back into the building so that the doors open out onto a covered space, enclosed on three sides; steps lead down from each fire-exit doorway to the street.

Most paying customers come out of the CIA the same way they came in, through the main entrance; the fire exits are for emergencies only. But they are in frequent use nonetheless. The recessed platforms onto which the doors (seldom) open make a very good place to bed down for the night. Climb up the steps from the street and turn around and you have a square of space all your own, almost a room: doors (closed shut, emergencies only) behind you, walls either side and a canopy on top; enclosure and shelter, and vantage – a clear view over and across the street, which you are *by* but not *on*. If you get there early enough of an evening you can even take your pick, working around the perimeter to whichever doorway has its back to the prevailing wind and weather. Most of the doorways are large enough to accommodate two or three, lying down side by side.

Of course, the fire exits must be kept clear of obstruction and so they are tidied by cleaning and security staff most mornings. But not before the Breakfast Run has called. Which is what we are doing this morning, working our way around the building. Doorway No. 8 shows signs of occupancy – bags and blankets – but there is no one home; a chalked notice on the wall reads 'Gone to Spar. Inky.' In Doorway No. 7 there are two figures curled up in sleeping bags, neither one too responsive to Jeff's cheery 'Good morning. Good morning, Breakfast Run.' 'Urghh,' says one. 'No thanks,' says the other, wriggling deeper into his bag (from the sound of his voice we reckon it's Steve Harris). Around the other side things are busier: two in Doorway No. 5; two more, plus one dog, and Inky visiting, in Doorway No. 4; and Phil and Chrissie together in Doorway No. 3 half obscured by a blanket they have strung across the top of the steps to give some privacy. Jeff passes along briskly, shouting up at each doorway: 'Morning. Morning. Breakfast Run. We'll be over at Iceland in five minutes if you want anything.' Some stir and some don't. Chrissie sits up, shouts hello and shoves Phil. We walk over to Iceland and start arranging the flasks and cups and Tupperware boxes (boiled eggs and bacon sandwiches inside). We don't do breakfast at the CIA anymore, not on the steps themselves; only over here, a short walk away. The reason being that the CIA management recently contacted the local authority to ask for help in dealing with its homeless problem, and the CCT has duly has been asked to oblige by dispensing food and drink only to those prepared to come away from the building. This way there should be not so much mess (eggshells, polystyrene cups, food scraps, spilt coffee and sugar; though the real problem, for the CIA, has been used syringes and excrement), added to which if people have to get up to get breakfast then the hope is that this will have them moving off and about the city earlier, sparing CIA cleaners and security staff the chore of rousting those who might otherwise 'lie in'.

Phil comes loping over. He is in a fine and vigorous mood (no mention of his row with Jeff yesterday) and has a story he is keen to share. Last night two of the girls, Mandy and Fiona B., committed a street robbery – £200 they are boasting of, taken off a passer-by under threat of violence says Phil. He thinks this was foolish; a foolish thing to do and foolish to boast about it, and more foolish still if they think they are going to get away with it. 'Wait till they check the security cameras,' he says. In any case, the robbery has really stirred things up. The police have been up and down all night. The victim has misidentified his assailants – at one point fingering Phil and Inky (but the police didn't buy that, knowing the two of them) – and exaggerating the amount taken. 'Stupid,' says Phil. But he is a little gleeful at the turn of events. It has really got things going, got people talking. No one knows where Mandy and Fiona spent the night.

Jeff asks Phil if Chrissie is OK. 'What do you mean?' asks Phil, suddenly hostile. Jeff explains that he saw her on High Street last night begging, barely conscious it seemed, blowing down a tin whistle in a derisory attempt to pass for a busker. Phil laughs. 'That's her medication,' he tells us. 'She made £1.50. Took her two hours. Ha, ha, ha.' We give him breakfast to take back to Chrissie, even though we have agreed to give food and drink only to those who actually get up and walk over.

Most doorways are recessed and so present a sort of niche, but a niche is more than a nook or alcove, a niche is also a set of opportunities or conditions combined in such a way as to make life possible, one way of doing things (among many) within a wider environment. If Cardiff's homeless occupy a niche within the wider urban environment, then they do so in ways which combine both senses of the word. They find little wrinkles and nicks in the city fabric in which to retreat and rest up, and combine their particular knowledge of these places into the more general practice of getting by. On its own this is good reason enough for any passer-by, busy with his or her own city life, to miss what might be going on with Phil and Chrissie, say. Other people's niches are, after all, their own, and none of anyone else's business. In this the homeless are little different from any other urban grouping, each with its own routes, sites and scenes. But different doesn't have to mean equal. The niche settings Phil and Chrissie rely on and know a lot about are not those they would have chosen, and if the two of them seem to fit right in there what with everything they know about making do in the city centre, that is not because being homeless in some fire-exit doorway is what or where they want to be.[6] Their urban niche is what is left over once almost everyone else has laid a claim. As such it might go unremarked not only because niches do – almost anyone's, glanced in passing – but also because its utility is hard to appreciate even when attended to. Some of the uses to which rough sleepers put parts of the urban environment do not so much take place behind the back of whatever else is going on, as subvert intended functions. This can further obscure any niche existence the homeless might cobble together in the middle of Cardiff or any other

---

6. It doesn't hurt to be very, very clear on this. Among other things, a niche can be taken to refer to a comfortable position in life. But there is nothing comfortable or satisfactory about anyone spending the night in a doorway outside the CIA because they have nowhere else to go.

city; it can be hard to see a bed when it looks, to anyone else, like a bench, or a step or a doorway.[7]

Walking round the CIA, Jeff is looking out for those for whom fire-exit doorways afford shelter and a place to lie down overnight. The place looks different from Jeff's perspective, not because its physical qualities are inconstant but because the same stable configuration of materials that makes a fire-exit doorway also affords enclosure and resting up and keeping warm (or at any rate out of the wind). More than this, fire-exit doorways afford outreach; a cloistered doorway has outreach-ability and is perceived as such by CCT workers. You can step off the street into a recessed doorway and crouch down next to someone without drawing too much public attention, you can take a look and see who it is and how they are doing, if they'd like a cup of tea, if they want to talk.[8]

What neglect affords

I began this chapter by looking at lost space and asking what it might take to see it. Among other things, lost space can look damaged or the worse for wear. Sometimes the damage has been a part of what has led to the space becoming lost, though it doesn't have to be that way. Where this is so – where damage has played a part – it can take two forms. One is sudden and intended: demolition of a building or buildings can create lost space overnight; this sort of damage is usually inflicted as a prelude to reconstruction, but for as long as a clearance site is left empty – there is often some significant interregnum – there is a gap in the city fabric, a nothing much of anything where there used to be a something.[9] The

---

7. 'Perception is economical' writes James Gibson (1986: 135); we see what we need to see, or rather we see according to our nature and needs.

8. Which makes it a shame that the CCT have temporarily agreed (having been told, more or less) to offer services only at a distance from the CIA building – so as to get clients up and about each morning and off the premises. Telling people to move on from where they are in order to get the things you were supposed to be bringing them doesn't seem quite right, doesn't seem quite like outreach.

9. Demolished ground in the city centre tends to stay that way for at least a few weeks before rebuilding begins. Perhaps the delay is necessary. But weeks very quickly become months, and months can add up to something longer still. A case in point would be the clearance site alongside Central Square. The office block that used to stand here was once home to Cardiff's planning department and was briefly repurposed as a media centre for the 1999 Rugby World Cup and then left vacant. In 2005, having stood empty for five years (though variously occupied in the meantime by the city's homeless, distributed on

other sort of damage creeps up slowly, as a patch of land slips from use and attention over time. Some lost spaces only start to register – with outreach workers and others who have need of them – once an unspecifiable tipping point has been passed and the space, whatever it once was, has edged over into something else, an absence.

Two sorts of damage then, demolition and neglect. Each is indifferent to the city as it stands. Demolition is violent, and a spectacle. The sorts of damage brought on by neglect are different, at least to begin with; disrepair can creep up on you – on a building or a plot of land; indifference here is a sort of unseeing. Until someone does take notice. At which point neglect shades over into the visible spectrum of things and becomes unsightly, an eyesore.

All of this takes place at almost any scale. Embedded within the long cycles of renewal and decline operating at the level of the wider cityscape there are more modest developments. Some of these are 'developments' proper – an empty warehouse gutted in preparation for conversion into luxury apartments (but no part of any wider renewal scheme). Some are confined instances of decline, a patch of ground ill-fitted to use and grown over with weeds, but wedged between two perfectly viable commercial premises – lost space, to return to Trancik's coinage. At a still smaller scale there is the daily labour of cleaning, tidying and making good (much of it abrasive – scraping and scouring), set against the continuing erosive and corrosive work of rain, wind and oxidation and the build-up of litter and dirt in this or that corner or fissure.[10] Which takes us back to Nigel Thrift, and repair, an act of kindness – well intentioned – that needs doing, but might well hurt (as anyone who has tried to clean out the dirt from a cut or graze knows only too well). The city is always

---

several floors inside and around the building's perimeter too – Phil and Chrissie were there for a few months), what was still being called 'the media building' was demolished to make way for a £50m development, the 'glass needle' skyscraper. This was to have been Cardiff's tallest building, housing luxury apartments the swankiest of which were to sell for (reportedly) £500,000. Work was due to begin within a couple of months – the usual interval – but took longer than that and was delayed in 2006 when a fibre-optic cable was discovered running through the site. Building work was rescheduled to begin in 2008, but never did. Plans to build the glass needle were axed and new plans submitted to build two hotels instead. Those plans have been superseded in turn (see Chapter 9).

10.   Journalist Alan Weisman (2008) provides a detailed and colourful account of just how quickly the city might come unstuck in the absence of ongoing repair and maintenance in his book *The World Without Us* (see also Hall and Smith, 2015).

being worked over, tuned up and repurposed and at the same time always being run down, disposed of and let go. As a result, its shape and arrangement changes, constantly – spreads, shrivels, scars over, revives, discolours – like any living thing. Outreach workers make their way through this shifting terrain, not just as observers of change, some of it sudden and some slow. Every new development (abandonment, decline, construction, makeover) has the potential to signify, to open up some new space or close it off, to push or pull the shape of a morning's patrol off to one side or the other. The most obvious and immediate way in which this happens is when some established location, long ignored and unattended by all but outreach workers, comes back to notice as a site for construction. This can happen quickly, from the point of view of those with most at stake in the space (i.e. those living there). The area is cleared of all accumulated debris and fenced off (again) in a matter of hours, portacabins are delivered and the homeless are dispersed. When this happens outreach workers must disperse too, looking for those that have gone, or, as with Phil and Chrissie, waiting for them to settle again somewhere else. Which Phil and Chrissie do, in due course, finding an affordance in a fire-exit doorway at the CIA along with others already established there. But not for long.

Outreach: There has been a change of scene. The CIA management has had enough and clamped down; cleaners and security staff, working together with the police, have broken up what had become an established and conspicuous encampment. The fire-exit doorways have been cleared of any sign of occupancy; leftover belongings have been binned and all surfaces jet-washed clean. Clients the CCT has been used to seeing at the CIA are now somewhere else, or nowhere in particular. It can take time to find somewhere new and a few of those who were CIA regulars are still unsettled, moving from one spot to the next, from one night to the next, trying to gain a new foothold. In turn, the Breakfast Run has lost its shape a little and become restive, workers moving here and there from one morning to the next, testing out reported sightings and plausible locations, trying to locate the missing.

Phil and Chrissie have not gone far, although it takes a few days to find them; they have set up camp in a small hut in a yard behind the (derelict) York Hotel, just down the road from the CIA and only a stone's throw from Cardiff Central station. We call there this morning at the end of a couple of hours spent circling the city centre (19 'sleepers' found, four or five still 'missing' or unaccounted for, from what was the CIA scene). We carry drinks and food around to the back of the building, shuffling sideways through a tear in the chain link fence to one side of a padlocked gate, taking care not to draw attention. Around the corner there is another obstacle, this one cobbled together by Phil, a sort of barricade of assembled objects – traffic cones, plywood and a rusted washing machine, a wisp of barbed wire strung along the top. We negotiate this blockade and reach the hut – the boiler room we have taken to calling it, though I am unsure that it ever had this function. The little yard in which the hut sits is bordered on three sides by the elevated railway line running into Cardiff Central and the walls of the old hotel; a rusted metal staircase leads up to a fire-exit doorway on the first floor, boarded up. Phil has secured the hut from inside, so we must knock. Jeff hammers on the door: 'Hello? Anyone home?' Nothing. Jeff hammers some more, and out comes Phil looking much the worse for wear and complaining of the cold; he has a small dog with him, running around and nosing into the Tupperware boxes we have brought. Jeff hands over all the remaining bacon rolls and eggs as we are now at the end of the run. Phil takes two teas, loaded with sugar and slips back inside. We don't get to see Chrissie.

One way of looking at this sort of thing, all the way down from city-wide redevelopment plans to the hosing down of a set of steps, is as a reassertion of ownership, a re-privatisation of space gone briefly public; although, again, the words public and private do not quite measure up to what is going on in every instance. In one very important sense, a place like the yard alongside the Johnston's building is only ever private property, in use and in dereliction. Someone, somewhere, owns it, on paper; and in due course they make good on that entitlement, selling the plot on for redevelopment. All private property is liable to be reclaimed in this way, making its interim use precarious. The same will happen – does happen – with the hut behind the York Hotel.[11] Properly public space, on the other hand, might seem to offer some surer respite. If private space belongs to someone, whatever temporary incursions others might

<hr/>

11.   Outreach workers returning from anything more than a week away from work – annual leave or sickness – typically find it takes a day or two to realign their confidence as to who is where and what is going on on Cardiff's homeless scene. If only briefly, they are unsighted, like novices. Not only because things will have happened and clients will have moved around in the meantime, but also because the places in which things used to happen and where clients were once to be found will have moved along too. Some will have vanished altogether. Nor does it take a week for this to happen. Places can go missing in an afternoon: a hedge is cut back and the once familiar muddy space behind it is no longer a space behind anything, no longer a space at all.

make while no one else is looking, public space is always for anyone and can be relied on as such; it tends to stay public too. Yet things are complicated here as well. The principal public spaces of Cardiff's city centre, designed for public and pedestrian use and guaranteed as such in several ways are just those through which CCT outreach workers pass most briskly, their attentions cursory. Why? Because these are the places in which they least expect to find a settled client – holed up, bedded down, established. Phil and Chrissie have never once tried to make a space for themselves on the Hayes, for example. Why not? Because this is a setting in which things that come to rest are briskly removed or *seen to*; a setting that is conspicuously managed and maintained, patrolled by street cleaners, safeguarded by security staff and CCTV. And it is a space all too obviously already in use, with one of the highest retail footfalls in the city centre; which makes it a goodish spot in which to sell the *Big Issue* – there is an established pitch here, secured by agreement with the City Centre Management (provided vendors behave themselves) – but a very poor one in which to beg for any longer than five or ten minutes;[12] and it is no place at all in which to unfurl a sleeping bag, at almost any hour: you would be seen, and shooed off, or worse. My point is that if the most obvious thing about the look of private property is that it looks like someone else's, then, for some of the homeless, the same goes for almost any set piece public space – these look like someone else's too.

Disused public space, on the other hand, is as amenable to provisional occupancy as any (private) derelict yard, grounds or premises. When the toilet block behind the National Museum is decommissioned and bricked up by the local authority it does not pass into private ownership, nor is it any longer a 'public' convenience; instead, because set aside and not in use, because no longer overseen, it becomes available. A couple of the breeze blocks hastily cemented across one doorway are worked loose, without anyone seeming to be any too concerned by the breach. Soon several rows are gone and it is possible to scramble up and squeeze inside. A grille across one window corrodes and is left sagging, banging in the wind. Weeds grow, unchecked, around the base of the building and sprout from the roof. And Ralph is in there, having dragged a salvaged mattress inside, keeping to himself, glad to have '... got off the street, somewhere private, like.' And once Rees is established it is only a matter

---

12. For details of the City Centre Management see p. 103n.

of days before an outreach worker is there too, in the early morning, with a cup of tea: 'Nice place you've got here, Ralph,' says Jeff, brushing cement dust off his knees.

What emerges in all this is a cross-coupling and occasional inversion of public and private. Neither one seems to offer the homeless what they are after until it starts to come apart at the seams; each is liable to be experienced as something like the other, if only temporarily. A certain looseness and loss of function seems to matter most; inattention too, and more than anything neglect.[13] The Flemish architect Wim Cuyvers has made some of these same connections in research conducted with his students in the Dutch city of Eindhoven. 'Before accepting a difference between private space and public space,' he suggests, 'one has to acknowledge that every space is to a certain degree public and to a certain degree private.' (2006: 34). Agreed, of course. Even so, these two are not so always intersected or mutable as to be indistinct. Nor does Cuyvers propose as much:

> Yet I do see a difference. For me, private space is a space owned by somebody who has the money or the power, while public space belongs to nobody and hence does not fall under anyone's control. Public space can be defined then as 'non-economical', while private space is 'economical'. (2006: 34)

Agreed again; this is a more or less familiar framing – one sort of space secured in ownership, the other available to anyone. But then Cuyvers moves on to a more interesting and original conception, suggesting that '[r]emaining garbage or dirt offer good indicators of the spaces I consider public, because in a world that is directed by hygiene, garbage is always taken away in private places' (2006: 34). And next, this remarkable passage:

13. Herman Hertzberger, in his *Lessons for Students in Architecture*, offers the following classification: 'public: an area that is accessible to everyone at all times; responsibility for upkeep is held collectively. Private: an area whose accessibility is determined by a small group or one person, with responsibility for upkeep' (2005: 12). What is interesting to me here is the way in which upkeep and maintenance figure twice. Places, be they public or private, are, it seems, always *maintained*. Does that mean there is nowhere that isn't? Obviously not. What, then, are we to make of places that aren't? Perhaps the very word repair lends an answer, of sorts: neglected space is unrepaired, and such unrepaired spaces are just those to which the homeless then retreat.

Furthermore, I regard public space as a 'space of transgression', that is, a space where you can go to do something that you cannot do in private, because it is controlled. When a child wants to do something without its mother knowing, for instance, it leaves the private space of the house. My definition does not imply that the public space is a space of anarchy, but rather, it is where you go for a moment to escape … This is where I relate public space to the space of 'need', the space where you go to do something that, despite all the rules of society, you cannot escape from and where you have to go for a moment. It is also a space of 'need', or the place where the garbage is; not garbage as dirt, but as the groups of the population that are in a position of 'need'. As such, public space for me is the space of vulnerability. (2006: 34)

Cuyvers is precise on the very point that I have suggested Phil and Chrissie intuit inexactly. Public space, he argues – an inversion of a sort, but not in the direction one might imagine – is only ever space that has been disregarded, in which there is dirt and litter, and in which those who have no other recourse than to do so can at least find somewhere to be left alone with their need. City spaces about which no one seems to care are precisely those in which need escapes attention, and comes to rest. Elsewhere – and this could be 'public' or 'private' space as conventionally defined, as these two are more or less the same in Cuyvers' thinking – it is the very fact that attention has been paid to a setting, and evidence that care continues to be taken, that discourages the needy and unkempt; their presence is unwelcome.

Neglect, then, affords a sort of tolerance, and makes some room for the homeless in the middle of the city; upkeep and repair of the sort that keeps the Hayes swept clean does not. Of course, it is not a good thing that Phil and Chrissie are sleeping on the floor of a damp and unheated hut squeezed between a railway line and a derelict hotel. Even so, a damp and unheated hut is better than no hut at all, and, more than that, it is *somewhere*. For as long as Phil and Chrissie are there and established in residence, outreach workers know where to find them and are in a position to call by twice daily and check up on things, to help Chrissie with her medication, to deliver food and some other basic services and work away at the longer-term goal of reaching agreement on what a more suitable arrangement for the two of them might look like. This is to recognise that outreach workers are to some extent implicated in the shifting transposition of public and private, inattention and care. Neglecting to spend any time at all in the civic centre during daylight hours, the CCT confirms this as a non-place so far as need and homelessness goes. Working their way along rear access lanes late at night they corroborate the likely whereabouts of their regular clients. Making a house call of an awkward scramble – 'Nice place you've got here' – Jeff affirms Ralph's 'privatisation' of a decommissioned public convenience. Waiting for a passer-by to do just that, before slipping around the back of the York Hotel, outreach workers are co-conspirators in an unofficial city, intimate knowledge of whose niche affordances is the mark of their expertise.

Agreement with Phil and Chrissie as to what a more suitable arrangement might look like, in terms of accommodation, was something that took the CCT a very long time to reach. In large part this was down to Phil's sustained refusal to consider hostel or emergency accommodation of any sort, or to have anything to do with the local authority Housing Department (a poor enough starting point for negotiations, made no more promising by his rejection of benefit entitlement, and his significant drug use). Over 18 months, these two moved through more non-place and lost space settings in the centre of Cardiff, more spaces of need, than any other existing or remembered client. And not because they were themselves unsettled or fickle in their residency exactly. Quite the opposite, if anything; they were very much to be relied upon once established somewhere, hardly ever moving on unless made to do so. As and when this happened – as it did, of course, repeatedly – Phil would always take pains to carefully scout out their next location, tending to the derelict and hard to access wherever possible. He was acknowledged to have a particularly good eye for this sort of thing. With a move in prospect, as when the skip was first delivered to the yard beside the Johnston's Building, he would become particularly animated and could be seen up and about early, rifling through the city centre for likely replacement sites, somewhere he and Chrissie could rest up again and *stay*, not just overnight but around the clock and for weeks at a time. Moved along and fixed up somewhere new, which is to say somewhere run down and unrepaired, they would hold on (again) as long as they could, on occasion managing several months undisturbed, though sometimes only days.

Outreach: Early morning on Clare Street. We leave the night shelter for Central Square and then head directly to the civic centre. The RHS Spring Flower Show is in town and opening today, and the CCT has received what Jeff, feigning sensitivity, describes as a 'very rude' email from the 'Head of Parks', the second such in a week. Some of the homeless have been causing trouble in Bute Park and the decision has been taken to ask, or instruct, the CCT to stop going there in the mornings, as it only encourages them. 'I do know where they're coming from, I suppose,' says Jeff. Even so, he is not particularly happy. He has been told by Steve that it will be best to skip the park, not just today but for a little while longer, certainly until the Flower Show is over, and then maybe a few days more, just to let things ease off a little. In the civic centre there are bollards out across the road, restricting traffic and parking; these and (presumably) other precautions are in place for Princess Anne, who will be here later this morning to open the show, apparently. The civic centre proves busy, however, bollards being no obstacle to the homeless: nine in all on the museum steps plus Len Goodyear moseying about in the gardens opposite. Jeff shouts over to him but cannot make himself heard above the noise of a motorised sweeper doing loops in front of the museum. I trot over to fetch Len and we walk back together. I ask him what he's doing in the gardens. 'Looking for dead bodies,' he says, moodily. 'They might as well be dead, some of them – mostly dead'.

We stand on the museum steps for half an hour, doling out hot tea and bacon rolls as more and more turn up. It is a clear morning, bright, but windy and cold. Every time we seem just about ready to go someone else comes around the corner, lugging blankets and bags and shouting 'Wait!' A young woman called Ceri comes over and Jeff has a quiet word with her. When things finally dry up we head directly to Iceland and the CIA. We are all a little chilled and this gets Jeff to talking about how, mid-week, he and Nicy were caught out in a downpour, hail and heavy rain and thunder and lightning. They got soaked. This was during an evening patrol, followed by outreach work with the StreetLife Project. They had wondered if they might find the red-light areas empty, in such appalling weather, but instead it was very busy, with all the women standing around in not much at all, soaked through. Ceri is a sex worker, as well as being homeless, and this is why Jeff called her aside at the museum steps. There was an attack on one of the women last night, and Jeff has a description and a partial number plate. He wants Ceri to be careful and to spread the word.

We cover Queen Street, the Hayes, the CIA and Iceland and then move on to see Inky, who responds to our knock and steps outside the cage (see p. 147n). He tells us he was woken this morning at 'an ungodly hour' by someone strimming the grass outside – a council worker, presumably. He takes food and drink for two and disappears inside, barefoot; in the gloom we can just make out a figure wrapped in blankets sitting in front of a candle by the rear wall.

Phil and Chrissie are no longer on Central Square, having been well established under the eaves of the media building for over three months (even if they were still there we would not have called for them until now, as Chrissie likes to lie in). The building has been cleared in preparation for demolition; access to what used to be Phil and Chrissie's spot on the balcony is now blocked by a plywood barricade. They are now inside the Central Hotel, two hundred yards away, also derelict (gutted by a recent fire) and secured by plywood hoarding but not yet scheduled for demolition; others removed from the media building have joined them there. Around the left-hand side of the perimeter hoarding a panel has been prised back and we lean through the gap to shout for Phil. He shouts back after some delay and we then walk around to the right-hand side to meet him (he is bedded down inside by the prised panel, which is where we shout for him most mornings, but has some way of actually exiting the building around to the right, which we haven't figured out yet.) We wait five minutes but there is no Phil. We wait another five minutes and then I walk back around to shout through again. Phil sticks his head out, remonstrating that he can't walk all the way around to the right hand side because of his hip and all the 'shit on the floor and missing floorboards'. I pass him two eggs and then two coffees (five sugars for Chrissie). He doesn't say anything about anyone else being in there and we decide to leave it at that today.

Demolition of the media building was delayed, though only briefly, following reports that some of the city's homeless had reoccupied the site in defiance, or ignorance, of the warning notices posted around the perimeter – which indeed they had. At this point, CCT outreach were brought in on the act and asked to circulate a revised date around the local homeless scene(s), and to help search the premises to locate, and then relocate, any clients in residence. Right up to the morning on which demolition work began, outreach workers were on site confirming the whereabouts of clients known or likely to have used the building previously. Eventually the demolition crew was given the go ahead and the media building was brought down. Sometime later the Central Hotel was too (as before, the CCT were asked to help confirm it as untenanted before work began). Given notice, Phil and Chrissie moved on; not far.

I will move on too. Spaces of need are an important part of the landscape of outreach: a patchwork, unofficial city variously braided together with set-piece and commonplace public spaces and private property of different sorts (and the disputable verges running between these, shading one into the other). The connection here, to which this chapter has been addressed and to which all outreach workers are sensitive, runs between neglect and need and inattention. If the rough-sleeping homeless can be said to have gone public with their troubles then this is not to say that they do so only in plain sight and in what we might most readily call public space. Where are they then, and in what sense have they gone public with anything? This circle is squared by Cuyvers, though there are other ways to square it too: things and people go missing in settings that escape attention; they end up where they must needs go.

Dirt, already a theme, has been a part of this chapter too, because that is the way in which we so often think about leftovers and leavings – as dirty, if we consider them at all. We are generally uneasy about things left over, and prefer them tidied away. The streets in Cardiff that are most frequently and repeatedly littered are those in most common use, but they are also, in consequence, the most frequently and repeatedly cleaned, spruced up again each morning and maintained throughout the day. The leftovers are elsewhere. If one wanted to seek out the dirtier corners of the city centre, one would go – of course, where else? – to where the cleaning wasn't getting done. Which is what outreach workers do, because their clients are onto this already, in the grip of this logic, necessarily.

7

Coming Across

I have referred to Nicy's encounter with Cindy several times already, having first described this point by point in Chapter 2. The encounter is instructive but nothing so very out of the ordinary so far as CCT outreach goes; there have been any number of outreach encounters since, each one particular in its own way, more than a few as wretched as those few hours spent trying to get anywhere at all with Cindy. Nothing all that new then, for an outreach worker;[1] added to which, coming across Cindy that one morning was all that happened – nothing came of it and no one saw Cindy again. This happens often enough with outreach patrol. Off to either side of the principal characters the CCT has had to do with and helped over the years there are countless others with whom the team has crossed tracks just the once or twice and never seen again. Accident and eventuality put all sorts of people in the way of outreach one early morning (or evening) but not the next, and it can be hard to tell, at first encounter, if you have come across someone whose circumstances are such that you are likely to see them here again – in a doorway by Burger King, on a bench in Bute Park. First encounters happen all the time, but only a few come to stand for anything and are remembered.

Outreach workers only ever know those clients they get to know; those they meet once or twice they hardly know at all. This might seem an unnecessary statement, but it is the word client that matters. Some first encounters with clients are easy to recall, not because they were memorable in themselves, but because they led on to continuing contact and support, and perhaps, here and there, to something accomplished. There are a number of ways in which an outreach worker might tell the story of a particular client – to a community psychiatric nurse called to make an assessment, to a social work student on placement – but most of these involve some sort of account of a first meeting. Every story has

---

1. Even so, the incident had something about it, and stuck around for months, and longer still in outline, as an outreach story (see p. 226n).

to start somewhere and although outreach workers come to know quite a lot about some of their clients – where they were born, where they went to school or used to work, how long it is since they were last in prison, who they used to be married to – most of the accounts they give of the clients they work with begin with the time they first came across them. 'When I first met Ryan he was sleeping in a tent under the Penarth Road bridge and half his stuff had been kicked into the river.' Or, 'That's Stacey Reed over there, with Wayne and Jackie. She was on crutches when I first met her, with this huge pack on her back and this tiny little dog. She'd come all the way from Birmingham.' Or, 'You'll like Roy. He's changed, mind. He was round the side of the Central Hotel when we first found him, in a hole, basically. And he wouldn't speak, to anyone. We weren't sure if he *could* speak. It was a couple of weeks before he'd even take a cup of tea.' These first encounters assume significance and find a place in memory because the individuals have become known, as clients. Other first encounters are likely to fade because that is all they ever were.

And it is ever so easy for a first outreach encounter to come to nothing, because there is so little at stake, so little invested at that point; either party to the encounter, each a stranger to the other, can simply turn or walk away. An offer of help made out of doors in the middle of the city is a delicate thing, easily declined; and once declined there is really nowhere else to go, other than away. It might help to persist, but doing so could just as well harden the recipient against future advances; it could be better just to leave alone, today: 'OK then. No problem at all. We're here every morning, early. Maybe see you tomorrow.'

What is being postponed in such instances, accomplished too, is a first small step in what outreach workers hope to build into a client relationship. They see need, or its possibility; they want to help; they have goods and services to offer; they want to reach an understanding; they want to bring about some sort of a movement – forwards, upwards, off the street. One way or another outreach workers are always working at *coming across*. Chance encounters, visual appraisal, the management of appearances, reaching an audience, the (reciprocal) provision of goods, services and information: each of these is a sort of coming across. So too is the eventual goal of winning clients over to a recognition and agreement that homelessness is a step too far and it would be best to come back on side, indoors. This takes us back to Michael Rowe's description of homeless outreach work and its essential territory:

Homeless encounters take place at a border that divides one world from another. This border is physical, in the sense that it is staked out by emergency shelters, soup kitchens, and the streets, and it is social and psychological, in the sense that it is staked out by experiences and perceptions. For each party, the act of crossing the border is physical, social and psychological, a movement of identity as well as of place. (1999: 1)

Outreach thus defined is all about coming across, about movement across a border. The measure of the work becomes the number of those brought back from the edge, and perhaps the way in which this is accomplished. Outreach work itself appears as a sort of frontier endeavour.

In this chapter then, I want to return to the outreach encounter, to the sorts of contact outreach workers have with those they come across in the centre of Cardiff, wherever it might be that they come across them, and the sorts of assistance they are able to offer. But I aim to do more than describe this contact and assistance; I want to look at the work of outreach as directed towards an end, as having a trajectory. Surely, at some point, outreach clients stop being so – stop being clients; some of them because outreach work is no longer necessary, because outreach work is done? What does that look like, when it happens? And how is it accomplished? The answer to this last question is, not easily and not often, and not without with a great deal of work, and seldom in ways that can be separated out from the mundane and (seemingly) negligible contacts that outreach workers keep up with those they call their clients. Even so, outreach has as its ambition a migration, perhaps of attitude and frame-of-mind, and certainly of circumstance, on the threshold of which those who were once strangers, and since then 'regulars', find that they no longer need the support of the CCT in quite the way they used to. Outreach workers hope to see their clients come across: the work is supposed to lead somewhere.

Is she working?

Coming across. The work begins with an encounter with a stranger, and before that with the sighting of a stranger, about whom almost nothing is known. Is the figure stretched out on the grass drunk, sleeping, sunbathing, in any kind of difficulty at all, or none? Is the woman on the corner working, or just waiting for a friend? There is no need for an outreach worker to reach out to someone who is not in need of outreach. But it can be hard to be sure.

First impressions surely count, but they can also be misleading; not everyone looks like who they really are, and not everything that needs seeing to shows on the surface. The possibilities for confusion and misreading are at a particular pitch in the evening outreach patrols that the team undertake as part of the StreetLife project. Outreach work with street sex workers gathers together a tangle of possible (mis)iden-tifications. Most of the women are looking to be seen, and some dress the part. But not all of them. A few dress down, in jeans and t-shirts, keeping it casual. Still others have made arrangements by phone and are waiting for one of their regulars to pick them up – and are not really looking to be seen in the meantime at all. Those who are too young, or young enough to look too young (and liable as such to draw police and social work attention) are made up to look a little older – just old enough; meanwhile those in their twenties are tricked out in the other direction, dressed as teens, and those in their thirties are mostly trying to pass for twenty-something. Almost everyone is trying to look a little different from the person that they are. Street sex work is a hurried, fretful, mundane business; even so, the outfits, makeup and accessories can give an air of performance and intrigue combined. Everyone wants attention, but only of a certain sort and only so long as they are working.

So too the outreach workers. They want to be seen and recognised, at least by the women they are there to reach out to. They drive slowly around the same few streets, slowing down and speeding up again, pulling over and parking, getting out to mosey around. But they don't want their services to draw a crowd, and don't want to come to the attention of local residents (who may object to having prostitutes on the corner of their street, and to outreach workers too, by extension). From time to time the CCT agrees to keep away from certain areas or not to park on certain streets, having been asked or told by the police not to do so following complaints and the suggestion that the service 'encourages' the women to work where they do rather than somewhere – anywhere – else. Circuiting the city centre and a familiar knot of roads, outreach workers trace out more or less the same circuits of movement as do those looking to buy sex; they see the same cars again and again, doing the same thing as they are: circling round, trying to decide who is working and might be worth stopping for, hoping not to run into the police.

Misidentification has consequences, some comic and some serious. More than once, though infrequently enough to be remembered as particular occasions, outreach workers have walked over to introduce themselves to a woman they have not met before, who is clearly working, only to discover she is not working at all – apologies, discomfiture, a hasty retreat. On a couple of occasions outreach workers driving up and down the same sequence of streets have been pulled over by the police. And why not? They are more or less kerb-crawling after all. The stakes are highest for the women, whose personal safety and evening's income depend on getting it right when they show themselves off and when they don't. Standing on East Moors Road in her short skirt and boots, Bryony is dressed to be looked at, but she is also a careful observer of just who it is that is doing the looking and why it might be that they want to catch her eye. As a car drives past, slowing up a fraction, she must make a rapid assessment: Is this trouble? Or business? If the latter, then further, particular care has to be taken here, because not everyone who wants business is a safe bet or worth doing business with. Some punters are unreliable, a waste of time; some are dangerous – and may be taking pains not to seem so. Making out who is who and what they might be up to – which is what some of those behind the wheel are trying to make out too – is not always easy.

Outreach: Hot all day, a heat wave; it is just about pleasant by 10pm and beginning to get dark. I have been out with Jeff and Den on evening outreach and we are now beginning the StreetLife patrol.

We are using Den's car, driving up and down the same few streets, parking up whenever we see the need or think it might pay to take a nose about. Before we get underway, Jeff passes around photocopied snapshots of two girls. One picture shows a teenager in school uniform at the top of a flight of carpeted stairs, the other shows a group of young people in jeans and t-shirts sat together on plastic chairs in a back garden, one face has been circled in red pen. They are ordinary-seeming photos, both girls, the one on the stairs and the one circled, looking cheery and unaffected. One is 15 years old, the other 16, says Jeff; they are both in local authority care (though as often 'missing' as actually there) and both are thought to be involved in prostitution. Nicy saw them together last week on Ocean Way, or thinks she did - this was before the photos came through to the team. She had them both down as in their early twenties. 'Just goes to show,' says Jeff. Given their actual ages, there is concern for the girls' safety and wellbeing; a series of multi-disciplinary meetings involving social workers, the police and the CCT has been held over the last couple of days, and we are to keep a careful look out for both girls tonight.

We drive up and down Ocean Way, round through Splott and along Tyndall Street, looking to see who is or might be working. Other cars are doing the same. It is a little hard to tell who you are looking at, not least because of the hot weather, which has brought everyone out in short skirts and skimpy tops (even Den is wearing shorts!). We park up on East Moors Road to speak to Dana and Maria. There is no sign of Bryony, who usually works this corner. We don't show Dana and Maria the photos, but we ask in a general way about the two girls, hoping not to arouse too much suspicion. Maria thinks she knows them, or has seen them.

Further up Ocean Way there are two young women in a bus stop together. They wave at us at first then turn away. Are they working? 'Not sure,' says Den. 'Could be. Doesn't look like the girls in the photos though.' We decide we will give it 20 minutes and then come back and see if they are still there.

We drive over to Penarth Road, across the river and down Clare Street, making a number of stops along the way, then along the Taff Mead Embankment where we find Becky coming out of one of the lanes that run behind the terraced houses. She wants condoms and a can of Coke, and chocolate, and crisps. She says the police are out tonight, in unmarked cars, so she is being careful. Debbie Stevens zooms past on the back of a motorbike, waving and shouting. Becky rolls her eyes. Driving back over the bridge and around Callaghan Square Den slows to a crawl alongside Leah Pearce, all dressed up. She draws her hand across her face in a sort of faux-casual gesture, to avoid catching his eye. Is she working? We decide to put her name on the outreach log, even though we can't be sure.

Back on Ocean Way we pull over for Lorraine (no sign now of Dana and Maria). She takes condoms and a cigarette and we stand around and chat for a while. The police are out, she says, and have already given her a warning. She tried to tell them she was 'allowed' to work Ocean Way (having been moved on in this direction by the police on previous occasions, as a compromise of sorts, away from the residential streets) but was told no: 'No one's allowed. You've had you warning. Next time you'll be arrested.' Jeff asks about the two women in the bus shelter. Yeah, Lorraine says, they are working; they were dropped off half an hour ago by a guy in a car – maybe he's pimping them. She's not seen them before and she thinks, from the way they were, that tonight might be their first time. Lorraine has not worked for a few months but is out this week because the methadone prescription she was on has been withdrawn. She went to Liverpool for a funeral and in doing so breached the conditions of her treatment order.

She is in court on Friday where hopefully all this will be sorted. Till then she is working for (money for) heroin.

We spot the two newcomers again, walking up Ocean Way together. We overtake them and turn left into a car park to wait. There is only one other car in the car park; a man is sitting behind the steering wheel, watching us watch the two women. Den makes a note of the licence plate, scribbling it on a pad on the dashboard. He may follow it up later, ask a favour from the police. We get out of the car and cross the road on foot. Up close, the two women look much younger than at first, unlikely to be out of their teens. Jeff makes introductions and starts to explain about the project and the CCT. The girls giggle and play dumb and scandalised. Are we saying they are prostitutes? Not exactly, says Jeff, but this is a '… known area, and you're not in any trouble, not with us anyway'. Neither girl looks anything like the two in the snapshots. Den asks for their names. They want to know why he is asking - which is fair enough, and rather stalls things. 'No reason,' says Den. The girls insist they are just waiting for a lift and will be gone in five minutes. Jeff shrugs and tells them it's not the best place to be at night. We head back over to the car and drive off. Are they working? 'Course they are,' says Jeff.

Driving back along Tyndall Street, Wendy flags us down. We pull over into Ellen Street and drive around the corner into the industrial estate to wait for her there, rather than park right in front of the Novotel Hotel. Wendy walks over and takes condoms, a panic alarm and a cigarette. She is looking so much better than last time I saw her. 'Off the gear, that's why,' she says. She wants to know if the police are out tonight and we tell her yes. Unmarked cars? Yes. She gets a call on her phone and jogs off back towards Tyndall Street to meet someone. We walk around to the footbridge to see what happened to a young woman dressed in bright pink who walked past us when we were talking with Wendy. Just a hunch Jeff had, which comes to nothing: no one there.

Half an hour later we are walking along Trade Street. Jeff spots a woman getting into a car. We don't chase after her.

'Put her down as 'seen', though,' says Jeff.

'What's her name?' I ask.

'Chloe.'

'Yeah, but which one? asks Den.

'Good point,' says Jeff. 'Chloe … errr. Can't remember. It'll come to me in a minute. Not Chloe Parker, Chloe … Chloe … errr. Just put Chloe for now.'

Turning the corner onto Trade Lane we almost bump into Lucy Hannighan. She is pushing a wheelchair in which a thin, elderly man is sitting, hands in lap. Lucy looks no more than 16 years old - though we happen to know she is 20; she is dressed young too, on purpose. She swings the wheelchair off to one side and lights a cigarette. 'Fucking hell,' she says in an excited whisper. 'Fifty quid for a wank. Not bad is it?' She has lots of gossip and allegation to share, mostly about a falling out she has had with Kylie and Carole. She wants Den to take her phone number so he can ring her up tomorrow and help move a sofa into her new flat. We stand together talking for about five minutes, throughout which Lucy idly strokes the head of the old man in the chair – sat silently, facing away from us, looking back down Trade Lane.

No night out in Cardiff is representative, whatever you might be doing; each is its own occasion. This was a fairly busy shift, for Jeff and Dennis, at the end of which the outreach log recorded a total of 14 women 'seen' – several more than appear in my abbreviated account. Some nights the StreetLife patrol sees only one or two women, all told. Some evenings there is all sorts of what Dennis would call drama: arguments, distress, conflict, incident. And then there are evenings when nothing much seems to happen at all and everyone seems fine and says they want a few condoms and a bag of crisps but don't have time to stop for more than a couple of minutes; street sex work is pedestrian, and hard on the feet, just like homelessness (and outreach work too). The numbers of women 'seen' varies according to the day of the week, the weather, recent police activity in the area, the time of year and more besides and is very hard to predict with any accuracy at all. There is an encompassing scene associated with sex work just as with homelessness, and particular scenes within that, smaller coalitions, factions, friendship groups; and these too wax and wane over the weeks and months.

There is also a continual supply of new arrivals. Some of these just appear one evening – at least it seems that way to the CCT; never seen before and now standing under the flyover eyeing up the passing traffic. Some start to show up on the fringe, as it were, not so obviously working at first, maybe accompanying a friend who definitely is; but then, over time, becoming a 'regular', waving down the van and rushing over to grab a handful of condoms before rushing off to a car parked around the corner. Many of those 'known to team' on the StreetLife patrol are known as homeless too, or as having been homeless; the whole hostel circuit (and scene) is there in the background too. People cycle in and out.

Rose, by any other name

To repeat, this sort of work – outreach, coming across – begins with an encounter with a stranger, and before that with the sighting of a stranger, about whom almost nothing is known. And the aim, at first, is to get to know at least a little something; enough to establish whether or not this is the sort of person that outreach workers might usefully reach out to. What comes next, if the answer to that question is 'yes', is a process of courtship almost; the careful, incremental cultivation of trust and familiarity. Workers come as friends of a sort, or concerned emissaries from a world of housing, health, care, employment, normality. They are looking for clients who are not clients yet, some of whom have just about stopped being clients anywhere else or are among the most problematic as such; and they do so out of doors and office hours, away from the more conventional frameworks for welfare engagement. For Dennis, Charlie, Jeff and Nicy, getting to know a possible client means making a tentative connection on (at best) neutral ground, without prior arrangement or invitation, with someone in seeming need but with good reason to be wary, skittish and cynical, maybe even hostile. You have to be careful how you come across.

Getting to know another person, under any circumstance, can begin without words, with a glance, a look exchanged and (briefly) held.[2] But following this some spoken introduction, perhaps a name – names differentiate and identify. Here is Nicy, talking about making that first connection:

'If I saw somebody begging I would probably want to make contact … I mean you've been with me when I do, and I generally say *Hiyah mate how are you?* and you get a bit of hello and whatever and just try and strike up a bit of conversation … I introduce myself and who we are and say, look, we're working with the rough sleepers and, you know, *How long have you been in town mate? What you doing? What brought you here?* I mean you judge it really by the kind of response you get, because quite often people don't want to talk. They're nervous, or they just don't want to talk, full stop. I mean, you might get a first name, you might get a life history.'

Some people don't want to talk, and some (far fewer) are hard to shut up once they get started; you might get nothing at all and you might get a life

---

history. And between the two you might get a name, which is not very much on the face of it, perhaps, but counts for something. After two weeks of repeated sightings and some minimal interaction, getting a name can feel like a real breakthrough – which in a way it is; because names make things personal, and have to be volunteered (no one can *see* your name). Nicy opens every encounter with a potential client with the offer of her name; it is almost always the first thing she says. She wants people to know who she is and that she is approaching them, is here, in the rain on Central Square or halfway up some fire-exit stairwell, as a person rather than a uniform;[3] and she hopes they might do the same: offer a name, give up who they are. Needless to say this is disingenuous, or would be if Nicy were to offer unconditional friendship. Nicy is an employee of the local state, paid to care for and keep tabs on a shifting collection of its most difficult and vulnerable inhabitants; she doesn't do outreach in her spare time and none of her real friends is homeless. Concerned attention offered kindly, one person to another, is something she works at in order to meet targets set by her line manager (who has had those, in turn, from his). But this is no more a case of double standards than can be found across a range of social care and public-service professions. Nicy knows she is paid to care and be nice; her clients know it too, and most would agree that she is the right sort of person to be doing that sort of work – you wouldn't want just anyone.

You can be 'seen' by outreach on the Crown Court steps a dozen times before anyone knows who you are. But nothing much really happens until the CCT has your name. Not because names are necessary just yet – strictly speaking, names can wait until everyone is ready to talk about registering with a GP or getting on the waiting list for a council house. But names are a signal that a person is ready to be acknowledged and addressed, ready to engage. Nicy's *Hiyah mate how are you?* might be the first of repeated attempts to engage, variously greased by offers of hot drinks, a cigarette, a sleeping bag. Patience rewarded, one week on, perhaps this not-quite-yet-client introduces himself as James. Now Nicy and James can take things forward on that basis, which is to say a

3. The CCT outreach 'uniform' is a low-key affair: work boots, dark blue trousers, a polo shirt and/or fleece jacket bearing the Cardiff Council logo and embroidered *City Centre Team*. It helps to have work clothes, not least because they are liable to get so mucky; looking just official enough is also useful on occasion.

first-name basis – no national insurance number, no date of birth, no surname either; none given, none asked for. When Dennis and Jeff meet James for the first time he asks 'Where's Nicy?', because it is Nicy that he knows. When there is a ruckus on the Bus, Nicy shouts out 'James, no! Come over here and stay out of it'. And when he does calm down and starts to talk, for the first time, about his children Nicy can say 'James, if you wanted to contact them I can help with that.'

Names are easy enough to offer and in one sense cost nothing, and most social encounters can only get so far without seeming awkward if no one says their name or asks another's. In this way it is not so very unusual for outreach workers to come away with a name at least on their first encounter with someone new; it doesn't have to be a big deal. Even so, they always play it carefully. The very last thing an outreach worker would do is walk over to someone they haven't met before and say 'Morning. City Centre Team. Can I have your name, please?' Much as they want names, they don't want to come across as being in the business of collecting them. When Dennis asks the two girls on Ocean Way for their names (p. 176) he goes in a little too quick and his enquiry backfires. Why does he want to know, they ask him. 'No reason,' says Dennis; and that is pretty much that, until next time.

Asking for a name is something best finessed, wrapped up as incidental chat rather than enquiry: 'I'm Jeff, this is Tom, and these here are hard-boiled eggs. Want one? How about some hot tea? What's your name, anyway?' All this accomplished as Jeff busies himself with organising the flask and a polystyrene cup that keeps falling over, looking away from the man he is talking to. No pressure. Who could refuse? And what is there to refuse, really? In the early mornings, making your way around the CIA fire exits, most people are still under blankets, huddled up or zipped away inside a sleeping bag, which makes it easy to shout out 'Morning! Breakfast Run. Is that you under there Wayne?' (knowing full well it isn't but hoping someone will pop their head out from under the blankets and say: 'No, who's Wayne?' To which the ready reply is: 'Sorry friend, thought you were Wayne. What's *your* name then?'). Nicy has her own strategy, explained to me one afternoon in the CCT office. When someone has been around for week or more and looks to be staying, and has run into CCT outreach a few times already, she'll catch them unawares: 'I say *Hiya ... oh ....* [feigning absentmindedness, clicking her fingers] ... *No, sorry, it's gone. What's your name again?* And they usually tell you, they say *John* or whatever, cos they think you already know.' Sometimes this scenario plays the other way around and outreach workers do already know a person's name, having had the information from one of the hostels or a social worker, but prefer to act as if they don't. If outreach workers don't know for sure who a person is but have a pretty good idea, a hunch or suspicion, they may conceal this too. There are cases in which this gives them a particular edge or advantage: a man they *are almost sure* is called Roy Lee and who was kicked out of the night shelter last night for fighting is telling them his name is John and that he wants a place in the Huggard and does not do drugs – only Roy Lee *does* do drugs, lots; a woman who looks *just like* Denise K., who is HIV-positive and whose case was discussed in detail at a recent team meeting (her photo passed around the room), says she is called Katy and wants a bandage for a cut on her finger. The most general point here, irrespective of particular knowledge with utility in the context of this or that encounter, is that outreach workers prefer not to show their hand too soon.

Unlike most of us, outreach workers write down the names of people they meet on the street; they keep a daily record of who they have seen and where, jotting down additional notes relevant to the encounter – 'referred to night shelter', 'will call at office later to collect food parcel', 'in court tomorrow'. They do this because they meet a lot of people and it helps to have some notes to refer to; also because their encounters with others are supposed to add up to something, progress towards which can monitored and reviewed in team meetings, and the outcomes of which are a demonstration of the team's purpose and a measure of its efficacy. Outcomes of this sort, quantifiable end results, are hard to come by because the work of outreach, so often, just goes on and on, spooling out across the city and through the lives of those with which it is entangled. But outcomes matter, not only in terms of reporting upwards to senior management and service directors who must calibrate the CCT's value within annual budgets, each one tighter than last year's: they matter directly, to the team. It is good to have a result every now and then, no matter who gets to hear about it; something unequivocally accomplished that has made and now marks a real change for a known and named client.

Outcomes can be counted, and count for something; every time the team gets someone indoors or into rehab they can claim to have made a difference (and can maybe even say goodbye to a client). But another reason outreach workers write down names is that doing so allows them to quantify the work they spend most of their time actually doing, precious little of which delivers an 'outcome' there and then or can be linked to any such just around the corner. The work itself, the messy stuff of repeated excursions here and there around the city centre doing this and that and generally keeping an eye out, is too hard to count, and (for that reason) sometimes hard to see – too much happens, a lot of it having the appearance of nothing much at all, little of it occurring in convenient integers of action or service delivery. But the people on whose account outreach patrol is undertaken – the clients and could-be-clients – are much easier to quantify. They come in ones and twos. One rough sleeper 'seen' by Nicy is just that, *one*; and another is *two*, and so on. Never mind for now what 'seen' means. This way you can actually put a number on the work that has been done one mid-October morning even if at the end of two hours' patrol no one is demonstrably any further on or anything other than they were when you started – homeless, that is. *Breakfast Run, 19th October. Total: 17.* But this only really works if you know names. If an outreach worker's log shows that he or she has seen 17 people out on the Breakfast Run but without a single name recorded then who is to say that three of these sightings weren't of the same person, spotted first on Central Square, then given a cup of tea on the museum steps and then seen once more on Queen Street? If the total at the end of the week is 54, is that 54 different homeless people or some smaller number, seen repeatedly? You can only be sure of any of this if outreach logs record who has been seen in a way that identifies and individuates. Names help with this difficulty. Without names, everyone is or could be anyone else; no one is someone in particular.

Getting a name is a breakthrough, but the need for names is such that the team is not always willing to wait. If someone isn't ready to give their name just yet, then outreach workers will, on occasion, make one up, a stand-in for the real thing. And they are not the only ones. Some clients do this too, operating with two or three assumed names and aliases, switching between these as best suits their purpose. Names, it turns out, are not so neatly fixed. Sometimes a whole sequence of monikers and nicknames is worked through before anyone's *real* name is properly established. This is a particular feature of work undertaken on the evening StreetLife patrol. Just one example will do. Outreach workers start to see a young woman on Ocean Way most evenings, obviously working. She is wary at first, but after a few weeks of not quite doing so she finally comes over to Dennis's car to take a handful of condoms and a bag of crisps. She doesn't stay around to talk. This establishes itself as a pattern over a period of weeks: condoms, crisps, nothing much to say. No one knows her name or has yet found a way to ask her that might not unsettle the fragile confidence she has started to show. So as to be sure that they are all talking about the same young woman – building a picture of who she is and what she gets up to, and 'counting' her as seen on such and such a night and not the next – the team decide to call her Blondie. She is marked down this way on the log sheet: *Blondie, Tyndal Street flyover, took condoms*. Then, a few weeks on, Blondie lets on that her name is Zoë. As there is already one Zoë on the books, Blondie is now called Blonde Zoë, or sometimes Zoë B (because the other Zoë is Zoë Archer, Zoë A). No change for a month, then Zoë B disappears. Two months later and she is back, staying in a flat on the Taff Mead Embankment with Lucy. Her hair is now dark brown. Zoë and Lucy work together most nights and because Jeff and Dennis have known Lucy for a long time Zoë is a bit more comfortable around them than she used to be. But Lucy doesn't call Zoë 'Zoë' at all, she calls her Rose, and when Dennis asks the two of them about this 'Rose' says that Zoë is not her name, she just made that up. So Rose it is. Six weeks later Rose asks Dennis for help making sense of a letter she has had from the council. The letter is addressed to Sioned Evans. 'That's me,' says Rose. 'Sioned Evans. Only sometimes I go by Thomas. That's my dad's name.' Rose, she says, is her street name, the name she works under. The whole chain of names has taken almost half a year to work through.[4]

A bit of story

Knowing Rose might well mean knowing her real name(s), and in the end it has to mean that (Dennis cannot help with her letter from the council

---

[4]. All of which can be compressed into the briefest commentary as Dennis drives up Penarth Road late at night gesturing ahead and to the left: 'Over there. That's Blondie by the bridge, with Lucy. She's Sioned Evans, Tom, but put her down as Rose so we know who it is. Put Zoë B in brackets. Jeff, if I pull up here do you want to walk over and have a word?' Strings of names like this, delivered rat-a-tat, a whole sequence for only one person, can be confusing if you are not in the know. But they make perfect sense to Jeff and Dennis and are a sort of lexical trace of the development of outreach familiarity over time, steps along the way in which they have come to know this young woman.

without also knowing that Rose is Sioned Evans). But what an outreach worker really wants to know is the person named, who they are and how they came to be here. Thus, a name is not nearly enough, even as it stands for the whole thing. 'Yes, we know Paul,' says Charlie. 'We've known him for years, the whole story.' The question an outreach worker really wants to ask, but cannot always, not at first, is: *What's the matter?* And the sort of answer they are after in (not) asking such a question is not so much a report on what is immediately wrong – *that* may be obvious enough, visible even – as an account that enables the way things are right now to be seen as entailed by what has gone before. What outreach workers want is a narrative into which they can then insert themselves, as helpers, (re) directing and deflecting a course of events, helping their clients to turn things around.

Getting to know the whole story takes time, almost always. Nicy's suggestion that 'you might get a life story' on first encounter is not inaccurate. But the chances are that you won't. And on those rare occasions that outreach workers do, the story is liable to be over-rehearsed, too readily told to be relied on just yet. More commonly available are scraps and indications, little bits of information and background, some volunteered, some winkled out or let drop inadvertently (and quickly seized on). The *whole* story has to be built up from *bits*. This was the most that Nicy wanted to get from Cindy, if only she could have removed her to the night shelter and got a coffee down her; one or two details and some sense of who she was dealing with, 'a bit of story' as she puts it. Again, as with names, there is something a little surreptitious in all this. Outreach workers proffer cigarettes and idly enquire about something or other, as if it doesn't much matter to them. 'Ever been married, Tony?', or 'You know Bristol, do you?' Over time, incidental chat and mild enquiry of this sort can shake loose quite a bit of information, often more effectively than direct questioning. Building a picture in this way – 'picture' is a word as commonly used by outreach workers as 'story' in describing the information they are after and the way in which it might be assembled into something they can use – requires a manner and approach consistent with, and affirming of, the way in which CCT workers move around the city. Outreach as spatial enquiry, just like outreach as a line of questioning, appears offhand and undirected not because it actually *is*, but rather because this is the way that careful outreach work looks when it is being done well. Out on patrol in the early evening, Jeff and Dennis meander around the city centre with no apparent objective other than to indulge what seems an occasional curiosity, pausing here or there, then tracking back, or circling around to take another look, without ever seeming – without wanting to seem – really all that interested or officious. This is the spatial equivalent of 'Ever been married, Tony?' Outreach workers would no more march direct from Marland House to the disused toilet block behind the museum than they would stridently cross-examine anyone they found there.

Assembling bits of picture or story into something bigger is an indefinite process, at various stages of incompletion with any number of different clients; in truth it never ends. One reason for this is that contact with clients is ongoing and the time it takes to get to know someone, bit by bit, becomes as much a part of the developing picture as whatever else has been learned about what went before. When Phil and Chrissie first arrived in Cardiff, the CCT knew nothing about either of them, who they were or why they were homeless or what they wanted to do about it. Phil in particular played things very close to begin with, giving nothing away beyond an enigmatic insistence that he and Chrissie would not consider moving into any sort of accommodation because doing so would mean names and dates of birth and housing benefit forms and the rest, which would allow unspecified others to catch up with the two of them. Two years on, by which time Phil was just about prepared to talk about moving in to a hostel (to which Chrissie had moved six months previously), the team had assembled a good deal of information about his past, and Chrissie's too, most of it having come in dribs and drabs, nobody rushing in with questions. But in addition to this, and in its way more significant, was everything the team also knew, by then, about everything that had happened to Phil and Chrissie in the considerable meantime: 18 months spent sleeping rough in Cardiff, followed by six more with Chrissie indoors and Phil in and out of short-stay and overnight accommodation, still very much a part of the street scene, ministered to by the CCT throughout. Getting to know someone (anyone at all, this doesn't have to be outreach) doesn't stop at having them tell you things about who they are; it involves them doing so over a period of time sufficient for the two of you to then be said to have a history. 'Tony? Oh, we go way back,' says Nicy, in lieu of any more detailed explanation as to how she has so confidently (and accurately, it turns out) predicted that he will be sleeping under the Penarth Road bridge having started drinking again last week and quit his hostel bed.

Yet going way back with Tony is never quite all the way back, and in any case signifies an understanding that is moving forward. Knowing Paul for years and years, 'the whole story', is nothing quite so definite or conclusive. There is always more, and almost every outreach patrol nets a new catch: snippets of information, inadvertent disclosure, admissions, confessions, bits of story.

Outreach: StreetLife patrol with Nicy and Den. Up and down Clare Street and along the Taff Mead Embankment, then Callaghan Square and under the railway bridge, parking up on Tyndal Street for a nose around Ellen Street and the industrial estate, where we find Susie Hindle. Susie is someone we are used to seeing every night, but has been missing from the outreach logs for a few weeks now, so it is something of a relief to see her. She has 'not been right' and in and out of hospital (for tests). All she needs is £40, 'and then I'm off,' she says; only no one is stopping. She decides to give it a rest and have a coffee.

Suzie sits on a low wall with Den beside her. Nicy and I stand some way off but within earshot. Susie has never been particularly shy of the team and she gets on well with Den, but she is not a great one for talking about herself. She can be quite close. Not tonight though. She sits on the wall for the best part of half an hour explaining to Den about the visits to the hospital and how they thought it might be cancer but it isn't, then about the problems she has at home: she has a baby girl, her own, to take care of, and a grown daughter, pregnant, whose boyfriend has just gone 'inside' and won't be out when the baby comes; she will be a grandmother soon enough, and only 34 years old. We knew none of this. Her drug use, which she has managed so much better than most over the last few years, is getting away from her again she feels, and she owes too much money, to too many people, some of them 'not nice people at all'. A couple more women come over for condoms; Nicy and I make small talk and keep them away from Den and Susie.

Den stands up to reach in his pocket for a pen, and writes down the phone number Susie is giving him, then the two of them walk back over to join Nicy and me. Susie has been crying, but is cheery now. Nicy tells her how good it is to see her and how we were starting to worry, not having seen her for a while. 'Bloody police,' says Susie, by way of explanation. In all the years she's worked she has never known it so bad as now. 'Police everywhere. Plainclothes, uniformed, vans. So I just stopped coming out.'

We say goodbye and walk back over to the car, Den telling Susie he will ring her tomorrow as agreed (Den is going to set up a meeting with someone from the drug advisory service and speak to Susie's social worker too, if she can be found – Susie hasn't heard from her in a long time and can't remember her name exactly. We climb in the car and close the doors. 'Did you get all that?' asks Den, meaning the whole half hour. 'Drive round the corner and I'll write it down.'

One hour later we are turning out of Sanquhar Street. A young woman standing on the corner waves to get our attention and I point ahead and left to show where we will park, away from the houses. This is Josie, only recently appeared on the scene; she is in her early twenties we think, not much of a one for talking yet. She takes condoms and a cigarette and then heads straight back to her street corner. We move along Ocean Way. Up ahead and walking away from us is a large woman, stepping unsteadily off the pavement into the road then back onto the pavement again; she seems to be signalling to oncoming cars but we can't be sure; none of us recognises her, at least from the back. We slow up alongside her and Nicy winds down the window, to say hello and explain and see if she can't get some idea of who this is and what is going on. But the woman is not particularly coherent and more than a little hostile. 'Who? Who!' she shouts. 'I don't know you! Who are you?' Nicy cuts it short and starts to wind the window up. 'Just drive on, Den,' she says. As we move off, the woman throws something at us, a bag or purse perhaps; in the wing mirror I see her stagger onto the road to collect whatever it was, sending a passing car swerving.

Sometimes, as happens here with Susie, a flood of information and confidence, a long time coming, comes all at once and relations between the team and a client take a big step forward. Susie wants help and has said as much, for the first time; the meeting with Dennis might actually lead somewhere (if she turns up for it).[5]

---

5. Which she did, and it did lead somewhere; relations with Susie were different from this point on – only a little different perhaps at first and on the face of it, but the shift was significant. Dennis was on the case now, always enquiring about her finances, health, drug-use and domestic situation (so much easier to do now that Susie had brought these things to the team herself), and this prompted further disclosures and then an admission, or something like it, from Susie, that she was looking to stop working and get off the street. This made it that much simpler to see where working with her was going, and the team, sensing movement, started to concentrate its efforts. Further meetings with Dennis helped sort her dire financial situation, which remained dismal enough but no longer desperate; a referral to a guidance and mentoring service, and support attending her first meeting, saw Susie paired up with a keyworker and fast-tracked to drug treatment; Nicy helped clear up some outstanding police matters. Multi-agency plans were worked up to secure Susie new accommodation, away from the domestic difficulties she had only begun to share with Dennis on the night in question but which she later revealed to be more convoluted still, and abusive. The move, to a new flat (not just new to Susie but brand new, a real find)

And where is all this information held, and how is it shared and shown to others? There are files, of course, upstairs in Marland House as in any office; sheaves of outreach logs in trays and boxes, and folders on desks. Almost any client who starts to come across to the team – with information and a request for help – is likely to trigger a good half inch of paperwork. There will be a housing application, medical and legal forms, a benefit claim and associated correspondence, and more besides, some or all of which may be kept indoors on behalf of clients with nowhere to keep it clean and dry and in any sort of order themselves. But this is paperwork in process and mostly clients' paperwork at that, open files held *for* clients. What the CCT outreach does not have is its own archive of client files. It doesn't *hold* information in that way at all. Team members know what they know about clients either because they are currently working with them, or because they just know them, in the sense that they see them every day, out on Central Square or the museum steps. Most of the team's outreach workers carry notebooks in which to jot new and significant information about clients, along with 'to do' lists or reminders of things they have promised to sort: travel warrant, food parcel, court appearance. These notes can be a source of reference for a day or two, up until the next team meeting, but the information recorded, the sort of thing Dennis scribbles down following his half-hour chat with Susie, doesn't get transcribed into a CCT file. Because there isn't one.[6]

---

became a point of focus and finishing line in relation to which other matters could be organised and sequenced – new furniture secured, benefit entitlement settled, methadone prescription down to an agreed level (and no longer topped up with occasional 'gear'), and an end to working: 'Once you move, we don't want to see you out anymore. OK?' All of this took lots of time and was not accomplished without setbacks and distraction, but in the end Susie did take up her new tenancy (Dennis helped with removals) and stopped 'working'. This took place over two years ago and the team has seen very little of her since, though they get the occasional report. Susie speaks with great fondness and appreciation for what was done for her: 'always being there for me … and waiting till I was ready, like.' Hers is a success story, and precious as such.

6. There are, however, files held by other agencies, to which the CCT has access. Two of these, each computer-based, are worth mentioning. The first is an online register called e-roof, which is managed by the housing department; e-roof shows the accommodation status of Cardiff's homeless from one day to the next, as recorded by staff in participating hostels and accommodation units. Outreach workers make little use of the system for information purposes. On the whole, they know better than e-roof where their clients are or have been staying or sleeping, or trying to. Then there is CareFirst, an extensive social services client record. This provides an occasional means of cross-checking information, not always reliably.

If outreach knowledge isn't exactly held anywhere, at least not on bespoke CCT files, how is client information shared? The Friday team meeting is important. Once a week, without exception, and for a couple of hours, desks in the CCT office are vacated, phones left to ring or switched to answerphone, and the whole team (shifts are arranged so that almost everyone is or ought to be in on Friday mornings) assembles in a meeting room along the corridor from the main CCT office space. Team members sit in a circle of chairs, teas and coffees to hand, the door closed, and together rehearse the events of the week gone, and look ahead to the week to come. Steve, the team manager, runs the meeting. There is no set agenda and no minutes are kept. Working around the room each team member lists the jobs of work they have 'on the go' right now and the clients they are working with. All current clients are discussed, 'current' meaning not the several dozen that team members might reasonably cite as those with whom they have been in some sort of contact of late (though these may be mentioned), but specifically those with whom the team has been actively working over the last few days, and/or those who might be barely even clients yet but about whom team members have particular concerns, those for whom *something needs to be done*. Among other things this is an exercise in getting the story straight, so that, for example, everyone knows the answer to the question 'Where are we up to with Bernard?' The answer being that Bernard is still uncommunicative, but seems to know a few words of German (according to Dennis), that the weather has turned cold again and he seems unprepared for this (there have been phone calls from at least two concerned members of the public), that his mental health is questionable and surely in decline (all agreed), that he can be found in the bus station most mornings and will at least take a hot drink (he did from Jeff, on Tuesday), that the police have been called to remove him from the bus station during the day at least three times recently (according to the bus station security staff, says Nicy); also that his case should be prioritised (all agreed), that outreach workers will really push with him next week and see if they can't get any further along with getting him in somewhere (and get him a sleeping bag in the meantime at least), that Nicy will speak with the Huggard Centre staff, where Bernard has stayed on occasion in the past, that Rosie, the nurse, will come out on the Breakfast Run on Monday and take a look at his feet – 'his nails are *this* long' – and that Steve will organise a multi-agency meeting to try and get some co-ordinated action, and a mental health assessment if at all possible. Updates on particular individuals and agreed plans of action are supplemented by discussion of general issues likely to affect some or all clients: the scheduled demolition of the Central Hotel, the bad batch of heroin in its second week of circulation, a complaint from City Centre Management about the mess around the back of Marks and Spencer.

The team meeting is where various bits of outreach story, garnered over recent days, are assembled and matched to what is already known and remembered and to the team's current resources and priorities and the wider context of whatever might be going on – at Tŷ Gobaith or the night shelter (both full, no vacancies), or the Cardiff Addictions Unit (Paul Short kicked off the programme, his methadone prescription withdrawn), and across the city centre, insofar as any of this is known for sure. The result is a bricolage of latest developments, updates, reports and concerns, and conjecture, that will just about hold together long enough to see the team through the week ahead (although there are some weeks when just about everything agreed on Friday morning is out of date by mid-afternoon of the same day, overtaken by events). The Friday meeting is never cancelled, brought forward or held back; but any significant development in the meantime will trigger some smaller *ad hoc* assembly, in Steve's office more than likely: Charlie and Dennis conferring with the team's mental health social worker about a new client 'discovered' that morning sleeping under a sheet of tarpaulin in Bute Park and not at all lucid or well. Discussion of client cases is not only a matter for the office, however. Out on the street, every outreach patrol is accompanied by, and the occasion for, a more or less running commentary on who is or might be where and in what sort of condition and what the team should do about it (or could do about it if other cases and clients weren't just as urgent or important). Jeff tells Charlie who he saw last night and why this spells trouble; Charlie tells Jeff what happened this morning when she tried to take Tony Harris along to his JobCentre Plus interview. Nicy gives Dennis the latest on Liam and Donna; Dennis rehearses the sequence of events that led to Swansea Nick's arrest six months ago, all of which started just over there by the subway stairs. Every patrol is an opportunity to go over old ground – doubly so; out loud and on foot.

If the question is how do CCT outreach workers hold and share information about their clients, then the answer is not that such information is held (in a file on a desk, or on a computer) in order to then be shared. Rather, the sharing of information *is how* that information is held, at least among themselves. Team meetings are important, but outreach workers know what they know – about what happened yesterday, or this time last year, or anywhere in between – because they are forever talking things over, out on patrols that criss-cross much the same territory as they did the day before.

By hook or by crook

To come across is not only to discover but also to yield, to give something of yourself to another. Outreach work requires both. Workers have to find the people they hope to work with (whose needs may be more or less visible, who may not be asking for help, or have long since stopped asking), then they have to engage these people as clients of the team. There is to be no paperwork; no one signs on the dotted line as a CCT client; strangers encountered become clients if it proves to be the case that they are in the sorts of need that the team suspected they were *and* they are or become receptive to the team's advances. Clients take what the team is there to give, and in return they give what the team is there to gather up and accomplish – some of them do.

No activity that takes place either side of a line and is organised around eventual movement across could be said to be one sided. Outreach is a reciprocal undertaking, from the very outset and throughout. It takes two, and there is give and take between them. Nothing quite comes for free. That this might be true may be clear enough already, despite the fact that I have on occasion described the help that workers give as unconditional. The Breakfast Run, for example, makes hot food and drink available to anyone who presents or appears as homeless; there is no charge and no strong expectation that this help be gratefully acknowledged. Free, then? Possibly. But not for long. There *is* an expectation that those who take breakfast for anything more than a few days should engage in some way with those handing over the coffees and teas; should exchange hellos at least and perhaps answer a question or two, lightly put; ought to give the team at least something to go on. If this minimal reciprocity fails to materialise then there may be a problem. Not at first, but before too long. 'We're not there to just give and give and give,' says Nicy. 'That's not helping anyone.' Under such circumstances, workers may feel they are being played. This is a matter of judgement. If someone comes in from out of town seeming savvy and practised, a new face but not at all backward in coming forward, keen to have a second cup of tea thanks, and will the team please make sure they call by the museum tomorrow, and make sure they bring a sleeping bag if they've got one spare, and can they have brown sauce instead of ketchup tomorrow … none of this will go down too well. 'We're not bloody caterers,' says Jeff. But with Bobby Renton and John, who greedily seize on bacon rolls and hot tea most mornings having spent all their money on booze, things are different. The team know these two, have done for years, and with both of them out of the hostels right now, and not likely to make it back in any time soon, it is a case of making sure they get something to eat and exchanging a few words just to see that they are doing OK. With Bobby and John the team are playing a long game and the payoff may be some way down the line. Nothing too much is expected of them right now, with the two of them drinking heavily again. So the cup of tea comes more or less free. Even so, an exchange of words with a couple of alcoholics in the early morning is still an exchange 'We always want something, even if it's a *No thanks* or a *Get lost*. That way at least you know that they're alive, that they heard you,' explains Nicy. The smallest shrug will do for starters.

Outreach: A cold morning, frost on the car windscreens, still dark. Jim and I are in the night shelter kitchen sorting eggs and rolls for the Breakfast Run; it will just be me and him today, as Den's car has not started (Jim works at the night shelter, which leaves me standing in for the City Centre Team). There is a quick discussion in the staff office over coffee and cigarettes as to whether or not we should book in Paula if we see her (she and John Reynolds are sleeping rough, having been kicked out of the B&B they were placed in only last week).

We drive over to Central Square and park up at the back of Marland House. There is a body visible in the covered walkway leading through to Central Square, laid out on a grubby blanket and wrapped in a sleeping bag. We walk over to see who it is but can get no response; whoever is inside has pulled their head and shoulders into the bag so we really have no idea who is in there. Jim puts a cup of tea down on the pavement to one side of the body in the bag. We stand there. 'Cup of tea for you there,' says Jim. No response. 'Is that you, John?' he asks. It clearly isn't John, who is much bigger and could never get his head down inside a sleeping bag like that, but it is something to say. No response. We stand there some more. 'Just give us a bit of movement will you my friend,' says Jim. We wait. 'There, he moved,' says Jim. Did he? I didn't see anything. 'Yeah, he crooked his legs a touch,' says Jim. Satisfied, he heads off through to the bus stands and the station forecourt. We spend 20 minutes on Central Square, jogging back over to the car when we hear a horn: there is a bin lorry waiting for us to move as we are blocking them in.

One hour later, outside Iceland, John Heron comes over for a bacon sandwich. Jim gives him one grudgingly, not wanting to argue the toss though it is a long time since John was actually 'out'. John asks if we have been over the Central Square yet and have we seen the guy in the bag by Marland House. He says the same guy was there, in the same place, tucked away inside his bag, at midnight last night. No one could get a word out of him then, either. We ask what John was doing out in the city centre at midnight and he just shrugs and says he went along to the Bus in the early evening and then the soup run and then he thought he might as well stay out a bit. He has been home since midnight, but was up again at six and has been waiting for us here at Iceland since 7am. Jim shakes his head.

Andy Saville is still out on Crwys Road, and has started to engage with outreach again. 'It was the snow that broke the ice,' says Jim, pleased with this wordplay. Den and Jeff went to see him on Monday afternoon, to check he was OK in the cold weather; Andy was gruff, but pleased enough to see them both and took hot drinks and a sleeping bag - peace offerings.

I will come back to Andy Saville and his falling out with Den and Jeff. For now, there is the still the question of who is giving out what for free on the Breakfast Run, or any other outreach patrol come to that; and if not for free then in exchange for what? What is it that others, with nothing much at all to hold on to, never mind hand over, are nonetheless giving in return? They give the same thing that outreach workers are themselves attempting to accomplish: some sort of contact and connection. Or they may do. Bearing gifts wrapped as necessities, outreach workers have to hope that at least some of those to whom they are reaching out will in fact reach back. What sort of outreach worker would you be otherwise (see p. 129)? To watch Charlie pick her way down the basement steps at the back of a vacant building, making just enough noise to be sure to be heard, and then place a cup of coffee on the ground beside a prone figure, and then back away, judging it best to leave it at that, for today, is to witness an ever so delicate first step in what it might take to build a relationship between two strangers. Of course there are plenty of times when things appear rather more familiar and brusque:

Jeff: 'Morning! Breakfast Run. Wake up you lazy bugger, I know you're in there.'

Paul: 'Is that Jeff?'

Jeff: 'No it's Avon calling. Who do you think it is? Course it's me. And Dennis. Hurry up, we want to get on.'

Paul: 'You can fuck off, the pair of you.'

Jeff: 'Charming.'

But this is only the same thing a few months on, premised on give and take.

Friends make gifts, but it is clients that outreach workers really want and in this they are instrumental. 'The Breakfast Run is about more than a bite to eat,' says Nicy. 'That's just the hook.' A first exchange, tentatively accomplished, paves the way for further negotiation. A good outreach worker lets this build slowly: rushing in won't help; it makes no sense to shower goods and services on a new client before either of you really knows what the other is after and prepared to accept. Some outreach encounters fizzle out within a week or so, at no great cost or embarrassment to either party. Having come across a young man on a bench in Bute Park one morning and then again later that week, the team loses track of him; he reappears at the Bus but only the one time – said his name was Darren (no surname given, or asked for), took tea, expressed passing interest in a place at the night shelter, but never really looked like going there (and never did), seemed to know Paul Short; he has not been seen now for over a month. This may be for the best – Jeff thinks so. CCT services are free of charge, but not indiscriminate. Outreach workers only want to make clients of those whose apparent needs warrant the effort. This makes them something like border guards, as well as scouts into the territory beyond.

If a bite to eat is a hook, only the homeless can take the bait; the CCT has no authority to enrol clients as it pleases, workers can only tender assistance and then see what happens. And to take is also, in this instance, to give – to yield, and admit a need: *Yes please: a tea, please. Three sugars.* And there may be a bit of story, and there may be a name; and to let somebody have your name is a surrender of sorts. To say *Tea? Yes please. Thanks. My name? It's Paul* is to give up something of who you are. A moment ago you were no one (to outreach), or could have been anyone; and now you are Paul. And two months on, following a whole sequence of greetings exchanged, services rendered and accepted, disclosures and conversations, it may be that Jeff will be in a position to vouch for Paul at the night shelter, persuading the manager to hold a recently vacated bed in reserve, on the grounds that Paul has been on at the CCT for a couple of weeks now to get him in somewhere and seems serious about doing so (and is drinking less, and has his benefits more or less in order having spent an entire afternoon with Dennis sorting this out, and is too frail to be out now the weather has turned). All of this, the repeated contact week after week, the time expended, the attention paid and rewarded (first a name, then further details, then bits of story, admissions of need), each small step and the whole thing taken together, and now the possibility that Paul might step across the threshold of the night shelter, off the street ... all of this validates the work of outreach and was Paul's to give as much as it was Jeff's to deliver. Being an outreach worker only works if others are prepared to take what you are there to dispense, and to come across in turn.

Mostly, outreach workers see such opportunities coming. A client like Paul starts to look good for a place indoors and the outreach team, registering as much, sets to, actively weighing the possibilities and making plans. One month ago it was all they could do to keep tabs on him, two months ago no one knew his name for sure. Now he seems ready – says he is, wants to quit the drinking or at least cut down, wants to get indoors (and not just as a couple of days' respite until his next benefits payment comes in); wants, in short, to make a move away from the sorts of need and circumstance, places and times of day, that would have him running into outreach workers. Others don't; don't want to make that move, at least not yet and perhaps not ever. Yet they remain clients: they will have a cup of tea in the morning and will spend time talking amicably enough with Nicy or Jeff; they will take blankets and food parcels, letters and such – whatever the team chooses to bring them. Although there is no movement with these clients, no real *give*, outreach workers are pleased to exercise a duty of care and maintenance, *in situ* (in the hope that things may change, one day). Some are a little closer to making a change, and may acknowledge as much to the team. In such cases the team's efforts are concentrated, but nothing is rushed. Clients who begin to indicate they might consider something different are treated with great care and delicacy, in the hope that the balance can be tipped the right way. Stubborn clients, set on keeping as they are, require no such subtle attention.

The CCT aims to work *with* its clients, respecting intransigence where that seems best for now, and elsewhere moving together with those who want to make a change. But there can be disagreement. Clients fall out with the team, having first got along. Outreach workers, for their part, lose patience too sometimes. One way in which this happens is when clients in receipt of daily visits and ongoing assistance start making additional demands that are not exactly to do with stopping being homeless, or are construed as such by the CCT: a new pair of shoes, another sleeping bag, a lift to a friend's house in Riverside, an extra food parcel tomorrow evening. All of this and more is available, but outreach workers cross-calibrate requests for help and a client's willingness to work together with the team. Clients who ask too much and offer too little may be told as much. 'We can help. We're here to help. But we need you to work with us,' Nicy tells a disgruntled Wayne Daley, having refused to drive him around the corner to the off-licence. Sometimes the boot is on the other foot and a client insists that they do want what the outreach workers are there to accomplish, that they want to change and get off the street, but that the CCT is not doing enough. Not all such allegations are misplaced. Outreach workers put themselves out for their clients, sometimes taking on more than the job description might specify, but they are always operating a triage of sorts, even with those clients who look ready to come across. Workers must weigh up what they have to offer a client against the probability that such help might actually *stick* if taken up, might make things any better in anything other than the very short term.[7]

Outreach: Early morning in the middle of what will be three bad days in a row for Andy Saville, established for some months now in a doorway on Crwys Road, where he can be found buried under duvets and blankets, surrounded by newspapers and cast-off bottles of booze. The CCT have lost patience with him a little of late, in part because of Andy's repeated complaint that no one really wants to help him and that the outreach workers aren't doing anything for him. 'I want a flat,' he says. 'I'm ready to move in somewhere, but no one's helping me. This lot aren't helping me. Useless, they are.' The CCT see things differently; they would rather have Andy in a hostel first, with some supervision and support on site (Andy won't have this, hates hostels), and drinking less (Andy won't have this either). The team did actually manage to get him into a flat not so very long ago, a rare achievement, but the place was a wreck within a matter of weeks and Andy was duly evicted; the team lost a bit of money there and

---

7.   Again, this is territory that Michael Rowe has covered, perceptively. Outreach workers' reluctance to move some clients into the first available vacancy can be tinged with the dim awareness that what is actually on offer is not much more than 'second-class citizenship'; indeed, this prospect 'haunts both parties' (Rowe, 1999: 113).

some credibility with the landlord – no more CCT clients in his properties any time soon, thanks. This morning Andy is at it again. 'What about my flat?' he wants to know. 'What about it?' asks Den, pouring hot water for tea.

Andy stands up to stretch and look about, rubbing his face; his left leg is soaked from groin to knee with spilt drink or urine. He tells us Badger woke him up half an hour ago: 'He knows I've got paid yesterday, you see. He thinks there's a drink in it for him. "Fuck off," I told him.' Badger is nowhere to be seen. Jeff listens with ill-concealed irritation while Andy recounts (with relish) how he came to be evicted from Marland House yesterday, having lost his temper in the Housing Advice Unit. 'All the immigrants and asylum seekers, jumping the queues. All they have to do is twitch their fingers,' says Andy. 'And I was *born* in Cardiff. If I went to their country and asked for a house they'd think I was having a laugh.' (There will be work for Den and Jeff to do today then, smoothing things over back at Marland House.) 'You're not helping us really, are you Andy, with that sort of thing? You're not helping *yourself*, either,' says Den. Jeff asks if Andy would like to hand over some of his money for safekeeping. Andy says no.

Midnight. Andy is raging up and down City Road. He left his doorway half an hour ago to buy a take-away supper only to find, on return, all his stuff (blankets, bags, letters and documents) 'kicked all over the fucking road' and his bottles of drink gone. He thinks some students have done it and has already confronted a crowd of them. We grab hold of him before he accosts another group and sit him down with a cigarette. 'All the Henry's and Henrietta's,' shouts Andy. 'Oh it's all a joke to them: *Oh, it's OK, Daddy will sort it out.* They're out drinking in clubs until two in the morning. But I can't afford that. Picking on the most vulnerable, that's what it is. Very funny, yes. Very funny. I could murder someone. I'll do it. I am going to kill someone, if I find who did it. The most vulnerable! All my stuff all over the road. And now there's no way to get a drink. So that's me fucked for the rest of the night. If I want a drink in the night I'm fucked.'

He is a little calmer after a second cigarette, though far from happy, and weaves off determinedly down City Road intent on persuading the staff in the 24-hour Spar to sell him a few cans. He is clutching what he says is the very last of his money, all the rest gone.

Morning. Andy back in his doorway, the Breakfast Run in attendance.

'I need to get in somewhere,' says Andy. 'No one is helping me. I'm homeless.'

'There's a place in the night shelter,' says Den. 'I could make a call.'

'I won't go there. I want a flat. That's what I keep telling you.'

'It's not as easy as that, Andy. You know it's not.'

'Well, sort it out, can't you. I thought that was your job.'

'We'd need to get a deposit together, to start with. What about your money, from yesterday?'

'That's gone. I drunk it. I need help. No one's helping me.'

This exchange has become wearyingly familiar, stale – though it must be a daily agony to Andy. The team are dead set against finding him another flat, certain that this is not the answer; and there are other clients right now whose needs and vulnerabilities rank higher, desperate though Andy's are. Which means he gets his cups of tea and bacon rolls, his blankets, his offers of a place at the night shelter – if only he would take it. But nothing more. Jeff and Den are committed to helping, but also irritated, not least by the repeated accusations of neglect.

Evening: outside the Bus, working the milling crowd of drinkers, one or two of them too drunk to be allowed on board. Andy is there too, rehearsing last night's events and the injustice of it all, and, then, the fact that he is sleeping out in the cold: 'I've got fuck all and no one is helping me.' He has been drinking most of the day (was on Central Square earlier, with friends) and is now really winding himself up: 'No one is helping me!'

I am busy with Jeff and Nicy trying to keep a couple of teenagers, a girl and her boyfriend, away from the Bus. The boy collapsed half an hour ago and may have had a seizure; he is up now but confused and belligerent; the girl tells us he is staying at Tresillian House, which is where we are keen to get the two of them. We don't want them hanging around the drinkers. Nicy has her car around the corner and is manoeuvring the two of them towards it, brisk and motherly now that we are nearly there. 'Don't be sick in my car,' she says. Andy shouts at our retreating backs: 'No one is *helping* me! No one!' He keeps it up as we move off, but the emphasis shifts: '*No one* is helping me.' What was an allegation of neglect becomes a giving of notice: '*No one* is helping me. Nobody. Forget it. And I don't want you coming round anymore and fobbing me off with a bacon roll in the mornings. Leave me alone!'

Having known and worked with Andy for a number of years, having helped him into housing – hostels, bedsits, flats – and out of difficulties, having watched him slip back to the street, repeatedly, having supported and advised him, shared time, food, cigarettes and conversation on countless early mornings, outreach workers can perhaps shrug off one evening's ill-temper; Andy's disavowal is understandable, if not altogether reasonable – he's angry. But his outburst was also an indictment: outreach work isn't helping, outreach is a sop to the homeless. Jeff and Nicy were visibly stung.

Ending up

Stories have a beginning and then a middle by which time some things have happened and the principal characters have moved on into the narrative. By the time the middle has been reached, the beginning marks a point from which distance can be measured and progress appraised. 'We've come a long way with Leon,' says Jeff. 'When you think about how he was when we first met him.' Having come this far there is now a story to tell, and the point at which it all began allows that to happen. If asked to account for the work he has done with Leon over the years, Jeff can reply 'Leon? Where to start? Well, when I first met Leon ...' When an outreach worker talks about having come a long way with a client, they may mean that things are different now than they were before, and that it has taken time to get there – also that there may be further to go. For outreach workers, as for the rest of us, time moves forward, always. Stories do too – they move forwards in time. But the distance travelled since the story began can be in either direction, forwards or back, or (more likely) a mixture of both. Overall, there may have been progress. Leon has come a long way. Others have too. Roy, not in a hole anymore but indoors, in a hostel bed (though still part of the street scene and still drinking). It took some time to get him the room, and longer still to get him to want to take it, but there he is, indoors and better fed and healthier looking than he was when Jeff first 'found' him (which makes his an outreach story with a beginning, a middle and something that looks a little like an end, though no one is claiming it as such just yet). However, there are also cases in which the story seems to have moved in the other direction. Stacey was in her late teens when she arrived in Cardiff and full of life and a vigorous sort of nuisance and complaint. Her story since has been chequered and unhappy and mostly downhill, at least to hear Jeff tell it. No one is giving up on her, but things do not look good; progress has not been made. Stacey was in a hostel for a while, a year ago, but is back on the streets now and looking worn down by it all, by the company she keeps and the heroin habit she didn't use to have.

Either way, the CCT are still in contact, with Roy and Stacey both, still working with the two of them, or ready to work as and when the work needs doing and can get done. Getting work done with someone like Stacey can be frustrating and takes time whether or not anything is accomplished at the end of it all. The same goes for Roy of course, and Leon, and so many others; but Stacey is a particular worry – her story has sagged back below the point at which it started out, or seems that way sometimes.

If CCT outreach workers have come any distance with Stacey, this is to be measured more in the growth of familiarity and understanding between them than in any concrete progress in seeing her housed and settled.[8] And this familiarity has developed at something like the same rate at which her contact with other support services has shrunk. Stacey is banned from more than one of the city-centre hostels, is no longer registered with a GP and is in danger of losing her benefits, having failed to respond to recent letters (delivered to her by the CCT). It is almost as if she were disappearing, over an edge. Only not quite – because the CCT are still in contact and see her most days, stopping to talk, minding how she is, making sure she eats. And Stacey seems ready to tolerate that and will chat and confide if she is in the mood, so long as, and because she knows that, no one is going to tell her what to do. 'We're not there yet with Stacey,' says Jeff. 'Nowhere near it. But she knows who we are and she knows we're here for her.' Which *is* somewhere further on from where the story started back when Stacey first pitched up in Cardiff, monosyllabic and suspicious and (for the first few weeks) wanting little or nothing to do with outreach. 'It's a bit of a waiting game right now, with Stacey,' says Dennis.

---

8.   Measured literally – spatially, that is – the distance covered would amount to almost nothing at all; sitting with Wayne and Jackie on Central Square she is only a few yards away from where Jeff first met her.

8

Learning to See

Movement and territory, lines of travel and thresholds of accomplishment have been at issue throughout the previous chapters. I have been working on the assumption that to see and understand where outreach work with the homeless gets done is to see and understand what that work is and why it might matter. The CCT works in the middle of the city with those whose needs and difficulties overlap and combine with being on the street, with needing to be there, with having nowhere else to go. CCT clients are 'out', and the job of the team is to get them 'in', or might be described that way (indoors, into treatment, into hospital, into work, onto a waiting list). Stability is important, or will become so – arrangements, appointments, accommodation secured, problems *fixed*. But so too is movement. Clients are encouraged to move forward and make changes; obstacles to progress are done away with or worked around; outreach work is supposed to lead somewhere. The landscape of outreach is one in which clients are found, either stuck and tucked away or vulnerably exposed, and then helped in ways informed from the outset by the ambition that helping might lead to them being somewhere else and better off. The CCT can count as an outcome a client no longer in the same extremity of need out of doors as they were when the team first found them.

Michael Rowe's analysis of the outreach encounter frames this as a sort of edgework, a series of negotiations practised across a border on one side of which society stands waiting. Persuading those on the far side to cross back over and come home is the outreach task, and it is not an easy one. For some clients, the stakes are too high; there is too much to lose (too little to gain). Put another way, they do not want to play. Here is Gerald Egan, whose thoughts on skilled helping I first considered in Chapter 5:

One reason it is difficult to give a clear-cut answer to the question 'Does helping help?' is the collaborative nature of the enterprise. Helping is not like fixing a car or removing a tumour. Helpers do not cure their patients. Helping is at minimum a two-person *team* effort in which helpers need to do their part and clients, theirs. If either party refuses to play the game or to play it well, then the enterprise can fail. Helpers need to give their best to the enterprise. But giving their best means, to a great extent, helping clients tap their own resources: not just getting clients to play the game, as it were, but helping them want to play the game. (1994: 10; italics in original)

Helping people *want to play* the game is a rather more evolved proposition than simply helping them along once play has begun; not so candid an exercise in care. Outreach workers must edge their way into others' confidence, winning trust on the basis of support offered free of charge. In doing so they aim to secure objectives their clients may not yet share. Hard bargaining must wait until the game is in play, and even then it may be best conducted as if it were not bargaining at all. Outreach workers coax and finagle, conceal their hand and up the stakes; '[t]he line between negotiation and manipulation can be hazy at times' (Rowe, 1999: 87). Clients hold their own cards and have it in their power to accept or decline an outreach worker's advances. The outreach offer is intended as holistic, but this can make it an offer to be accepted or rejected entirely. There will be all sorts of incremental assistance, certainly; but there may come a point at which one or other party – or both – comes to feel that helping isn't helping anymore.

Homelessness is *not* a game, of course; nor are homeless persons inhabitants of any other world than this one, the one we share. None of which disqualifies Rowe's *as if* analysis. He shows us outreach work as border-crossing; this is one way of seeing and, as Rowe acknowledges, it can both sharpen and obscure our understanding.

How might we see things differently? A first step could be to ask if the scrutiny Rowe gives to the figurative landscape of outreach, to outreach work as the crossing of a border, isn't a little immaterial. Perhaps outreach work does take place across a border, in some sense. But where else? Where can we trace homeless outreach in the physical landscape of the city? I have already made answers to this question a part of my account, tracking between the physical layout of Cardiff's city centre, the locations, routes and intersections that combine in the mobile practice of outreach patrol, and an interior geography of ups and downs and movements back and forth that are (for me, as for Rowe) important to any proper understanding of the work. In Chapter 6 I paid particularly close attention to certain sorts of space or setting that might be said to escape attention because 'lost' or leftover. Such locations are elusive perhaps, and sometimes hard to see; but they are real enough and only ever material.

What might we learn, then, from looking at the concrete landscape of outreach? I think there are two ways in which to ask this question, the first of which I will set out (and look to answer) in this chapter, the second in the next – if briefly. Here is the first – it requires a little re-ordering. Rather than asking what we might learn from looking, we might instead ask after the ways in which looking is something an outreach worker has to learn.

Outreach: Early morning outreach, mid-June, damp and muggy weather; a fine drizzle in the air. Very busy yesterday, says Jeff. Over 20 on the Breakfast Run. 'But you know how it is. We'll probably see no one today.' We pack up the food and drink and head off to Central Square, where Jeff thinks he saw someone or a bundle of stuff, or something, at one end of the bus station on his way in from Splott. Sure enough on aisle number two we find a man stretched out on the floor half asleep, wrapped in cardboard, head on a rucksack. Not anyone that we recognise. We say a loud good morning and the man turns over, sits up, rubs his eyes. His name is Graham. Doesn't drink, doesn't smoke – he is very keen to tell us; doesn't want any trouble. Would take a coffee, if it's free. Nothing to eat, thank you. We pour out hot coffee (three sugars) and talk a little more, Jeff handing over a CCT leaflet and pointing out Marland House just across the square from where we are gathered, but not open for another couple of hours yet. Graham yawns and lies back down.

Ten minutes later we are in Bute Park. We make our way to the footbridge at the back of the College of Music and from there we climb the railings and push into the undergrowth, between trees, to where we hope to find Michael and Hayley (Michael having let slip they were camped out this way at the soup run last night). We cast about for a minute or two then pick up and follow a trail of trampled scrub, footprints and litter, confirmed soon enough by wood smoke, to find two tents by a small campfire. Monty is outside one tent, emptying a can of lager; Michael and Hayley are inside the other tent, he says. We spend five minutes here but don't hand out food and drink. Hayley pokes her head out to ask why not. There have been emails from the parks and gardens department complaining about rough sleepers making a mess and outreach workers 'delivering breakfast'. Steve has asked us to make contact with anyone in the park, same as always, but to 'do breakfast' elsewhere. We tell Hayley we'll be outside the toilet block at the back of the museum with hot tea and rolls in twenty minutes. She ducks back in the tent and tugs the zipper shut.

In the civic centre Len Goodyear is there already, waiting by the toilet block, which has become a regular stop for us over recent weeks. Len is still housed, so far as anyone knows – he says he is, though he won't say where; but is always out early for the Breakfast Run. As we pour out hot water for tea (four sugars for Len), Adam and a young girl appear from the bushes by Alexandra Gardens and make their way over the road to join us, both of them looking very much the worse for wear, the girl wearing her sleeping bag as a shawl. A car slows to let them cross, then beeps. 'It won't be long until we're getting complaints here too,' says Jeff. 'From the office workers. You know, *I don't feel safe with them there*. That sort of thing.' There is a tent pitched behind the toilet block (Where are all the tents coming from?). Adam says that Paul and Lizzie P. are inside. Can he take them a couple of coffees over? Jeff hums and hahs then says yes OK. 'But no food, unless they come and get it themselves. It's not breakfast-in-bed we're doing here.' The toilet block has been breached again, having been bricked up by the council some months back. It must have taken some work, with a pickaxe or similar. Jeff clambers his way over the scattered breeze blocks in the doorway and steps inside, clearing his throat: 'Anyone home?' No answer. 'There's no one in there,' says Adam.

We make our way back past the museum (no one there, nor any sign) and then the Crown Court (remains only – a sodden blanket, cigarette ends and crumbs), then along King Edward VII Avenue past the Glamorgan Building where I glimpse some sheets of cardboard stacked along one side of the building, behind a pillar. 'Well done,' says Jeff as we walk over to take a closer look. 'You see? You've got outreach worker's eyes now, Tom.'

Praise indeed, though Jeff is also making fun. What we have here is something that can be seen, a combination of locations, indications and settings. Much of which you might miss if you didn't know what you were looking for, or were busy with something else; but a city through which a working practice can be threaded, through which outreach workers *find and pick their way* in a manner which marks out what they do as outreach rather than anything else. A landscape then, and a physical one, knowledge of the layout and configuration of which provides the grounds for movement, observation and assessment even as such repeated practices establish and confirm that knowledge.

Reading for sign

Looking out for the (hidden) homeless is a skilled activity and involves the ability not only to know a homeless person when you see one – or a sex worker, or a drug addict, or anyone else in any of the many categories of need to which CCT outreach workers respond – but, prior to catching sight of anyone at all, the ability to identify and follow up on indications that there might be someone to hand, as yet unseen but worth looking out for. How is this done?

How does anyone track down or gather up that which they are after, in pursuit of their livelihood? The question goes a long way back, as do some of the answers; we might leave the city behind altogether. Yet looking for clues and indications *is* also a very urban occupation, as any reader of detective fiction knows. And if the hope is that such clues and indications will be found, then it generally pays to have someone undertaking enquiries who knows the territory; moreover, someone whose working knowledge of that territory is aligned to whatever sort of 'missing' has prompted the search in the first place (and who can readily recognise a clue in this context, should they come across one). Setting out to find a vulnerable client gone missing from Tŷ Gobaith, outreach workers may have little or no further information about the circumstances of his departure and no clue, no indication, as yet, as to where he may have gone. Even so, they are not exactly in the dark. For one thing, they know a good deal about the sorts of places it might pay to start looking. Trying to locate anyone in particular, they can always start out from what they already know in general – about homelessness, about Cardiff, about the daycentres and the hostels and the drop-ins, about Central Square and the city-centre car parks, about this street and that street, about the North Road subway, about the derelict York Hotel. They are not *clueless*. Particular enquiries are informed by a general understanding, in this way. And so too the other way around. General enquiries, out on patrol are informed by a prior knowledge of particular locations. Some places are not to be missed, are worth taking a look around every day; others are much less likely to reward inspection. And an experienced outreach worker knows the difference between the two.

Some of the settings and locations that matter most on an outreach patrol are apparent enough; anyone can see the Crown Court steps or the fire-exit doorways around the CIA (although their express significance to outreach may not be evident to the casual observer). Others are beneath notice and look like nothing much at all unless you already know what you are looking at (and for). Still others are hidden away, are concealed. You would need to know these places existed, and be prepared to discover them for yourself, before you could begin to sift through them for signs of occupancy; they are not at all apparent, and some are camouflaged. Outreach workers can include knowledge of all such settings in the know-how they already hold (reserving pride of place and a particular satisfaction perhaps for the last category, the hidden settings and hideaways others don't even know are there). If they are the ones that know the territory when it comes to homelessness in the centre of the city then this is one of the ways in which that is so.

Outreach workers know their way around, and they know the sorts of places in which to start looking – and keep visiting. They are clued up, and this is enough to get enquiries underway. An outreach worker leaves Marland House and heads towards, circles around and spends time in the right sort of place: already, there is a proficiency at work. But what will they find there? Perhaps the very thing they were looking for, a client. Perhaps nothing at all. But quite possibly something in-between, some trace or indication that someone is or has been here, that the space is in use, even if there is no one to be seen. One inconclusive fact is communicated when an outreach worker (re)emerges from a basement stairwell and says to her colleague, with a shake of the head, 'No one there'. Something more definite would be put across were she to climb the stairs and say 'No sign'.

Places, even likely places, showing no sign of occupancy or use, slip down a rung or two on the ladder of outreach priority. Out on patrol there are always more places one could go than there is time in which to visit them all, and some internal calibration, constantly revised, sees the shape of outreach patrol contract, flex and distend accordingly, each day a little different from the one before. If there is no indication that a familiar spot is in use right now it will be that little bit less of a priority tomorrow.[1] Alternatively, signs of use discovered somewhere the team

---

1. Or it may be that there *are* signs, but the signs are that there is no good reason to come back anytime soon. Sodden blankets, wadded down in a corner, half frozen and bearing a patina of undisturbed street dirt tells almost the same story as no sign at all: no one is here, nor has this space been in use for some time. So too an empty bottle of pills under a bush in Bute Park, the prescription label bleached white by the sun. Finding nothing at all in the

has neglected for a week or two – a neatly rolled sleeping bag beside a wooden pallet wedged into the far corner of a supermarket car park, a litter of cigarette ends visible between the slats – will prompt further enquiries and a second visit later that day, and again the following morning. This is to move from a knowledge of the sorts of place in which to look, to the sorts of things you might find once you got there; not the lay of the land so much as the indications distributed across it, the provisional leftovers and traces that all outreach workers soon enough learn to see.

Outreach: February, Breakfast Run. Robbie and Jim are on duty at the night shelter and are together in the office smoking cigarettes and slurping coffee (bacon frying in the kitchen along the corridor); Carl is in there too, catching up. This is the first time in a long time that Carl has done the Breakfast Run. Roles in the CCT had a shake-up just before Christmas and Carl has been moved from the Bus Project and onto the morning shift. New arrivals at the night shelter include Wayne Daley, apparently kicked out of the Bridge Project (a residential treatment service for substance misuse, run from the Salvation Army hostel). 'Still, it was a good try,' says Carl, meaning Wayne did well to get as far as he did.

We drive off in Carl's car, hot food wrapped and packed in a box on the back seat; 200 yards on, half way along Tudor Street, we pull up and get out to explore. Carl has a hunch about the lane running behind the houses on the Fitzhamon Embankment. He has seen drinkers gathered here during the day. There is a private car park at one end of the lane, secured with a retractable grille; Carl says that if you are quick you can roll under this when a car goes in or out, which gives you a lovely spot to spend the night – dry, secure, out of the wind. We peer through the grille but can't see any sign of occupancy other than a splash of what looks and smells (strongly) like it might be urine against one wall. Carl calls hello, not too loud. No answer. We make our way along the lane, warily. There are puddles of water and heaps of litter and rubble, a discarded television set. It is still dark and we both stumble at points. The lane dog-legs left and here the rear wall to one of the adjacent properties has more or less collapsed. We step across into the overgrown garden beyond. It is too dark to see anything much. There has been a definite trampling down, though – of weeds and grass;

---

sorts of spaces in which outreach workers look most carefully is actually rather unusual and in itself a sign, as and when it does occur. When there is *absolutely* nothing in the rear stairwell of the Wood Street car park, the intermediate landing a few steps up from street level scoured clean and smelling of disinfectant, this is a sign not only that no one is using this space right now but, more than that, that no one is allowed to: the space has come to notice and been *seen to*, is being looked after.

and there are bottles and cans of strong cider everywhere. The house is unlit and possibly empty, the windows are mostly broken but secured with boards on the ground floor. 'Let's check again in an hour, says Carl. 'When we can see better.'

We walk on to Central Square and make our way, methodically, up and down the aisles in the bus station and then around the concourse. No one. We press our noses up against the padlocked entrance to the construction site along the far side of the square. There is an expanse of open ground beyond, dotted with cairns of rubble; along one side there are railway arches in one of which Carl thinks he can see a blanket – someone's bed maybe; we are not sure, maybe just a pile of overalls or a tarpaulin or something. There is no one there, anyway.

Carl suggests a walk through the Wood Street car park. By the pay station on the ground floor we find Rudy, a regular on the city-centre scene, resident at the Huggard at the moment but out and about and begging, most days, as now. 'Can you help me?' he asks. 'Got no money, sorry,' says Carl. 'But there's tea if you'd like some?' Rudy says no thanks, but gestures vaguely towards the lifts. 'More up there,' he says. We go to take a look. A scribbled notice suggests that the lifts are out of order and although one arrives, with a ping, and opens, we decide not to chance getting stuck in there for the morning, and walk up the stairs instead. Towards the top we start to find chocolate bar wrappers, lots of them, not yet trodden down or tidied up. 'Thought so,' says Carl.

At the top of the stairs we step out onto the open deck: more chocolate bar wrappers, discarded chocolate too. We cross the deck to stand at the far edge and lean on the barrier and look out across the city. Carl suggests we stop here, just to see if we can't pick out anyone down below on Saunders Road and Great Western Lane. 'Best time of day, this,' says Carl. We wait ten minutes then cross the deck to the rear fire-exit stairwell and descend that way. We've not seen anyone. The stairs are conspicuously clean. 'Someone's been here before us,' says Carl. We step out onto Great Western Lane.

Twenty minutes later we have done Bute Park and are with Gavin E., who is tucked up in a sleeping bag by the College of Music. All we can see is the top of his head, but we know it's him by his rucksack. He doesn't respond to our hellos. Carl puts a cup of sweet tea and a hot roll in foil on the ground beside him and steps back, quietly. We head across to the civic centre and then Museum Place and a little look down Park Lane where there is a set of cellar stairs at the rear of an office building. Vinny sleeps here when he is in Cardiff, says Carl. On inspection we find cardboard, but it is damp and rotten; it doesn't look like anyone has been here for days. We turn onto Park Grove and off again to search the car park at the rear of another (vacant) office building, backing onto the railway line. No sign of anyone there. On we go. St Andrew's Place, Park Lane again, Stuttgarter Strasse, Queen

Street, the Hayes, Bute Terrace and then Mary Ann Street. We take a look around the back of Toys 'R' Us, where Carl and Den found some blankets on evening outreach last week. We don't find any blankets, but we do find Pete Farnworth, huddled in a ball on the pavement, cold and shivering but uncommonly cheerful. He gets up and walks with us over to the CIA. We circle the CIA anti-clockwise, and find an encampment half way around. Carl recognises the occupant, from years back: Danny, and a girlfriend. The two of them have spent the night in Cardiff because Danny has to appear in court today. We move on. A cardboard screen further round hides two figures, under blankets; one is resident at Tresillian House but has taken a night off, as he does every now and then when it gets too much for him in there. We stay to talk things through a little. Pete Farnworth waves goodbye and moves off down the road, checking the doors on all the parked cars as he goes.

Clues and traces: discarded bottles, trodden grass, sheets of cardboard, blankets, splashes of urine, cans of cider, belongings, boarded windows, chocolate bars. Plus what Dennis reported last week and what Carl already knows (some of it from years back). Rudy's tip-off too. Car parks, stairwells, rear lanes, doorways, arches, parks, gardens; empty houses, vacant offices. Climbing, stumbling, circling, stepping over, backing off, moving on; views across the city in the half-light; close inspection of what might be something, or nothing; searching, high and low.

Learning to see, for anyone involved in the procurement of a livelihood within a landscape, is, as Tim Ingold has it, 'a matter … of acquiring the skills for direct perceptual *engagement*'; for those so engaged, '[k]nowledge of the world is gained by moving about in it, exploring it, attending to it, ever alert to the signs by which it is revealed' (2000: 55; italics in original).[2] For outreach workers stirring about down Great

---

2. Ingold is writing here about hunting, gathering and perceiving among the aboriginal Pintupi of Western Australia (and the Koyukon of Alaska). I am not. Rather, I am concerned with Nicy, Charlie, Dennis and Jeff, of central Cardiff. Yet theirs is a circumambulatory knowledge too. Is the comparison far-fetched? Not really. Nothing is being fetched at all in the sense of being carried across from somewhere else, to which it properly belongs. Everybody has it in them to look around in search of what they are after. My point is not that stone-age subsistence isn't one thing and urban welfare services quite another; that can be agreed. But there has to be some essential resemblance if only sufficient for us to have coined the words to indicate skilled activity *of this general sort*: tracking down, gathering up. Outreach work requires and proceeds by way of an attuned, receptive perception and careful movement through known surroundings that may yet surprise. So too other livelihoods.

Western Lane in the early morning the signs by which their world or livelihood is revealed are peculiar to it, even as those signs are part of the same city centre that everyone else knows and sees – or thinks they do.

This coincidence of knowledges, and the gap between the two – the things that outreach workers know about the city centre and the things that everybody (else) does – is most apparent on those occasions when the team has company: journalists wanting to do a homeless piece, or students writing a dissertation. Taking visitors out on patrol, as observers, two or three things almost always happen, and reveal something about where, and the way in which, outreach work gets done. Someone will almost always say something about how they *never realised this place was here*, or how they thought they knew the city centre, or how they *always wondered what was behind there*. Outreach workers, who may have taken pains to go just that little bit further off the beaten track than usual for just this reason, can take this as affirmation. Next, in counterpoint, someone will ask (as outreach workers move briskly past some rear access lane or entryway seemingly identical to the one they spent the last ten minutes rummaging about in): *Shouldn't we take a little look down there as well?* The answer is no, but it is harder to explain quite why. Why one lane and not another? Why around the back of that building but not around the back of this one? It is just that some places are a better bet than others, depending on what you know about them already and can see of them today. Some indications can be explained easily enough: 'See those orange plastic cap things? Those are for syringes. Like a lid. So we're just going to have a little look here. Mind where you put your feet.' Others are harder to spell out. It is not so much that a plank of wood has been pulled away from a fence. That might mean anything, or nothing at all. Rather, it is the way that the loose plank has been left there, propped upright, concealing the gap its removal has afforded – on purpose? You wouldn't notice it, ordinarily, unless you were looking. Or an even vaguer feeling, a hunch, that it might be time someone took a look around the side of the Johnston's building, even though no one has been (bedded down) there for weeks and the Breakfast Run has stopped making regular calls.

Because being homeless is dirty work and goes together sometimes with dirty places (so too other sorts of street life and vulnerability), litter of almost any sort warrants closer inspection by outreach workers, if only a stride or two closer and then a wheeling away again: 'Nah. Nothing.'

Figure 8.1

Again, it is not always so easy to make plain to an observer exactly what it is about this or that little collection of boxes, coat-hangers and food wrappers over there by a drainpipe that makes it worth a second look. Some piles of litter look like they are supposed to be there, put out for collection; others look less reputable somehow – gone over, gathered together, in some way suspect.[3] Outreach workers' explanations as to how it is they know what it is they are looking at, especially in more

---

3.   When it comes to litter as a sort of clue, there are two broad categories. The first comprises objects that others have set aside, dropped or thrown away, things no one else wants but which can prove useful if you are homeless and might be assembled to some purpose: a wooden pallet, a plastic chair, a sheet of cardboard, leftover food. Discovered, gathered together – behind the York Hotel, or in the far corner of a supermarket car park – these are sure indications that a site is in use, and worth coming back to. The second category includes the waste that the homeless themselves produce: forsaken sleeping bags (too wet to dry out by tonight, or soiled), cigarette ends, blankets, cans, medication, grubby paperwork. Different sorts of homeless litter can signify different sub-categories of the CCT client group – emptied cider bottles (drinkers), used condoms and cigarettes (sex worker), pins and foil (drug users).

marginal cases (not a sleeping bag in a doorway, which no one is all that likely to miss), are not always so helpful. It is hard to explain, easier to show, again and again, until a new volunteer or team member starts to get a feel for the work, an eye for the right sorts of detail.

One of the surest signs that they are on to something comes when outreach workers recognise *their own* leftover goods: a boiled egg trodden into the gutter, torn wrappers from mint-flavoured condoms – Ceri took a huge handful on Tuesday – polystyrene cups and sugar sachets carried away from Central Square only this morning and now here, in a pile, half-way along this strip of muddy ground behind the workshops on Tyndall Street. Whatever such signs might be taken to mean, in terms of who has been where and under what circumstances (and how recently, and what the chances are that they will be back), they are not the sorts of thing the team is generally keen to have seen by anyone else. Signs that only outreach workers really see – not too much and nothing too obvious, not out in the open – are best of all. That way things are kept intimate between the team and its clients. Otherwise there will be problems. Unattended urban space gives ground to the homeless; but the homeless can soon enough up the ante with their own exacerbating neglect,[4] and past a certain point such further inattention is likely to tip what may have been a scarcely noticed setting over into general awareness – as dirty. Suddenly everyone can see what the team would rather only they saw, and the likely result is that the site will be cleaned and reclaimed, leaving the CCT to cast about, waiting for someone they were working closely with only yesterday to settle somewhere else.

Three factors work counter to this tendency – mess and then more mess until a setting comes unhelpfully to general notice. The first of these I have referred to already as the *provisional* character of leftovers and traces. Doorways stay put, but litter is liable to move about, and some of the dirt and mess that comes with being homeless is no sooner dropped than dispersed. Cans clatter off around the corner in the breeze, spilt coffee gets washed away by the rain, cigarette ends and last night's cardboard are gathered up and removed by street cleaners on their daily rounds. All of which can take the edge off what would otherwise

---

4. Most of Cardiff's homeless and street drinkers are too hard pressed by any number of exigencies to make tidying up after themselves all that much of a priority (not that some of them aren't meticulous).

be a relentless accumulation. Some of Cardiff's non-space corners and hides keep just about unnoticed this way; littered repeatedly, occupied occasionally, but never quite enough of a mess that something needs to be done over and above what is already happening to litter in the city all the time. Then there are those clients who do actually work quite hard to keep things tidy; this is another way in which mess is held in check. Some consider it their civic duty, or say they do, but there is also self-interest, the desire to be left alone, not least by anyone in authority. The less litter, the smaller the chance that notice will be paid (even at the same time as mess may have been a sign that this was a place to which no one was paying much attention to begin with); you might win a little privacy, security too, the sort that comes with no one else knowing where you are or being able to see you as they pass.[5] Thirdly, outreach workers take a hand themselves and tidy up after some of their clients and on occasion chide them for making a mess. 'Don't leave all that stuff lying about,' says Jeff to a couple discovered in a doorway at the CIA. 'If you keep it clean you won't piss anyone off.'

Clues are provisional then, and can go cold, and the possibility that they might drives outreach on through the city. Early morning outreach is not to be rushed, and yet it *is* always something of a race against time. By 9am too much of what might otherwise have been seen and followed up on will be gone or obscured: doorways swept clean, steps and subways hosed down, litter dispersed or carried off; and the streets will be *busy*. Evenings are the other way around. Shops and offices shut up for the day and the streets thin out, leaving outreach workers to cast about for those things and people left behind and the beginnings of a reasserted occupancy: Andy Saville stepping down from the Bus, juggling sandwiches and a paper cup of soup and a cigarette, weaving his way into the civic centre, perhaps to the Glamorgan Building where

---

5.   The line of difference running between those too chaotic, or careless, or hard-pressed, to manage their spaces and those who keep things (sort of) tidy, is an important one on Cardiff's street homeless scene and gets braided together with other distinctions. Gavin E.'s place by the College of Music is not only his through repeated association but also by way of careful policing – his own. He won't share with anyone unless he knows they can be trusted to keep things clean, and he won't tolerate addicts under any circumstances: 'Smack heads? They don't give a shit, see? Just shit it up, wherever they are. And then shit it up somewhere else.' He keeps a length of metal pipe down one side of his sleeping bag at night, to see off any unwelcome visitors – and lets it be known that he does.

those sheets of cardboard were spotted this morning – worth checking out, but give him five minutes first, to get settled.

All clues lead somewhere, like a thread. But where? Most of the traces (of use or occupancy) that CCT outreach workers discern lead back to the same location, only later that day, or the next morning. If it 'looks like someone was here last night' or 'there's definitely been someone using round the back', then it will be worth checking the same spot again, adding it in to the next few days' fuzzy itinerary. If what has been left behind suggests someone in particular, related suspicions can be followed up in the meantime too: 'It says *Carrie Evans* on the label, only I thought she was in the Huggard. I'll give them a ring and see what's going on.' Other traces lead onwards, suggesting spatial adjacency, and can be investigated immediately. A breached security fence, one galvanised steel upright bent aside, and trampled undergrowth beyond: this invites further inspection. So too a makeshift toilet, or a stash of most likely shoplifted goods; you wouldn't want to bed down right next to any of that and be thereby (guiltily) associated, but you'd want to be close, perhaps just around that corner, or over that wall. So too a trail of discarded chocolate bar wrappers leading up the car park stairwell, like breadcrumbs.[6]

Not that the guessing game stops when outreach workers' spatial enquiries yield a find: someone in seeming need. Having noted a spread of flattened cardboard fringed with cans and cigarette ends under the railway bridge on Hope Street in the early morning, the team returns a couple of hours later to find most of this now gone but a young woman crouched against the wall in much the same spot. Success? It depends who she is and why she is here. Crouched, or collapsed? Or just tying a shoelace? Is she injured, unwell? Is she sober? Were the cans and cardboard, all of that, anything to do with her? Does she need looking after? Does she want help? What sort of help, if any? Does she match the email description of the missing girl, circulated yesterday? Answers to these and other questions require further scrutiny, and an eye for whatever hints and indications a person might present – the way they

---

6. The point about chocolate bars being that the silver foil wrap under the outer paper of some chocolate bars can be used to heat heroin; inhaling the resultant vapour is one way in which to consume the drug. In recent years a number of proprietary brands (of chocolate) have switched from foil and paper wrappers to crimp seal plastic; they are no longer the clue they once were.

look, the things they say and how they say them. Some of the team's most likely clients very much look the part; some you just know are going to be trouble – if you are an outreach worker, that is. Others are harder to read. And one must tread carefully in any case, in the making of enquiries, just as in the exploration of a patch of uncertain ground. Gathered together under the bridge the exploration continues, or may do. I have touched on some of this work already: the making of initial enquiries, the perils of misidentification, impressions given out and off, the development of relationships, disclosures and feigned uninterest, picking up on information let slip, building a picture.

Footwork

Searching for something is not the same as looking at it; searching for an object or person, we hope to set our eyes on it but cannot do this simply by staring or resting our attention. Instead we look around. We may do this standing still at first, but even so not without moving. Feet more or less planted, we look to one side and then the other, up and down; movements of the eyes and the head, neck and shoulders allow us to scope our surrounds. We turn on the spot and look the other way. All of this without taking a step – which is the very next thing to do if the search is not over and we still cannot see whatever it is we have mislaid or are looking for. To say of CCT outreach workers that they know their way around the city and know the sorts of places, in particular, in which to start looking for clients and clues, is not yet to attend to the ways in which they do so. How do outreach workers look for clues and clients? I have described some of the things they are looking for – traces, indications, trodden grass, broken bottles, dirtied corners – but not the activity itself. What does looking for such things look like? Before answering that question, it may be best to consider another, if briefly. The things that outreach workers look out for, the indications that are particular to this line of work, what do we learn from looking at them? What do we see when we are shown the broken bottle or the dirtied corner? We hope to see something of the way the work is, for an outreach worker. And perhaps we do. Perhaps to be shown the chocolate bar wrapper on the car park stairs is to be given something like a lesson: *There. See?* But it may take more than this – more than one occasion, more than simply having something pointed out.

Experienced outreach workers hold and share an understanding of the ways in which the look of the city, as they encounter this out on patrol, might lead them towards the thing they are after; they know a good clue when they see one, and it is possible to list some such: the things that outreach workers see and consider a good indication. Many (not all) of these are ordinary enough objects, but it takes an outreach worker to see them for what they are in the context of outreach work, or even to see them at all. Who really sees a stained sheet of cardboard and a couple of cans in a doorway? Such collections of objects become available, as something to see, only through an understanding of what they might mean. With other tasks to do, with different priorities (and modes of understanding commensurate with those), we might well pass by unawares. The problem is that the understanding that enables an outreach worker to see what is there for outreach, cannot, itself, be seen. Understandings are not visible objects, however hard you look. They can be seen at work, but not in themselves. Nor is seeing an understanding at work quite the same thing as seeing its workings. Walking in the early morning with an outreach worker bits and pieces of the city's general clutter are singled out and brought to attention, but every such sighting is the outcome of an understanding that was already in play long before anything was revealed. An outreach worker stops and points, and you see an object identified, as meaningful – you see the cardboard, or the discarded bottle or the trampled grass; you can see the work that an understanding has done, but not how. Put another way, seeing something is what happens when a search turns out the way it was supposed to, when looking for something comes to a happy end. To see the object, finally found, is to understand at least something of what was being looked for. But not how the looking was done, unless you were the one expertly doing it.[7]

---

7. Does an expert really understand what it is they have done and how they did it? Up to a point, obviously yes. But beyond that point, perhaps not. To be very good at something is not to be in possession of an extraordinarily detailed set of instructions – perhaps once held on paper but long since committed to memory – and a readiness to then execute these in careful, unerring sequence. If this were the case it would be easy enough to see and share one's own workings, as an expert. Instead, it comes close to being a condition of expertise that knowing how to do something and actually doing it run together, the one no longer so simply a precursor to the other. In this way understanding (knowing how) loses itself in action, and reveals itself only there.

So we are left with the possibility that we might see an understanding at work in the (eventual) identification of a clue or sign, and that we might share in that understanding, up to a point, once we have been shown what is there to be seen. But how did the outreach worker know that the clue was there, before it was there to see? The answer, of course, is that they didn't. How then did they move towards it? This is where expertise becomes opaque. Words, particularly, fail: a 'hunch', an 'inkling', an 'eye' for the sort of thing that matters, but seldom anything so candid as explicit deliberation, a figuring things out in which one can share. The same holds for experts in any number of fields. Yet there *is* something present and available about the deliberations that lead outreach workers to the things they are looking for, more present and available perhaps than expert deliberations in other fields. Outreach workers move towards the city that they see by bodily moving through it, and in this sense their deliberations – their workings – are available, at least to look at. So we are in luck. If the question is how does an outreach worker arrive at the things he or she sees, then at one level the answer can be seen and shared. You can watch them make their way there – to the sheet of cardboard, the doorway, the car-park rooftop; you can accompany them as they cast about for an answer to the questions that have set them going.

I am now back to the question with which I began. What does looking for something look like? And a first answer is that it looks like movement. When outreach workers step out of Marland House and into the street about to begin an evening's outreach patrol, they may pause briefly either to light a cigarette or zip up a jacket, but then they are off, moving through the city. It would make no sense to do anything else. 'Doing outreach' means taking a look around, on foot; it comes before any of the other work that the CCT gets done. True, both the Breakfast Run and the StreetLife patrol make routine use of motorised transport, in part because these patrols aim to cover a good spread of city-centre locations (at a time of the day when the traffic is thin); also to facilitate the transport of various goods and effects – flasks of hot water, coffee and tea, rape alarms, sandwiches, chocolate bars and crisps, condoms, blankets – that would otherwise burden and limit movement.[8] But the

---

8.   When I first began spending time at Marland House the outreach team used their own vehicles to run errands and transport clients around the city, but within a year they had acquired a works van minimally modified to the needs of outreach – driver's cabin up front,

point is always to park up, get out and take a look around; sitting behind the wheel is not doing outreach.

Night shelter: Half past nine in the morning, Clare Street. I am at the night shelter drinking coffee with Robbie, one of the staff at The Wallich; we are in the staff office (which doubles as a bedroom). The Breakfast Run is finished and I am about to make my way over to Marland House. Robbie is coming off shift and will be locking up shortly; almost all the residents are gone for the day, though John O'Mahoney is still shuffling around the place. Robbie has something on his mind. He has worked at the night shelter for years, and is as established there as some of the residents seem to be.

'You see the Breakfast Run needs to get back the way it was, Tom,' he says, drawing on a cigarette. 'It's got so that people are referring people to the night shelter and it's not appropriate to do that – because of the other people staying there and issues there may be, problems, with other people. And we know about that, cos we're the ones *working* here. So we know who it's right to refer and who not. Instead of someone referring someone they don't know anything about, and then there are real problems and we have to deal with them. The Breakfast Run has got to be like a bus route, and it's got to be like catering. And that's not right. It's not about a cup of tea and a roll, it's about making a connection with someone, finding out what their needs are – they may have health issues or other issues that we can help with, and you need to find that out. Not *there's your cup of tea and there's your roll and see you tomorrow*. And it's got too much like that. The run never used to finish until 9.30, 9.20[am] at the earliest. Now it's gotten that people want to get it over quickly. They want to go and do something else or get back to their offices. It's bad management and other people, when it should be the people that know.'

'And it's the same route every day,' he continues. 'No one is going out there *looking*. It's there's these people here, and these two people here, and so that's where we'll go tomorrow, the same places, and that's it. And maybe there will be people sleeping somewhere else. Maybe someone who's vulnerable and doesn't want to be with the others cos he'll get picked on, or whatever, and so they don't appear on the list. The Breakfast Run doesn't go to them – it's like they're invisible. And that's what the Run should be about, finding them people. You need to *look*, not just go to the same place every day. Look down the alleys and the embankment, get out to the cathedral. People sleep there, but it's like it's too far away for some people. That's not how it's supposed to be. It needs to get back to how

---

storage space and seating behind, rear doors opening onto a service worktop with cubby-holes for cups and spoons, coffee, tea, sugar and foodstuffs. Initially secured via funding for the StreetLife Project, the van soon came to be used for almost any CCT purpose.

it was to begin with. You need to *look*, that's what the Breakfast Run is all about. And if it takes three hours then it takes three hours. You need to look down the embankment and down this alley and up the cathedral. And if no one's there then OK, and you can look again tomorrow. That's what it takes. So it's going back to how it was, how it should be. You need to think: *Where would I sleep if I was homeless?* There's all sorts of places. And I know there are people out there the Run is not getting to. You see them in the day, and they're sleeping rough. But they're not on the list.'

I have heard this sort of thing from Robbie before, but nod along. John O'Mahoney, slips into the office from the corridor outside where he has been eavesdropping. 'I know Cardiff,' he says gloomily. 'Yes I do. I know every street and every garden, and every alley.'

So, what is eating Robbie? Some of the things he has to say, and the general tone of grievance, belong to a particular circumstance – a change in management at the night shelter and recent scrutiny of his own role in some of the above (in which context, he has lately fallen out with co-worker Carl, at whom the '… it's like it's too far away for some people' comment is directed). But he is also cross with the CCT, and Jeff especially, who has let it be known that he thinks the night shelter is sometimes not as willing to take on 'difficult' referrals as it ought to be. Robbie has taken this personally, as was perhaps intended. In this way, his monologue is a counter-assertion of expertise, a retaliation. *He* knows how outreach needs to get done. He knows what it takes and how things should be – others don't; Jeff doesn't. The jibe about people getting back to their *offices* is aimed at CCT outreach in particular and is meant to hurt. (When I talked this through with Jeff, later the same week, he was affronted and having none of it: 'Robbie? What does he know? He hasn't done the Breakfast Run for years … Idiot.')

Behind this particular circumstance, however, is as neat a statement of an outreach code of practice as one could wish for. A Breakfast Run that matched Robbie's taunt at all points would be no sort of outreach at all. *Everyone* knows that. And it is not the use of a car or van that is the issue. The essential point is that the movement has to be exploratory. No cursory rushing around the city dropping off hot drinks at scheduled locations then hurrying on to the next stop. No scurrying away from clients with whom a connection might be made or worked towards, half an eye on the next encounter. 'You need to *look*, that's what the Breakfast

Run is all about.' So says Robbie. Added to which, John's doleful suffix: '... every street and every garden, and every alley.'

So outreach workers walk, and must do so in order to see what is going on. Most of the places in which they spend most of their time are close enough to make this practicable, and in another sense it is only ever walking that is going to get you where you really need to be, as an outreach worker. Nor are they alone in this, as walkers; almost everybody walks in the course of any given day. But there are different ways of doing so. How a person walks depends to a considerable degree on what they are up to, perhaps where they are going but more importantly what they are doing. And in this outreach workers are set apart from many of the other pedestrians with whom they share pavement space, most obviously commuters, by which I mean anyone at all on their way from one location to another and aiming to get there directly in order to get on with whatever it is they can only accomplish once they arrive. Commuters are people with places to be. Outreach workers dawdle; they move along the city streets at something like what Cardiff's street cleaners call 'council pace'; there is no rush, because where they want to be is where they are already, out and about, looking around. They seem, at times, uncertain, moving in ways that give the appearance of someone not altogether sure of their location – which is, in fact, precisely how things are with outreach, but not as any index of unfamiliarity. Nothing stays quite the same from one day to the next in the middle of the city, and to attend carefully to such changes is to attend to the way in which the place continues to be itself. So, for seeming uncertainty read familiar consideration: very little is taken for granted, even as an outreach patrol moves down just the same rear lane as it covered only yesterday. Outreach workers also meander; they branch off and double back, convolute and muddy what might have seemed a simple enough task. They seem easily distracted.

I am not proposing that outreach workers move about on Cardiff's streets in any way that might draw more than a moment's notice. They just move a little slower than most other people, and look a little less like they have anywhere to be right now other than where they are. Perhaps they give the appearance of being up to something, but not brazenly so and not in such a way as to make it at all clear just what that something might be – rummaging around somehow; they have an air of off-the-cuff curiosity about them and their attention seems snagged in unlikely places.

Streetcombing

To rummage is to search, and to search is always to search for something, but whether one can say just what that something might be, in advance of finding it, depends on the sort of search one is setting out to do. Some searches are instigated by definite knowledge of what is not to hand: something or someone mislaid or gone missing. Such searches have a single remit, and can be brought to a completion – if successful; searching for something known to be missing, you know when you are done. Other sorts of search are never done, because they are undertaken not so much to find something missing as to see what is out there and might be going on. Outreach workers do both.

Outreach: January, late afternoon, already dark, and cold; Jeff and Nicy on shift, with me for company. Leaving Marland House at half-past six we cross to the car park to load supplies for the StreetLife patrol into the boot of Nicy's car, for later. We look in at the car-park stairwell and lift lobby, craning our necks to peer up and listen. Nothing. We head back to Central Square and make our way up and down the bus station aisles, me talking about having seen Bernard here on the Breakfast Run this morning, the point being that Bernard is back – in the bus station – having been shooed off by the police earlier this week, following some incident or complaint. His behaviour has been increasingly odd of late, and he was in poor shape this morning, looking cold and frail, hunched over on a bench with tissue paper stuffed into his ears. We stop to talk with the bus station security staff, outside the public toilets. They have lots to say about Bernard, not too much of it all that kindly or sympathetic, not too much of it anything we don't already know or haven't already heard. Even so, Nicy is all nods and smiles, careful to drop in a couple of asides about Bernard's vulnerability and the likely futility of just chasing him away every time he makes any trouble. She writes down the CCT office number on a sheet of notepaper and hands it over. 'Give us a ring next time,' she says. 'We've a better chance of sorting it.' (Bernard himself is nowhere to be seen. He was here mid-afternoon, apparently, but there has been no sign of him since.)

We head off along Wood Street and cross St Mary Street to walk up Caroline Street where I borrow £1 off Nicy to buy a bag of chips. Turning onto the Hayes, the two of us walk along together, eating chips, while Jeff zig-zags across from one side of the street to the next. We wait every couple of minutes for him to catch us up. Jeff is being the busy outreach worker, nosy, poking around; Nicy's attention, mine too, is not so obviously directed. Even so, we are, all three of us, looking around.

Although we are not looking for anyone in particular, or exclusively, we certainly have Bernard in mind, and keep returning to him in conversation and trying to match the look of him to figures we glimpse or pass by. On past St David's Hall where we briefly mistake a bundle of rubbish for someone's bag or belongings – Bernard's? We turn right, onto Queen Street and all the way down to the far end, winding around the benches and trees, passing from one shop doorway to the next, taking turns left and right where an arcade entrance, street junction or service lane permits. We wind along Park Lane and back. 'Which way now?' asks Nicy. We could go left or right. We turn right, onto Station Terrace and then Bridge Street. We take it very slow here. Jeff rummages around behind some bins for a couple of minutes picking through a stack of remaindered building materials. We go halfway along the lane behind the Cardiff Masonic Hall, and then retrace our steps. On Guildford Street we peer over the wall running along one side of Helmont House. There is some red grit, plastic granules or something, scattered along the top of the wall and in piles here and there. None of us has any idea what it might be. Odd. Jeff brushes it from his palms, then sniffs his fingertips. 'No idea,' he says. 'Probably nothing.'

At the library we turn right and head back towards Charles Street, for the soup run. Gavin E. is sitting on one of the benches and we join him to talk for a bit while the crowd gathers and the volunteers set out the trestle tables and the soup and sandwiches. Gavin tells us how he went to Edinburgh once having seen a tourist guide to the city and spotted a good sleeping spot in one of the pictures. He is thinking of going again. Where will he be tonight, Nicy wants to know. 'Same place,' says Gavin. 'College of Music. Don't tell anyone.'

We can't see Bernard. Not that we'd expect to see him here, as the soup run is not really his scene. Nicy gets up to work the crowd; Jeff and I walk off to one side. A teenage boy in a baseball cap swaggers over and asks Jeff if he will sell him a cigarette. Jeff says no, he doesn't smoke, and stares off into the distance. The boy can't seem to figure out if he's been snubbed. He stands there for a half minute, then turns on his heel and walks off. Jeff brings a lit cigarette out from behind his back. Nicy comes over with bits and pieces of information and concerns, various leads to follow up tomorrow; nothing about Bernard though.

Looking for Bernard figures here as something that Jeff and Nicy are up to and able to get done even as they cast about more generally. Most outreach patrols work the same way, with particular threads of individual concern woven into the shaggier fabric of general enquiry.

But looking out for Bernard can only be folded into the more general business of an evening's work for so long as concerns for his wellbeing remain imprecise and unexceptional. Should those concerns tip over into something more immediate and acute then the rummaging must stop, and finding Bernard will be brought to the fore as the only thing that Jeff and Nicy are up to, a job of work to be kept at until Bernard is found or the search exhausted. Plenty of outreach patrols end up this way, begun as a general reconnoitre but narrowing down to pursuit of a single client in particular need whose vulnerability has revealed itself and accelerated over the course of a very few hours. On occasion the whole thing has the (rather desperate) air of a game.

Outreach: Jeff and Den and me, on the StreetLife Project patrol; a wet November evening, dark already. We have been out for half an hour and have parked the van on East Moors Road by Ocean Way in order to walk back over to the corner of Sanquhar Street where we saw Kirsten standing (unsteadily) by a lamppost just five minutes ago. The corner is a regular spot for Kirsten although the police have warned her off repeatedly following a run of complaints from local residents. We cross the road and turn the corner, but when we get to the lamppost where we saw her just moments ago she is gone. This probably means she has been picked up, perhaps by the police but more likely by a punter. We will circle back in 20 minutes and try again. We are particularly keen to see her this evening as the feeling among most of the care professionals who have to do with her is that she is not in a good way at the moment and needs looking out for more than most. Her drug use has escalated over the last month or so and she is drinking heavily. At the same time, her general appearance has really slumped. She was at Marland House this afternoon to discuss her domestic situation, which is dire, and she left the building in tears. Some or all of the above also has to do with an incident three weeks ago which saw her admitted to hospital and then discharged wearing a neck brace and with one arm in plaster (there are a number of different versions of events circulating, most having to do with Kelly Williams and *her* boyfriend and either drug debts or infidelity).

We are about to walk back over to Ocean Way when Jeff sees something, alongside one of the houses backing onto Spruce Close: a crouched figure. We walk back over in an offhand way, not wanting to give the appearance of sneaking up on anyone. Kirsten steps out of the shadows. 'I thought you were the police,' she says, or slurs. We spend five minutes with her, Kirsten slumped, half sat, on the low wall running in front of the houses on Windsor Road. We would like to get her home but haven't quite said as much out loud as we know from experience that she can be stubborn if she ever feels she is being manoeuvred. She agrees to come over to the van, just two minutes' walk away, to get a cup of hot chocolate and a cigarette and maybe have a chat. We walk off together, but just as we are about to cross East Tyndall Street Kirsten ducks off to one side and jogs back towards

Sanquhar Street saying she has left her bag in the bushes. We wait for her, then wish we hadn't – she doesn't return. Walking back along Windsor Road to find out what the delay is all about we see her getting into a car, which pulls away from the kerb and drives back past us, all the way around the roundabout and past us again and then on over the railway bridge. Kirsten waves and shouts something out of the car window, pointing back to where we were stood talking moments ago.

Half an hour later, we see Kirsten again, in the same spot as before, visibly very much more drunk than before; she is having trouble standing and can't keep upright without tottering to one side and then the other. When we cross the road to speak with her she is barely coherent. She takes a cigarette from Jeff but has great difficulty lighting it with her broken arm and neck brace. We walk her over to the van, Den on one side and me on the other, holding her upright. Den offers to drive her back to her flat. 'It's not safe for you to be out like this,' he tells her. Kirsten says she can't go yet. She needs 20 minutes, then she'll come. Arguing gets us nowhere and Kirsten starts to get belligerent. In the end we say OK. We walk her back to her corner. 'Twenty minutes,' says Kirsten, laughing now. 'Don't forget me.'

We are back again in quarter of an hour. No Kirsten. We park up the van and take a walk around. Down Sanquhar Street and then cutting through Spruce Close and over East Tyndal Street, and on to Keen Road. No sign of her. Wendy is standing on East Tyndal Street, talking urgently on her mobile phone and tossing her head at passing cars. We ask her if she's seen Kirsten. 'Yeah,' she says, pointing back the way we just came. We retrace our steps. Still no Kirsten. We decide to spread out. I take the long way around to Sanquhar Street. Jeff and Den cut through Applewood Close. A couple of minutes later, at the sound of car tyres and some sort of fracas, we converge at a trot on the corner of Sanquhar Street and Windsor Road. Kirsten is shouting. We hear her before we see her, and then there she is, half in and half out of a car, involved in some sort of wrangle with the driver. She is just about sitting in the front passenger seat but with the door swung wide open and sprawled outwards, leaning over; she has her one good arm outstretched, the palm of her hand resting on the road surface. The car has the look of having been about to pull away, but is now stationary; the headlights are on and engine still running. With a heave, or possibly a tug from the driver, Kirsten rights herself and slams the door. The car zooms off. We are in two minds whether or not to call the police. Kirsten wouldn't thank us, but there are good enough grounds tonight: she is in such disarray and so vulnerable as such – not least because so liable to pick fights when drinking. Was she dragged into the car? Was she shouting for help?

We are about to make the call when Kirsten reappears. No more than five minutes have passed. Then she disappears again. How did she do that? Where did she go? We find her alongside the same house as before, on

Spruce Close. She is hunched over, trying to do up her trousers but having trouble with the zip, drunk as she is and with only one free hand. Den is stern with her now, which sometimes works. She has to go home, he tells her, and we are going to take her. Kirsten says OK. Den goes to fetch the van. Jeff and I wait with Kirsten, who announces that she's lost her bag. Perhaps she dropped it around the side of the house? I go back over to take a look. Kirsten stays with Jeff. I have a good look around but I can't find the bag. When I come back Jeff is on his own.

'Where's Kirsten?' I ask.

'I thought she was with you,' says Jeff, surprised. 'She went to find you.'

'But I was only over there,' I say, pointing.

Den pulls up in the van: 'Where's Kirsten?'

'She's gone – again,' says Jeff.

It is almost 10pm and we have given up on any idea of doing anything else with what is left of outreach tonight other than trying to find Kirsten. Wherever she is, she can't have gone far, at least not on foot. We spend the next half an hour combing the same very few streets, criss-crossing Spruce Close, Applewood Close, East Tyndal Street and Keen Road. We work our way around corners, behind hedges and bins, even, at one point, dropping down onto hands and knees for a rat's-eye view under a row of parked cars in case she has fallen and rolled under one of them. We repeatedly section the same small patch – not much more than a couple of hundred square yards – working back and forth, through every conceivable nook and corner. We stop short of shouting her name as we don't want to draw attention. But we whisper, urgently: 'Kirsten!' Back and forth, round and round. Nothing. We decide to stand still for ten minutes on the corner of Sanquhar Street, working on the assumption that she can't be hidden somewhere but must be moving about, one step ahead of us, if unintentionally (unless she really is trying to avoid us). If we stand still maybe she will walk by, eventually. We give up on this after ten more minutes. She seems to have disappeared so completely that we wonder if she hasn't slipped into one of the houses, though we are unaware of any connection she might have to anyone living here. If not that then, unlikely as it seems, perhaps she has managed to steal past us and cross East Tyndal Street, making her way towards the train station, or along Ocean Way. 'It's like hide-and-seek,' says Jeff.

We cross East Tyndal Street again, and walk through the car park alongside Keen Road. Ten minutes later we are back on Sanquhar Street. Suddenly, as if from out of nowhere, Kirsten appears. She wants to go home, which is where we take her, nice and quick before she changes her mind or anything else can happen.

The path of outreach on this particular evening threads across the city at first, but then gathers into a knot around Sanquhar Street and Windsor Road, pulled tighter and tighter as the three of us – Dennis and Jeff and myself – circle on foot, looking for Kirsten. Just another of those more memorable occasions when what might have been outreach as usual turned into something a little more particular and taxing. The same as with Nicy and Cindy (see pp. 44–8), only on that occasion not so much an hour spent searching for someone as an hour (and more) spent dealing with the consequences of having found them.[9] Added to which, a further distinguishing feature: Cindy was not known to be missing in the first place. How then was she found?

My theme has been rummaging around (the sort of open exploration that Robbie signals as the very nub of outreach practice), as a foil to which, I have been discussing *particular* searches, those occasions when outreach workers are after someone they know to be missing, someone not yet found. Movement in such cases might be described as exploratory too – to explore is to enquire into a possibility, after all. Put another way, realised in movement, these two activities share a characteristic uncertainty; a search *requires* uncertainty, so too exploration. But exploration is also more than this, or different. The uncertainty at issue when a search is undertaken is an uncertainty about where it is that a thing or person known to be missing and sought on that basis might eventually be found. To set about looking for Bernard is to have it in mind to find him, from the outset; one's movement can then be

---

9.   These two instances of outreach – an evening spent looking for Kirsten, a morning spent dealing with Cindy – share a passing resemblance. Each concerns a young woman found drunk and vulnerable, but stubborn too, neither one willing to go anywhere else just yet, each one suspicious and pleading by turns, neither one wanting the police to be called (only Kirsten got home without that happening). But there is a deeper resemblance, less to do with detail. Both of these instances are, or were to become, *stories*. Tried on for size back at the office, told and then retold first by those who were there and then by those who weren't (but could *recognise* a good outreach story when they heard one), Jeff and Dennis's difficult shift on the corner of Sanquhar Street became something more than an account of what happened to pass for outreach one Wednesday evening in mid-November. Nicy's difficult morning with Cindy did too. Both became outreach standards of a sort, taking their place alongside (only) a few other enduring and well-worn accounts – 'that morning when …', or 'that evening we spent …', or 'that time we tried to …' – each of these long past any practical application but remembered nonetheless, because now a story and, as such, worth repeating. And why a story? Not for reasons of wholly exceptional content. More likely because in some way illustrative of certain general truths about outreach: the way that clients seem to work against you sometimes – unintentionally, maddeningly; the terrible and desperate state in which some clients find themselves and can be found; the grim satisfaction to be had from doing, or trying to do, one small good thing; the coupled urgency and futility of the work.

organised accordingly. But there are others out there somewhere in the city not yet known to be missing, whose needs the CCT is nonetheless concerned to respond to and whom outreach workers are tasked to locate and uncover. Outreach encounters with these individuals are unlooked for yet essential. And this is where the word exploration properly applies, not only as indicating a diffuse sort of search directed to turning up something unanticipated, but also as designating a mode of enquiry that furnishes its own justification.

What I have tried to insist on as the essentially open and exploratory character of outreach has had a tendency to slip out of focus, not least in the accounts I have given of workers' practice – the empirical passages, detailing this or that outreach patrol. I hope I have insisted on it sufficiently – outreach as enquiry, as much a sort of looking as a sort of looking after – to have begun to make my point; but it has proved much easier to state the case than to show it. What can be shown easily enough and provides the seeming detail and content of most of the fieldwork accounts I have supplied, is where outreach workers go – here, then there, then on again to somewhere else – and what happens when they get there, in particular what happens when something actually takes place. Nicy goes to Central Square, and something happens, she meets Cindy; that is easy enough to show, along with everything that happens next. But it has been harder to show the sort of looking after that has to happen before anyone can be offered help. Not impossible, however: single remit searches can be described. Looking for Kirsten was something that happened too, and passed not without incident; it was, itself, an occasion, and can be related as such – and not just by me, but by Jeff, and by Dennis. But what outreach workers don't tell stories about is the business of just looking, which is what they spend an essential part of every working day doing. What is there to tell? This is just what they do, a practice they relax back into and perform with unconsidered fluency whenever things stop actually happening and it is time to return to the footwork that moves outreach along – not only as its necessary precursor, but as a job of work in itself, an exercise in care and attention.

This returns us to the account I have already given, of outreach workers moseying through the city alert to all sorts of possibilities but in ways that look a little like being lost or distracted, inattentive even. What is absent in such cases is not attention, but some or all of the anxious determination that might drive forward a single remit search.

Nor should the absence of any such anxiety be taken to signify a lack of concern. It is more the case that when looking for something inexactly, when casting about, anxious preoccupation doesn't get you all that far. If anything, it gets in the way and stops you seeing. Fixed ideas about just what it is one is looking for can make it harder to see what might be there already. Better to let one's attention sag, such that it might then catch on something; better a roving (in)attention paid to nothing in particular, but spread about, exercised in such a way so as to amplify the possibility that something of the sort you are after might come to notice. In this way, with no apparent urgency, but with purpose, on any given early evening or wet, Tuesday morning, lugging flasks of hot coffee and information leaflets, outreach workers move towards the things they hope to find, even as they do not know exactly what it is they are looking for. This is how to find Cindy, or Tony Adams, or a damp mattress tucked away in the far corner of a private car park off Park Lane. Nor is this a method – a sort of *streetcombing* – suited only or best to finding something or someone new. Certainly there are occasions when outreach workers set out to find a client they already know to be out there, and in certain respects such searches represent a different sort of activity, not so much exploration as pursuit. But my point here is that when casting about more generally Nicy might just as easily find someone or something she already knows about as someone or something she doesn't. She might find some combination of the two – Cindy, right by Marland House, and buddied up with Rolly from the night shelter. She might find all too familiar traces of drug use, but in some niche or corner that was empty yesterday. In this sense outreach workers have to start over again every day, setting off to see what might be out there even as doing so means going no further than they went the day before.

And the skill in all this lies not so much in an outreach worker's ability to seek correspondence between things seen and some notional directory of all those things, and only those things, that an outreach worker is supposed to see to. Rather, skilled outreach work explores a world in which everything matters, or might do; anything that catches the eye, according to the tenor and drift of one's enquiries – a tenor and drift aligned in this instance to possible difficulty or distress, to exposure, to damage and needy concealment. Cardiff's street cleaners are the same. They are tasked to see to the rubbish, on the street. No one has to tell them what the rubbish looks like, or what is or isn't rubbish, or what might have to do with the job of cleaning up. Nor do they leave their depot looking for any single instance of litter, an image of which they already hold in the head, like a swatch of colour to be matched to the spectrum of the streets. The litter is just out there, as it was yesterday. You don't have to know in advance what it will turn out to look like, or even where it is exactly (which will be that little bit different anyhow from where it was yesterday). All you have to do is move around in such a way as will bring it into view.

Street cleaning: Pete does more or less the same route most mornings, the streets he is supposed to cover are listed in the office upstairs at the depot on Millicent Street. 'The good thing is once you're out here no one can hurry you. You're your own boss, see? I can go round whichever way I want.' He warms to this theme as we make our way out past the casino and down Mary Ann Street to Bute Terrace. There are streets he has to cover, but doing the job right means taking time so it's not as if anyone can hurry you. Not that you could ever pick up everything that's been dropped, not that the street doesn't need doing again half an hour later. You've only got a couple of hours and you could spend twice that just on Charles Street. 'You've got to weigh it up,' says Pete.

We take a left up Churchill Way, skirting the CIA, then left again along one side of Bridge Street then back along the other to re-join Churchill Way, following this up to Queen Street, and then back, turning left onto North Edward Street as far as the Spar and back again, each side of the road; left onto Churchill Way again, to the lights, and left onto Guildford Street and Station Terrace. Slowly all the way, stopping every few yards to stoop and sweep. From Millicent Street to Queen Street station, where we are now standing, is five minutes' walk, but it has taken us the best part of an hour what with the roundabout route and the constant (purposed) distraction.

We stop for a breather – a cigarette; a car runs through a puddle and the splash of dirty water hits me though not Pete who has taken up position behind the two-bin truck. He rolls his eyes. 'Run you over if you don't watch out,' he says. 'Cos it's like they don't see you.' Pete tells me that Freddie, who does the civic centre, got chased down Park Lane by a wino the other day, shouting insults at him. This really tickles Pete: 'Imagine that, a fucking wino! Ha!'

The alley behind the Cardiff Masonic Hall is not so bad today, cans and bottles mostly, though there is a strong smell of shit. 'Don't use your hands for anything,' says Pete, nudging debris here and there with his feet. 'We'll find it in a minute.' We are saved by the bell: Pete's phone. Donnie, back at the depot, wants us to go to Queen Street, to the alley alongside Boots; he has had a call from City Centre Management asking him to make this a priority.

We head off to Queen Street by the shortest route and without stopping. We are not rushing exactly, but our progress is uninterrupted; there is no pausing and stooping, no looking around, no doubling back. We are there in no time and soon enough shovelling a pile of wet newspaper and paper cups and cans and dirt (also a soiled blanket) into the two-bin truck, which we fill to overflowing in short order. We head off to find a PCV,[10] repeating this trip a couple of times until the alley is swept clean. We are done in half an hour. Pete doesn't think it is worth going back as we are all out of sync now and won't get the full circuit done before his shift ends anyway. We walk down Queen Street and then the Hayes, then onto Caroline Street to get a tray of chips and gravy to take back to Millicent Street.

A tray of chips on Caroline Street is an occasional treat, and staple for anyone labouring out of doors in Cardiff – street cleaners, outreach workers, the homeless too.

Ways of seeing

There are (different) ways of seeing, and what we see and the way we see things 'is affected by what we know or what we believe' (Berger, 2008: 8; originally 1972). This is true enough, but there is more to the ways in which we see than the things we know and the beliefs we hold. Seeing is a practical accomplishment before it is anything else; it is something that has to be worked at, and as such is affected by what we are prepared to do. We make seeing happen. Perception is intrinsically active in this way; 'perceptual experience', writes Alva Noë, 'acquires content thanks to the perceiver's skillful activity' (2004: 3). Better yet, '[t]he process of perceiving, of finding out how things are, is a process of meeting the world; it is an activity of skillful exploration' (Noë, 2004: 164). This is outreach, as I have described it.

To see is to move then, or to be able to. Perhaps this runs counter to commonsense, which tends to equate clear imagery with stillness and contemplation. When we think in this way – commonsensically – the relationship between movement and perception appears instrumental, rather than constitutive. We do the one in order to then stand still and

10. PCVs (Pedestrian Controlled Vehicles) are large, powered carts, much bigger than a two bin truck, used to empty street bins or to collect bagged commercial litter; a street cleaner walks in front 'pulling' the cart by a grab handle, pressure on which activates an electric motor.

do the other, as if we were all photographers; only when we are done moving can we start to see.[11] But I have been concerned in this chapter rather less with what it might mean to look *at* something already available to view (to picture it) than with what it might mean to look *for* – something or someone in particular, but also anything at all that might meet the general tenor of outreach enquiry. Outreach workers looking to come across some instance of need, or person in difficulty, or sign or indication of such, do not find their vision obscured by movement. Nor is seeing something they do only when they come to a stop. Moving about, repeatedly, painstakingly but also inexactly – rummaging around – is how they come to know the city. The work is essentially piecemeal and open-ended. Outreach requires a raking over of the city's known environs, a daily re-engagement with familiar territory that *explores* even as it goes back over ground covered only yesterday.

What I have tried to do in this chapter is to move towards completion, towards a definitive account of what it is that CCT outreach workers are up to. It seems to me that outreach praxis, the thing that outreach workers have to do because of what it is they are tasked to accomplish, is more than anything else a matter of exploratory enquiries, conducted locally; it is the repeated probing of an environment for what it might hold (back) and disclose. To make enquiries in this way is to gather up and assemble, to *build a picture* of what is going on out there.

The next chapter is the final one, and moves away a little from close detail, at least in the sense that I use the chapter to look back on outreach rather than continuing to report, as in this and preceding chapters, as if from the middle of it. In thinking about outreach in Cardiff today, and looking ahead even to some of the ways in which the city will be changing soon, I do, however, come back to this question of the ways in which we see (and I mean all of us, not only outreach workers). In doing so I return to some of the sorts of seeing and blindness that I first signalled at the very start of this book.

---

11. Noë has it that, on this view, the relation between movement and perception 'is like the relation between the lugging around of a camera and the resulting picture. The lugging is preliminary to and disconnected from the photograph itself' (2004: 2). I am drawing here on Noë's excellent study, *Action in Perception*, the main claim of which is that any such divorce between what we do and what we see is not in fact possible.

9

Change Blind

Earlier in this book, thinking about where it is that outreach gets done, I described it as definitively street work. For outreach workers, I suggested, it is always the street that matters, and what the street stands for and says about the needs to which their work is directed. I hope to use this final chapter to think a little more about street work and outreach, returning, in conclusion, to some of the questions I raised at the very start of the book, about the ways in which we see, in the city, and what it might mean to look after someone.

Losing ground

In a short essay titled *Urban Spaceman*, written in the mid-1980s, Judith Williamson proposes the following: '[i]n urban life "the streets" stand for shared existence, common understanding, a place that is owned by no-one and used by everyone' (1986: 211). There is something to this, notwithstanding what I have had to say about lost and leftover space, notwithstanding Wim Cuyvers' transposal and reframing of public space as a space of dirt and need. Williamson's essay considers the arrival of the (Sony) Walkman as a clue to the direction in which modern urban life was headed back then. Her diagnosis is that such technology signals a retreat from public life, even as those who use it make their way through the city streets alongside others. No matter what they see, they hear only what is going on in their heads; they are deaf to others. This recalls Richard Sennett's anxious thoughts on urban individualism, cited in my opening chapter. Williamson suggests that the Walkman creates 'troops of sleep-walking space-creatures, who seem to feel themselves invisible' (1986: 209), and again I think back to my opening chapter. If the Walkman is – was – a symbol of retreat (into the head and away from the street), then the question is what happens to the street. Does it get left behind? Or will it will find such new life as it can, according to some other purpose? These questions have some bearing on Cardiff today, other cities too.

Times change and the 1980s are long gone, although in other ways still with us. I first came to Cardiff in 1997, a year or so before the CCT was established; I first sat down with Steve in his office in 2004, and much of this book reports on time spent embedded in his team throughout 2005 and 2006, though I have kept up more or less weekly contact ever since. It is now 2016, and in some ways the practice of CCT outreach in the centre of Cardiff today looks nothing like it did when I first got to know it. In that sense this book is already out of date, was already so even as I set out to write it. Steve is no longer the team's manager and now lives and works in Manchester; Nicy qualified as a social worker a good few years ago and has also left the team; Jeff has retired; others have joined (and left); the CCT is smaller today than it was, having had to cut its cloth in response to significant budget reductions. Charlie and Dennis are still at work. There is no CCT office in Marland House any more, no view across Central Square at a 'more or less invisible' client group; Marland House itself is vacant and boarded up, scheduled for site clearance as part of the phased *Masterplan* (2014–2017) for the regeneration of Central Square and its environs. (The CCT is now based in the Housing Options Centre, the other side of Central Station, next door to the Huggard Day Centre.)

What were once known and likely settings for outreach attention, and which figure as such throughout this book, are no longer the same, or gone, or have been made over. The Central Hotel was bulldozed and the site cleared to make way for new premises several years ago; the Clayton Hotel stands there now. Plans to demolish the York Hotel and redevelop for office and restaurant units are currently under consideration. The CIA is sometimes still called that, but has been the Cardiff Motorpoint Arena for years; overnight access to its fire-exit doorways has been brought to an end by the installation of metal security grilles. Iceland is long gone along with the wider swathe of the city centre that was replaced by the St David's 2 redevelopment (see p. 36). The industrial units off Tyndal Street are no longer there, and the cleared site, designated the Capital Quarter, has outline planning for an 800,000 sq ft new development to include offices, hotels and student housing. The Johnston's Building has also gone, demolished to make way for future redevelopment. Construction work is underway on what was to have been the site of the 'glass needle' (see p. 160n), but will now be One Central Square (a 134,000 sq ft office block with basement parking and on-site customer team, touted as 'Cardiff's No 1 Business Address'). This work, now significantly advanced, represents phase one of the above-mentioned *Masterplan*. Subsequent phases will see the bus station relocated and revamped as a 'transport interchange', the construction of the new headquarters of BBC Cymru Wales, the demolition of the Wood Street car park, and further site clearance and development, much of the latter earmarked for student accommodation, residential apartments and retail. The *Masterplan* aims to create a new gateway to the capital, one that will 'empower people, generate activity, foster belonging and promote civic pride'; Central Square itself is to be 'an exemplary location that will be regarded as clean, safe, well-maintained and managed; a place that is actively looked-after and cared-for'.[1]

The maps I once made of outreach practice no longer match the territory and would be no guide whatsoever as to where to put yourself in order to do outreach today, not that they ever were – which has been my argument throughout. Outreach workers themselves move through the new Cardiff much as they ever did, adjusting their circuits of attention day by day, following up on what they already know and hope to find out and think it might be worth taking a closer look at. Do they move as easily as ever? Not always – they never did move easily; they negotiate the same apprehensions, uncertainties and occasional prohibitions today as were a part of the fabric of the work ten years ago. Outreach workers continue to tread carefully: across uncertain ground, testing their entitlement, mindful of clients' privacy and sensibilities. Even so, it would be possible to argue that there has been something of a change here too, a narrowing of the prospects for outreach work. This process – a slow squeeze on outreach practice – was already underway when I began my time with the CCT. It comes tied together with, and is revealed in, those developments that make it possible to frame the city's ambitions for Central Square (as above) in a language of care and maintenance, looking after and cleaning.

---

1. See http://centralsquarecardiff.co.uk. The Central Square Cardiff *Masterplan* is led by Rightacres Property in partnership with Cardiff Council.

Non-stick streets

Ronnie is a cleaner, and we have heard from him before (see pp. 132–3); he comes on shift at 5am and does Mill Lane, Saunders Road and the bus station – with a motorised sweeper that gives the kerbs and edges a nice 'sharp' look. I have had a lot to say about edges and borders myself, borrowing at times from Michael Rowe's (1999) work. Borders supply a spatial arrangement across which certain moves can be made, and in the making of those moves the border is repeatedly constituted and might shift and flex. How far is an outreach worker prepared to go? Where might they draw the line? These are questions I have asked already, and perhaps answered. I have also insisted that any such notional border, along and across which outreach workers might be said to move, must also touch down in a material world, on actually existing city streets. Outreach encounters happen not only across a border of difference but also in a doorway on Crwys Road, and around the back of Marland House. Nor do such settings figure in the work of outreach only as a backdrop, across which the contours of a more telling geography flicker and contort. The cityscape also moves; it changes all the time and as it does so the possibility that Rowe's border might break the surface here and then there, might run this way or that, changes too. It is not just that the edge of outreach practice shifts according to the moves made across it; the cityscape through which that edge runs weaves its own way – it reconfigures, opens out and at other times closes up, tightens and contracts. Possibilities become available, and then foreclosed.

I have already discussed how it is that some of the settings in which outreach workers find themselves, and to which they make their way, fall in and out of use. There is nothing new in this. Outreach would be a very different exercise if the city's homeless were only ever in the same few places. Viewed up close this churning over of locations and occasions looks like nothing much more than just that – a churning over. The corner of a car park, the side of a building, a grass verge or doorway: any one of these might escape public attention long enough and sufficiently for it to come into homeless use. Only then, three weeks on, it empties out again. Richie had his gear stashed there but it all got nicked and now he's gone; or Katy was taking punters around the side, but it's been tidied up and the hedge cut back. Someone moves on, or is made to; someone else settles in, perhaps somewhere else; the whole thing comes out even. At least it seems that way, up close. The picture is thick with detail, and pixelated.

But at a distance, over time, a good part of this detail resolves into something rather more one-sided and systematic. One aspect of this has been the continued installation of deterrent measures of the sort I first mentioned in Chapter 2. There are more such today in Cardiff than there were ten years ago, and there were already more back then than when the team was first founded. Outreach workers duly note these developments, as one might expect; a newly installed security shutter is just the sort of thing that ought to catch an outreach worker's eye, just the sort of thing you would have to notice in order to then be able to answer that most essential and recurrent of questions: *Where are we at with …?* To which today's answer might be: *Well he's gone from Great Western Lane. We know that much. They've put up a shutter. We saw it there this morning.* Shutters, fencing, mesh, locks fitted, gates installed, also cameras and motion-sensitive security lights – these last two a particular feature of shop doorways. Surveillance and deterrence combined have squeezed the homeless city.[2] Perhaps it could be said that the streets – in the sense that Judith Williamson intends – have shrunk, or, if not that, have been in some other way diminished. But what might this mean? Shrunk? The city centre is no smaller today than it was ten years ago, and what gets called the pedestrian environment, or circulation space, or the public realm, has been at a premium for a number of years – repeatedly enhanced and expanded; open space and accessibility are among the new *Masterplan* priorities. Which is to say that there is something here that does not quite tally with the idea of Cardiff's streets as ever more securitised. There *is* that side to things, certainly, but it has come wrapped up together with something that looks a little different.

The issue is one of appearances. Some of the design and security measures installed to address unintended use in the centre of the city have a stark quality to them and are not that easy on the eye. This is no surprise, and (one assumes) would be just fine with those doing the deterring if they could be certain that the only people doing the looking were the ones they wanted deterred. But this isn't so. Plenty of other

---

2. So too other measures, such as the introduction of Designated Public Place Orders in 2008, giving the police in Cardiff powers to require persons not to drink alcohol in 'controlled drinking zones' (Central Square was the first such designated zone).

people are looking too, and are encouraged to do so, more so today than ever before. The city centre is supposed to be looked at, and is supposed to look good; its agreeable appearance is fundamental to what economic regeneration has come to mean in Cardiff, as in a great many UK cities besides. People – visitors, shoppers, tourists – are expected to come to the city and like what they see, and choose to spend time. Accordingly, the streets ought not to prickle and forbid. Better a smartening up, and, where necessary, a *smoothing out* of any possibility that the wrong sort of thing or person might lodge or snag or settle – and catch the eye.[3] Accordingly, the more general tone of developments in the middle of the city has edged away from (overtly) deterrent measures even as these continue to be introduced. Softer curbs predominate, easier on the eye. This new tendency is perhaps best illustrated – literally – by the design images circulated in advance of, and as advertisements for, the larger-scale renewal schemes that have enhanced and reshaped the city centre in recent years. The trend is scale-invariant, however, and does not require artists' impressions; it can be witnessed concretely and up close every time a rear entrance doorway is as good as removed – taken off the homeless map, so to speak – not by the installation of a security shutter but by a repositioning of the door itself, the entire portal brought forward and re-fitted true to the walls either side, leaving a blank surface of brick and steel. The *Cardiff City Centre Public Realm Manual* very much favours this approach, advising not so much prohibition as the 'designing out [of] recessed entrances, hidden areas and ... inactive frontages' wherever development opportunities arise (Cardiff Council, 2009: 85). Rear lanes are identified as a particular problem in this regard, liable to accumulations of dirt and rubbish; so too some pedestrian subways, for which enhancement opportunities include cleaner, brighter surfaces and the elimination of 'harsh building angles and recessed areas' (Cardiff Council, 2009: 87). As I suggested in starting out on this account, fading into the streets – if that is what the homeless might do, or once did – works best when the streets hardly matter to those hurrying along them, when no one really cares to be there. Steve says as much, looking down from his office window in Marland House back when the

---

3. Security fences and grilles are if anything a nuisance to street cleaners: litter gets trapped in the lattice. Much better no gap(s) at all, a smooth continuous surface, easy to clean, non-stick.

bus station was nothing much to look at. It remains to be seen how things will work out, with outreach and the city's homeless, on a redeveloped Central Square.

But this straining of the eye, if it can be put like that, this tension between the unsightliness of need and the look of the city, is nothing altogether new. It has been at issue since the CCT was first established, a familiar trouble, encountered over and over again. Clients who mess things up, for themselves and for others, mess things up for outreach too.

Outreach: Early morning, mid-April; just Jeff and me, as Dennis is ill. We have some housing benefit forms to deliver to Cowbridge Road, which we get done first, before the traffic builds up. From Cowbridge Road we drive to Cathedral Road to see if we can locate Badger, who has been sleeping along here at various points, but is proving elusive. We park up and nose about for 20 minutes, finding nothing much more than a likely-looking strip of carpet in the corner of a car park behind an empty office building. We check the church too, but half-heartedly: the spot here that Badger used to favour, a doorway round the back, was recently fitted with a security mesh, since when there has been no sign of anyone. Jeff thinks the carpet will have been Badger's and that we have missed him (again).

As we make our way along the rear lane, pausing here and there to take a closer look at things, Jeff tells me that he and Steve will be meeting with the head of City Centre Management (CCM) later today to discuss the future of the Breakfast Run. Commercial anxieties about the homeless presence in the city centre have escalated in recent months, and the CCM wants to see some changes. The Breakfast Run has been singled out for particular attention as a service that – it is alleged – encourages dependency, makes it easier to sleep on the streets and in doing so adds to the general untidiness (spilt drinks, discarded sandwiches, polystyrene cups, all of this strewn about in the early morning, mixed in with sodden blankets and leftovers from the night just gone). 'There's something in the litter bit,' says Jeff. 'But the rest is bullshit.'

We drive over to Bute Park and the civic centre, parking up to take another walk about. Pete Farnworth and Johnny P. are in the entrance to the music college, as expected. There are two young men on the steps of the Glamorgan Building, already rousted by security staff and now packing up their sleeping bags and blankets, ready to go. Making our way along Windsor Lane we find Paul outside the United Reform Church, his rucksack at his feet. He has been up for an hour, waiting for us. He takes a coffee but nothing else – no roll, no egg. We stay to talk for five minutes and then move along; Paul too. Waving goodbye, he drops his coffee cup in a bin. 'Thank you Paul,' says Jeff. 'We could do with a few more like you.'

One hour later and we are outside the Central Hotel, trying to make ourselves heard above the noise of the passing traffic and kegs of beer bouncing off the pavement as two men in overalls fling one after another from the back of a lorry parked outside the pub across the road. A young couple walk over, wrapped in blankets, dragging two large rucksacks. These two arrived in Cardiff less than a week ago and have been spending their nights in the Wood Street car park. Jeff eyes the line of cars stopped at the traffic lights alongside us and asks the couple if they wouldn't mind waiting five minutes, perhaps over by Marland House.

We work our way through Central Square, across and then back to Marland House where the young couple are sitting on the pavement being addressed by Andy Saville. We hand out hot coffees and breakfast and Jeff sets about talking to the two of them, trying to find out as much as they are prepared to share about where they have come from and what seems to be the problem. Meanwhile, Andy gets a bad boiled egg. The shell is broken and the egg inside discoloured; it is probably fine to eat, but doesn't look too appetising, and Andy complains to Jeff, interrupting his conversation to ask for another. Jeff pauses for a fraction then says, perhaps wearily, that Steve can probably have one more if he is that particular about his eggs in the morning. It is a slightly awkward moment, if only just. Andy is not sleeping out at present (he is staying with Andy Watkins in a bedsit on Salisbury Road) and so isn't a CCT priority. Jeff could have given him nothing at all – not that he would. Momentarily discomposed, Andy plays up, acting brash. 'And here's what I'll do with *this* egg,' he shouts. 'In the gutter, where it belongs.' He throws the bad egg into the road, where it splatters across the tarmac. Jeff loses his temper, and shouts at Andy: 'That's exactly the reason the Run is getting stopped!' He orders him to pick up the egg and tidy the mess if he wants another one. Andy's bravado is punctured and he sheepishly scoops up the remains of the egg. As he does so he asks what this is all about, the Run being stopped. Jeff explains. 'That's not good, Jeff. Not good at all,' says Andy, slowly shaking his head in a show of deliberation and concern. He starts to lecture the young couple about how important it is to tidy up after yourself. They should listen to him, he says, because he's been on the streets himself, '… for years, before you were born probably'. The girl is giggling behind her hand. Andy takes a new egg.

Not drawing attention, not messing things up for others: these are matters of daily importance and dispute among outreach clients, principally the homeless, but sex workers too. On occasion those who keep things clean fiercely disparage those who don't, although these categories are more clear-cut as allegations bandied about than as actually observable. And Jeff is not just sticking his oar in; all of this matters directly to the CCT, which was established to help with the look of things in the middle of the city, in sympathetic and concerned response to people in some or other sort of a mess, out of doors.[4]

So far as outreach goes, these two purposes – helping out and cleaning up – align often enough to allow them to be held concurrently (if not always comfortably). On such occasions as they do align, the assistance the team provides – the recognition, the advice and concern, the support and advocacy – leads to a disappearance of sorts, and they have one less client; someone they used to know and have to do with fades from the streets, not in the way of a non-person, but as someone who simply isn't around so much anymore, because clear of the public difficulties in which they were first found: the team stops seeing them. This happens in many more instances than I have recorded here. Outreach work amounts to something, in that way – clients disappear. But for every one that does, a new one is likely to surface, either that or a former client reappears or comes unstuck and the team starts to see them again. Nor is this unexpected or any source of frustration or disappointment. There is nothing about the work the CCT is tasked to do that suggests it might one day be over – no further need for it. No more than street cleaning could be considered a job that might one day be done.

But my point here, drawing back from the detail of outreach work as performed from one day to the next, has been that a wider change to the sort of city Cardiff looks like and is and wants to be has continued apace since I first knew the team, and things are tighter today as a result. Cardiff's outreach workers (and street cleaners) work in a smarter city than they did ten years ago, a city with ambitions to be smarter still. Lost space and leftovers in the middle of Cardiff are not left that way for long today – the appetite for urban renewal is rapacious, it seems, and it matters more today than ever before that no one is throwing eggs about on Central Square in the early morning, making a mess, looking troubled. And it will matter more tomorrow. In this sort of context, the question might be asked as to how much of the street – owned by

---

4. In an earlier chapter, I suggested that helping others and sweeping up might be considered rather different sorts of work, as indeed they are. Yet there are also similarities, and I have signalled these. I have given street cleaning a place in this book, mostly without explicit comment, in order to allow some of those similarities – and differences – to make themselves heard. Outreach is a sort of street cleaning even at the same time as it is something else altogether; each of these two activities says something about the other.

no-one, used by everyone – is really there anymore, if not everyone is supposed to be seen on it. Some would say less than there used to be. Glassiness and surface, café quarters, and an over-eager rush to renewal. Certainly, to follow the work of street-level outreach in Cardiff over the last ten years is to chart a slow squeeze and displacement, as space (and tolerance) for the homeless in the centre of the city has diminished.

The arguments here are familiar and lead where one might suppose.[5] That this is so does not stop them being important arguments. It very much matters the sort of cities we build, whether or not we build them all at once in great swathes of urban renewal, or piecemeal. Joseph Rykwert, with whom I began this book, has it this way:

> the feel and the fabric of the town or city is always present to the citizen as it is to the visitor. Appreciated, seen, touched ... and because there is constant interaction between society and the urban fabric, we cannot tinker with our cities without making some adjustments to society as well – or vice versa. (2002: 6–7)

If Rykwert is right then we might aim to build cities, and tinker with the ones we have already, in ways which would allow someone in need of a place to rest up and be left alone at night to find it, without shame, or difficulty, or hostility; without being driven off, designed out, messed about with. I don't see this book as making that argument exactly, still less winning it.[6]

---

5. See Anna Minton's (2009) book, *Ground Control: Fear and Happiness in the Twenty-First Century City*, which charts the transformation of Britain's city streets by urban planners and private developers over the last two decades. Concluding an early chapter – titled *The Death of the City* – Minton suggests that what is essentially at stake in market-led urban renewal and the corporatisation of cities, all the way down to street level, is the limit such developments set on our readiness to see and appreciate others, 'people become unaccustomed to – and eventually very frightened of – difference' (2009: 36). An early review by sociologist David Byrne opened as follows: 'I learned absolutely nothing from this book ... because if you are engaged in any serious academic way with the urban in contemporary Britain you should know all this stuff already' (2009: 336).

6. I am not against the argument, but if I were tasked to do something about homelessness I might start somewhere else. Then again, does it seem all that fanciful or naïve to suggest that a city might make room for those with nowhere else to go, might choose not to recoil architecturally from this possibility? Rykwert contends that the one 'ought' about the city is that justice be done by its citizens; taken further, the argument might be that such justice should be seen to be done (2002: 228). What would this look like? Perhaps something like

Perhaps, stepping sideways, I might say just a little more about gates and doorways, and Central Square. A gateway is a threshold, a station is a stop; each has a propensity to gather and snag and each says something about who we are or might be as we pass over and through, or end up there. The powers of the doorway, writes Simon Unwin, pervade our lives; like the wall, the doorway 'is an essential element in the organisation of space ... [p]assing through doorways affects our states of being; who we think we are as well as where we find ourselves' (2007: 3). This architectural commentary runs very close to Rowe's conceit – outreach encounters at a border. To arrive somewhere and step across is to experience a transition in state of being:

> You move away from being a 'person outside' into a 'person inside', from being a 'person at large' to being a 'person at home', from being a 'person lost' into a 'person who knows where they are'. The catalyst of this transformation is the doorway ... the doorway divides your world, and in doing so, provokes a sense of 'otherness'. (Unwin, 2007: 12)

What to make of this in a city that is slimming down on its doorways and making a gateway of its station?

Do outreach workers see this too? Of course they do. In some ways they are among the most acute and reliable reporters on changes to the physical look and layout of Cardiff's city centre. They have to know what is going on out there. But the cumulative effect, the general tendency? Again, yes – they see this too. But not so much *as* outreach workers. True, the time frame for outreach work runs into years sometimes with those of its clients that prove most difficult or vulnerable. Outreach sometimes takes the long view. But one cannot so easily *act* in that frame. With one's eye and focus on an individual client and his or her journey – possibly over months and more – the city's alterations and renovations blur somewhat. The streets still matter, but they do so in terms of their particular shape *this morning*, such that the client can be found (again)

---

this: 'In a society which nurtures people and fosters trust, the fact that people sometimes want to sleep in public is the most natural thing in the world. If someone lies down on a pavement or a bench and falls asleep, it is possible to treat it seriously as a need. If he has no place to go – then, we, the people of the town, can be happy that he can at least sleep on the public paths and benches; and, of course, it may also be someone who does have a place to go, but happens to like napping in the street' (Alexander et al., 1977: 458).

and seen to, today. How would an outreach worker make whatever sense he or she might have of the overall direction things have taken in the middle of Cardiff over the last ten years any part of what might usefully be agreed on as a plan of work for an individual client in the Friday team meeting? That is, or ought to be, more than a rhetorical question.

What else has changed? The toilet block behind the museum is currently bricked up and unoccupied. White Lightning cider (see p. 45) is no longer available in the UK. The outreach *Guide to Homeless People in Cardiff* is still distributed, but to a far greater number of EU migrants and asylum seekers than was ever the case when I worked with the team.[7] Pedestrianised space has crept along St Mary Street. New public realm enhancement schemes abound. The StreetLife project continues, but under the auspices of Safer Wales, an independent charity based in Cardiff; outreach workers still support the project, but given present staffing levels only once a week. The Bus Project still parks up by the museum in the evenings, and is busy, so no change there. Other things are similarly unchanged. The soup run continues to operate weekday evenings on Charles Street by Marks and Spencer and the Ebenezer Chapel (sold in 2012 and currently undergoing grant-funded restoration as a community, heritage and conference centre); outreach workers are usually in attendance. Crucially, the main hostels and emergency accommodation projects, including the local authority's Tresillian House, the Huggard Centre and the Salvation Army hostel, Tŷ Gobaith, are all still located only five minutes' walk from Central Square.

A fair bit of the city centre looks more or less the same as it ever did, certainly so if you are prepared to take one street rather than another, close an eye, open an umbrella. Outreach workers move around in much the same way as before: careful, casual, not really going anywhere – or not seeming to. There are sleepers(?) on the Crown Court steps most mornings, and elsewhere across the city centre in at least some of the locations I have written about here, and some new ones besides. I began this book, almost, with the following: *Cities grow and change, and sometimes die – or are said to. People do too.* Among those of Cardiff's homeless who have featured in these pages the following are all dead:

---

7. This has been a big change, only just underway when I began accompanying outreach workers on their rounds and hardly visible in the account I have given here.

Duffy, Len Goodyear, Wayne Daley, Jackie Harrison, Andy Saville, Robbo, Phil, John, Bernard, Liam Sadler, Kirsten. That is a very grim roll-call, and incomplete.

A tinkering trade

A city that has less space and tolerance for the homeless than it used to is also and necessarily a city with less space and tolerance for outreach (and for the look of outreach work getting done). It is not only that outreach workers suffer collateral damage with every action taken against any one of their clients. Curbs on homeless space are in themselves curbs on outreach space. If the city changes for those on the streets – shrinks here, narrows there – then it changes at the same time for outreach workers. A doorway can be a good place to spend the night and try to sleep, and it matters as such to the city's homeless. But a doorway can be all sorts of things to an outreach worker too: a kitchen counter, information booth, dispensary, confessional. Any such doorway brought forward and refitted flush to the wall into which it was previously set, not only says something like, *this is no longer and cannot be a bed*; it also says something like, *this is no longer, and cannot be anything, other than a door*. Spaces of need are at the same time spaces of care, or can be; and if you shrink and tidy away the one you are liable to shrink and tidy away the other.

I am not aware of any architectural or design intervention in Cardiff's city centre having been introduced with the express intention to limit the exercise of care. No one is targeting outreach work in that way. There are, however, occasions when outreach *is* directly targeted, in terms of where it is *told* it may get its work done. I have described a few such, at various points throughout the book: occasions on which outreach workers have had to (re)align their practice not in consequence of some movement on the part of a client, or to follow some new lead, but because they have been *told to keep away* – asked to keep out of Bute Park, put off from visiting the CIA.

What is being asked of the team in such instances is not only that its outreach workers stop going somewhere, but that they *stop making somewhere a place to go*. It is the look of the work getting done that doesn't sit so well, and, more than that, the suggestion that the work itself has somehow become tangled up with the very thing it was supposed to see an end to. Of course there should be outreach, but not if it draws attention, not if it is becoming a part of the mess it was supposed to tidy up. *Can't you take the work somewhere else?* This question was asked throughout the time I was most intensively involved with the CCT, not always out loud or directly, and continues to be asked today. And there has been a narrowing. If outreach workers in Cardiff today have enough of the licence they need to get a good enough job done (which they probably do), they don't have as much of it as they used to.

I want to return here, briefly, to the idea of repair, and to Nigel Thrift. Repair is an act that sees things patched up and made good, and Thrift suggests such acts might play a significant part in the life of cities, as a much underappreciated mechanism by which the urban fabric is kept going from one day to the next. Grand schemes for urban renewal are one thing, and bring new life in their own way, or are said to; but maybe the baseline resilience, the actual one-day-to-the-next *life* of cities is accomplished in less remarkable ways: minor interventions, making do and mending. Furthermore, given that the city is more than its streets and buildings, given that the city is also the people, perhaps repair has a role to play here too, patching up and helping make good, keeping us all going from one day to the next – again, more often than we might ordinarily realise, and in ways that might hold out more hope than grand utopian schemes for social renewal. Perhaps thinking about repair and what it gets done, and the limits to what it can get done, and recognising that work and those limits, might help us in reaching some settlement with a root urban misanthropy we cannot quite shake off. Perhaps it might. But things are complicated with people and repair; more complicated than with objects.

One significant difference between the repair of objects and the sorts of repair that outreach work might be said to aim at has been discussed already; it has to do with who decides what broken means and what ought to be done about it. Making things better for someone usually requires them to want you to. Under some circumstances even reaching that point can take work, and once it has been reached there may be still more to do, further negotiation and some mutual adjustment, before decisions are made as to how to proceed. For those whose lived circumstances have taken them some way down a line of difficulty, such negotiations can take time: weeks spent trying to win Lizzie P. round to attending a doctor's appointment, months spent chipping away at Martin; a cup of tea and sandwiches and another long late-night chat with Paul Short on the museum steps is necessary *because* he doesn't think he's ready to go indoors again, and the last time he tried it was all too rushed and people didn't really understand why he was finding it so hard, and then there was everything else that was going on at the time with Lotta, and then he lost the plot and kicked off in the TV room and the police had to be called and now he's banned. And while it is getting done this sort of work can look messy, or like it isn't making much of a difference, or like it hasn't even properly begun. And it can look this way to anyone – who cares to see, or can't help but notice – because it doesn't really have its own space in which to get done, only what it can find; it never did have much of its own space and has even less of what it once had now that the industrial units off Tyndal Street are gone and the site has been cleared – because that used to be a good little spot for Paul, and Jeff would come and find him there sometimes.

All of which signals a further complication so far as the repair analogy goes, a complication that has to do not so much with the necessarily reciprocal character of social repair as with what such repair looks like getting done. Repair and appearances or the look of things are very often linked, at either end of the process of getting something mended. A broken down this or that (to recall Thrift's phrasing) usually, if not always, *looks* broken, as well as being so; the look of something said to be damaged is often enough a clue as to what the damage might be; things that need fixing look faulty. It follows that an object repaired often looks better than it did when it wasn't working properly. But in such cases the appearance, the look of the thing once it has been mended, is only ever a subsidiary consequence of what has really been achieved. *That's better*, we say to ourselves, surveying a repair job well done; *looks better too*, we might then add. The point being that looking better wasn't what the job was all about. We have a word for those sorts of repair that get this relation the wrong way around and chase after the look of the thing purportedly fixed without properly addressing what was actually wrong with it to begin with. We call that sort of repair cosmetic. Such repairs are phony, if sometimes quick to do.

Outreach is not a cosmetic exercise; workers don't think about the work that they try to do in those terms at all. Outreach aims to make things better for those it is able to enrol as clients; its efforts don't always show, and such repairs as it is able to undertake are not always enough – not every fix sticks. Things sometimes look good or at any rate better, in the middle of the city, as a result of the work that outreach workers get done there, but not because appearances were what they were hoping to improve on.

How do outreach workers look after those to whose needs they are tasked to recognise and respond? And what does this work have to do with the look of things in the city? And what does it have to do with looking? These questions have been at issue throughout this book and were first signalled in the opening chapter, where I began by considering the needs of strangers and the ways in which seeing, and failing or refusing to see – a narrowing of vision – might be in some way bound up with city life.

Appearances, I have suggested, are at something of a premium in Cardiff today. Renewal and upkeep in the centre of the city – big plans and minor, everyday attentions – combine in such a way as to secure an environment that has the right sort of look: clean, safe, fun and open for business. Care has been taken and continues to be taken to see that this is so. Meanwhile, and in consequence, other sorts of care and attention, directed to the needs of those gone public with their troubles, struggle to find a place. Struggle is the right word here: there has been no final embargo on outreach, nor is there likely to be one.[8]

Even so, the team is mindful – has to be, more than ever before – of the ways in which its work rubs up against the newly minted look of much central city space in Cardiff today. Its practice is scrutinised in this particular context. What difference does outreach really make and, more to the point, does it have to make that difference – if there is any difference to be made – on the street, in the middle of things? Again, the question: *Can't you take the work somewhere else?*

Something like the same puzzlement can be put a different way. Think back to the novice or visitor, joining an outreach patrol for the first time (p. 210). I suggested that on such occasions two or three things can be relied on to happen, and I outlined (only) two of them: directed to some location all too familiar to outreach, the novice remarks that he or she *never realised this place was here*; next, passing what looks like

---

8. The Cardiff Council that is working in ready partnership with retail and commercial interests to see Central Square and its environs redeveloped wholesale is the same Cardiff Council that supplies emergency accommodation, supported housing, social services, and supports the continuing work of the CCT.

a promising spot, seeming to share qualities with the one just visited, the novice wonders if it mightn't pay to take a look there too (outreach workers say no, but find it harder to explain quite why). Number three doesn't happen every time, but it happens enough: the novice can't help but wonder out loud why the attention paid to those the team finds bedded down seems so cursory. A cup of tea, a few words exchanged, a reminder about that morning's court appearance, a loose agreement to meet later on to see the CCT nurse; and then off somewhere else, leaving behind a client or clients to all intents and purposes as homeless as they were ten minutes ago. Or so it seems. *Shouldn't we have stuck around and done more?*

The novice's mistake is to imagine that the sorts of needs that the CCT addresses can be fixed, if not in ten minutes then perhaps in an hour, surely in a day, given some more concerted effort: hostel bed, medical check, needs assessment, social worker allocated, benefit claim processed or straightened out. And things are just not like that with outreach and its clients. If things *were* like that, then outreach might not be needed; those who would otherwise have been outreach clients would have sorted themselves out – which is of course what happens all the time. There are any number of people who never come near the CCT because they get along to the Housing Advice Unit or the hospital themselves, or they call up their social worker and ask for help, or they are lucky enough to have had sufficient resources, or whatever else it might take, to have kept themselves off the streets. Outreach workers are left with the ones who don't, can't or won't do some or all of this, for all the reasons I have outlined.

Shouldn't we have stuck around and done more? might seem a different sort of question from *Can't you take the work somewhere else?* But what these two sorts of puzzlement share is the root idea that outreach might be better not to distribute its practice the way that it does, all around the city. It would do better to stop and get on with things until a problem has been sorted. In my view, this is fundamentally to misconstrue what outreach work is up against and what it accomplishes. The idea that care, in this particular context, might be done all at once and completely is, I think, mistaken in something like the same way that the idea that we see as if by taking a photograph – a snapshot, all at once – is mistaken; the idea that outreach might fix things by sticking to one client at a time is a mistake in something like the same way that the idea that we see by staring, by fixating on what appears in front of us, is mistaken. This brings me back to comments made at the end of the previous chapter, about moving and seeing and the ways in which outreach workers look to build a picture of their clients' needs, and leads to a conclusion.

The groping city

That perception and movement might have something to do with one another seems obvious enough, at least in the everyday sense that we need to be able to see where we are going if we don't want to trip up or bang into something. We are told to look before we leap, and perhaps it would be as well to look before making any move at all. How else would one know where to go and what one might encounter? Framed in this way the two activities, perception and locomotion, are sequential. We look to see where we are going and then we move; the one precedes and prepares the way for the other. More than this, looking and moving, can appear necessarily distinct, likely to compromise one another if undertaken in tandem. To see clearly and in detail one must stand still and focus; objects in motion are that much harder to make out. This is the commonsense (and orthodox) position I set out, and took against, in Chapter 8. Having considered the ways in which outreach workers look *for* as much as *at* their clients, I found myself inclined toward the idea that to see might be also and at the same time to move – even as this suggestion seems to run up against some of the ways in which we usually think about these two activities.

And what if we can't see? Again, commonsense, and to some degree experience, give us a ready answer: unable to see – in the dark perhaps, or blindfold – we find ourselves much less willing to move, much less able to do so with confidence. We are reduced to feeling our way. We reach out, spread our fingers and paw at the environment around us, tapping our way along. Our movement becomes hesitant and uncertain – or questioning.

What is most interesting to me about the movements described, the movements of a person in the dark or without sight, is that these movements, however we might characterise them, become a part of what it is for that person to 'see'. Movement (and touch) delivers perception, *is* perception. Stood still, the person in the dark – let us put them somewhere in particular, a city street; they are stood by a lamppost on a city street late at night, only the lamppost isn't working and all the other lights have gone out – a power cut perhaps; they are effectively blind, unsighted … standing still, the person in the dark sees nothing. There is nothing *to* see. And any movement is a hazard, because, unable to see, a step in any direction is a step into the unknown. Given this, they might be best-off staying put. Imagine the person in the dark is you, or me; we might prefer to cling to the lamppost, hoping the blackout will prove temporary and the lights will soon come on again. As things *stand*, we know nothing. Then again, perhaps more boldly, we could move. Fingers spread and arms stretched out, hesitantly at first but in a spirit of exploration and enquiry, we might ask questions of the way the environment is, the way the street runs, the arrangement of objects along the pavement and the sequence of buildings along its edge, by touch. We have been here before, almost, in Chapter 2, where I first considered what it might mean to be lost on a city street.

But now I have proposed a new thought experiment: the lights are off and we are not so much lost as blind; we cannot see how things are, with our eyes (a map would be worse than useless). Even so, the street can still be grasped. Doing so requires of us that we feel our way, and although feeling one's way might seem a rather different undertaking to looking where one is going, I am not so sure it is all that different from the sorts of looking *around* required of us when we don't know where we are in daylight. To feel one's way is to explore and understand even as one goes forward, not in advance of doing so. Going forward (or backwards or sideways) is what makes it possible for us to 'see' – to make out where we are; more than that, going forward is what 'seeing' *is*; movement *is* perception. Only in the dark? Actually, no. What do things look like with the lights on? The answer is that they never look quite as they are, from wherever it is we are standing. Instead, objects look the way they appear to us, from here, and then here, and then somewhere else again. Consider the deformation of appearance that happens as you walk along a street and past a building looking upwards. You don't ever see the building as it actually is, any more than you see a street the way it is shown on a map. What you see is a shifting perspective: the building swings into view, grows in size, looms, distorts, tapers, recedes. None of which leads you to think that the construction is unreliable or elastic, or that the building is alive – a monster perhaps, 'grotesquely inclined this way and that, like King Kong', as Louis Chevalier has it (1994: 3). Nor do you consider your vision defective. You saw the building. And know how the building is, or was, because of the way its appearance altered as you moved past it. I am following Alva Noë again. Here he invites his reader to consider perception by touch:

> To perceive by touch, for example ... the layout of furniture in a room (as a blind person might, by moving around and reaching and touching) is not merely to have certain feelings and sensations ... Your tactile impression that things are arranged thus and such consists not in the sensations in your hands and feet, but in the way those sensations result from attentive movement through space. (2004: 14–15)

I am taken with this example, and have had blindness in my sights since the first chapter of this book. But what does any of this have to do with outreach? I have already described outreach patrol in Cardiff as a crepuscular undertaking, inclined towards dawn and dusk as times of the day when workers and clients can hope to have the city centre at least a little bit to themselves. Outreach also gets done at night, in the dark. But not in an unlit city, not in the pitch black. Outreach workers can usually see what they are doing, where they are going and what needs to be done. Even so, I want to stay with the suggestion that this line of work might be best understood as an exercise in feeling one's way. To operate in this way, to feel one's way through the city streets, is to accomplish a different city vision from the sort of seeing that happens when one takes a photograph. When we point a camera at something and press the shutter-button we get a scene, within a frame, in sharp and uniform detail; but as Noë and others have argued, snapshots of others' lives notwithstanding (see pp. 7–8) it is unlikely that the process of visual perception happens anything like that way in humans. We are not cameras and we do not see in snapshots, even when the lights are on. We see through repeated interaction with the world, never fixing our vision but instead distributing it, working it back and forth across whatever it is we want to be sure of, never seeing anything all at once, but assembling content as we go. In short, it may be that we are mistaken if we think that seeing is anything like taking a picture; it may be that looking is a lot more like being blind.

I have reached a conclusion. In doing so I cannot claim to have added anything to the philosophy of perception and consciousness as such; I do not know how Jeff or Den or Nicy sees, any more than I know how I do so myself. But I think I know how outreach workers see to others on the streets of Cardiff, how they seek them out and keep pace with their problems and how the care they provide is accomplished. And none of these things, not the seeing, not the keeping pace, not the care – the looking after – is accomplished through a jealous and unswerving attention. Outreach workers do not fixate in their attentions, any more than we see by staring – instead, we look around; and care is the repeated touch.

Epilogue

Outreach: a blue sky and sunny, already warm; Nicy is at the night shelter with the bags all packed and the flasks ready, and we are off nice and early – the Breakfast Run. There will be a funeral today: Frank Bishop who used to be on the streets back when the CCT was first established but has been in a hostel for a good few years now, with one or two brief falls from grace. Frank died of an overdose. He had lots of friends on the street and homeless scene, which he remained very much a part of once housed. We are mindful that a number of CCT clients might be a little on edge and emotional today.

We start out on Central Square, looking for someone new, a man calling himself Bingo, who we met for the first time earlier this week and who has been spending his nights on the ramp by the Wood Street car park, where Phil and Chrissie used to stay. Nicy spoke to him yesterday (he was drunk) and arranged to meet him here this morning. The immediate problem is that Bingo, having appeared in Cardiff with his lower leg in a cast, has since for some reason best known to himself got someone to help him cut it off – the cast, not his leg. He is suffering as a result, and needs his leg reset. When Nicy saw him yesterday he could barely walk, but was refusing help. He did, however, promise to meet up today so that Nicy could drive him to the hospital. So where is he?

We can't wait around forever so we drive up St Mary Street, passing one of the old CCT regulars, Francis, no longer street homeless but still very much on the scene. Francis doesn't see us, though we wave frantically. He spends pretty much every day walking through the city centre, preferring to be out of doors than stuck in the room he has in a social housing project off Newport Road, secured for him by the CCT over a year ago. 'Francis always asks for a hug,' says Nicy. 'Strictly speaking, political correctness and all, you shouldn't probably – but I do.' Allegations could be made, is her point; but she feels it must be important for some of the team's clients to have a little human contact now and then. 'A hug's OK,' she says. Even so, she worries about nits and things like that, and tends to keep her hugs 'lite': a little pat on the shoulders, elbows tucked in, a little stiff in the upper body. She mimes this to me in the car, laughing at her own good intentions and discomfiture.

We park in the civic centre and walk along City Hall Road towards the museum. Others are there already, waiting for us, including Hayley who stays talking for 15 minutes after everyone else has gone. She is making a big effort to come off heroin, having recently secured a methadone prescription. It is hard though, because her boyfriend is still using all the time. Maybe she won't really make a go of it herself until he's ready too. Her teeth are in a bad way, and hurting; she keeps wincing as she speaks. Nicy promises to speak to the nurse about that, back at Marland House, and try to get an emergency appointment set up; she gives Hayley a number to ring, in an hour or two, for an update. 'If you don't ring, I'll find you,' she scolds.

One hour later we are back on Central Square. Chris Mellor is there, out last night and not wanting the same again. Nicy calls the night shelter there and then and books him a place: easy. There is still no sign of Bingo. Ron comes across and takes a cup of tea; he was in the EOS last night. Big Alan walks out of the train station and wants to know where Bingo is. We ask him why, and he tells us he has a job on, cash in hand, something Bingo is supposed to be signed up for. Nicy says she doubts that Bingo will be doing any work with a broken leg, but Alan insists that it is all sorted: supervisory work, bus fare arranged, Bingo knows all about it and was supposed to be here by now. It all sounds a little dubious. Big Alan is his usual self, affable enough, but also sly, not in any way forthcoming. The CCT would like to know a lot more about him than anyone seems to know right now. He is not homeless himself, almost certainly not; but no one knows where he lives exactly or what he is up to. He was at the soup run last night too, apparently. The team are just not sure of him at all. 'Mooching around the city centre. Hanging round vulnerable people, offering to help them,' says Nicy. 'There's something funny there.'

Bibliography

Ackroyd, P. 1993. *Hawksmoor*. London: Penguin.

Ackroyd, P. 2001. *London: The Biography*. London: Vintage.

ACPO. 2010. *National Policing Improvement Agency Guidance on the Management, Recording and Investigation of Missing Persons*. London: NPIA.

Alexander, C., S. Ishikawa, M. Silverstein, M. Jacobson, I. Fiksdahl-King & S. Angel. 1977. *A Pattern Language: Towns, Buildings, Construction*. New York: Oxford University Press.

Augé, M. 1995. *Non-Places: Introduction to an Anthropology of Supermodernity*. London: Verso.

Barber, S. 1995. *Fragments of the European City*. London: Reaktion Books.

Berger, J. 2008 [1972]. *Ways of Seeing*. London: Penguin.

Brighenti. A. M. 2010. *Visibility in Social Theory and Social Research*. Basingstoke: Palgrave Macmillan.

Byrne, D. et al. 2011. Review [*Ground Control: Fear and Happiness in the Twenty-First-Century City*, by A. Minton]. *Sociology*, 45 (2), pp. 336–8.

Cardiff Council (Regeneration Group: Strategic Planning and Environment). 2007. *City Centre Strategy, 2007–2010*. Cardiff: Cardiff Council.

Cardiff Council (Regeneration Group: Strategic Planning and Environment). 2009. *Cardiff City Centre Public Realm Manual*. Cardiff: Cardiff Council.

Chevalier, L. 1994. *The Assassination of Paris*. Chicago: University of Chicago Press.

Cloke, P., J. May & S. Johnsen. 2010. *Swept Up Lives? Re-envisioning the Homeless City*. Oxford: Wiley-Blackwell.

CRISIS, 2010. *CRISIS Policy Briefing: Introduction to Homelessness & Housing*.

Cuyvers, W. 2006. Reading public space in the (non-Western) city: a dialogue between Zeynep Celik and Wim Cuyvers. *OASE (Positions. Shared Territories in Historiography & Practice)*, 69, pp. 32–45.

Department for Communities and Local Government. 2010. *Evaluating the Extent of Rough Sleeping: A New Approach*. London: Communities and Local Government Publications.

Douglas, M. 1996 [1966]. *Purity and Danger: An Analysis of the Concepts of Pollution and Taboo*. London: Routledge.

Egan, G. 1994. *The Skilled Helper: A Problem-Management Approach to Helping* (5th ed.). Pacific Grove, CA: Brooks/Cole Publishing.

Engels, F. 1993 [1845]. *The Condition of the Working Class in England*. (Oxford World's Classics Edition) Oxford: Oxford University Press.

Finch, P. 2003. *Real Cardiff*. Bridgend: Seren.

Fitzpatrick, S., G. Bramley & S. Johnsen. 2012. Multiple exclusion homelessness in the UK: an overview of key findings (Briefing Paper No. 1). Multiple Exclusion Homelessness in the UK: Briefing Papers, Edinburgh.

Fletcher, G. 1966. *Down Among the Meths Men*. London: Hutchinson.

Frank, K. A. & Q. Stevens. 2007. Tying down loose space. In K. A. Frank & Q. Stevens (eds), *Loose Space: Possibility and Diversity in Urban Life* (pp. 1–34). London: Routledge.

Gibson, J. J. 1986. *The Ecological Approach to Visual Perception*. New York: Psychology Press.

Goffman, E. 1990 [1956]. *The Presentation of Self in Everyday Life*. London: Penguin.

Goffman, E. 1991 [1961]. *Asylums: Essays on the Social Situation of Mental Patients and Other Inmates*. London: Penguin.

Gray, J. 2007. *Straw Dogs: Thoughts on Humans and Other Animals*. New York: Farrar, Straus and Giroux.

Hall, T. & R. J. Smith. 2015. Care and repair and the politics of urban kindness. *Sociology*, 49 (1), pp. 3–18.

Hannerz, U. 1980. *Exploring the City: Inquiries Toward an Urban Anthropology*. New York: Columbia University Press.

Hertzberger, H. 2005. *Lessons for Students in Architecture* (5th ed.). Rotterdam: 010 Publishers.

Herzfeld, M. 1997. *Cultural Intimacy: Social Poetics and the Nation-State*. London: Routledge.

Højer, L. & A. Bandak. 2015. Introduction: the power of example. *Journal of the Royal Anthropological Institute* (Special Supplement Issue – The Power of Example: Anthropological Explorations in Persuasion, Evocation, and Imitation), 21, pp. 1–17.

Holloway, K & F. Brookman. 2008. *An Evaluation of the Women's Turnaround Project*. Pontypridd: University of Glamorgan.

Ingold, T. 2000. *The Perception of the Environment: Essays in Livelihood, Dwelling and Skill*. Abingdon: Routledge.

Ingold, T. 2007. *Lines: A Brief History*. Abingdon: Routledge.

Ingold, T. 2011. *Being Alive: Essays on Movement, Knowledge and Description*. Abingdon: Routledge.

Jacobs, J. 1992. *The Death and Life of Great American Cities*. New York: Vintage.

Joyce, P. 2003. *The Rule of Freedom: Liberalism and the Modern City*. London: Verso.

Katznelson, I. 1992. *Marxism and the City*. Oxford: Oxford University Press.

Leach, E. 1976. *Culture and Communication: The Logic by which Symbols Are Connected*. Cambridge: Cambridge University Press.

Lipsky, M. 1980. *Street-Level Bureaucracy: Dilemmas of the Individual in Public Services*. New York: Russell Sage Foundation.

Lovell, A. M. 1997. 'The city is my mother': narratives of schizophrenia and homelessness. *American Anthropologist*, 99 (2), pp. 355–68.

Lovering, J. 2006. The cultural transformation of Cardiff. In A. Hooper & J. Punter (eds.), *Capital Cardiff 1975–2020: Regeneration, Competitiveness and the Urban Environment*. Cardiff: University of Wales Press.

Mack, A. & I. Rock. 1998. *Inattentional Blindness*. Cambridge, MA: MIT Press.

Masters, A. 2006. *Stuart: A Life Backwards*. London: Harper Perennial.

Minton, A. 2009. *Ground Control: Fear and Happiness in the Twenty-First Century City*. London: Penguin.

Moretti, F. 1999. *Atlas of the European Novel: 1800–1900*. London: Verso.

Noë, A. 2004. *Action in Perception*. Cambridge, MA: MIT Press.

Pithouse, A. 1998. *Social Work: The Social Organisation of an Invisible Trade* (2nd ed.). Aldershot: Ashgate.

Raban, J. 1988 [1974]. *Soft City*. London: Harvill.

Reeve, K and E. Batty. 2011. *The Hidden Truth about Homelessness: Experiences of Single Homelessness in England*. London: CRISIS.

Rowe, M. 1999. *Crossing the Border: Encounters Between Homeless People and Outreach Workers*. Berkeley: University of California Press.

Rykwert, J. 2002. *The Seduction of Place: The History and Future of the City*. New York: Vintage.

Sayer, A. 2011. *Why Things Matter to People: Social Science, Values and Ethical Life*. Cambridge: Cambridge University Press.

Schout, G., G. de Jong & J. Zeelen. 2011. Beyond care avoidance and care paralysis: theorizing public mental health care. *Sociology*, 45 (4) 665–81.

Sennett, R. 2002. *Flesh and Stone: The Body and the City in Western Civilization*. London: Penguin.

Sennett, R. 2004. *Respect: The Formation of Character in an Age of Inequality*. London: Penguin.

Simmel, G. 1971. The metropolis and mental life. In D. N. Levine (ed.), *Georg Simmel on Individuality and Social Forms*. Chicago: University of Chicago Press.

Smith, A. 2002 [1759]. *The Theory of Moral Sentiments* (ed. K. Haakonssen). Cambridge: Cambridge University Press.

Thomas, H. 2003. *Discovering Cities: Cardiff*. Sheffield: Geographical Association.

Thrift, N. 2005. But malice aforethought: cities and the natural history of hatred. *Transactions of the Institute of British Geographers*, 30 (2), pp. 133–50.

Tilley, C. 2004. *The Materiality of Stone: Explorations in Landscape Phenomenology*. Oxford: Berg.

Tilley, C. 2008. *Body and Image: Explorations in Landscape Phenomenology 2*. Walnut Creek, CA: West Coast Press.

Tonkiss, F. 2000. Inner city. In S. Pile & N. Thrift (eds), *City A–Z*. London: Routledge.

Trancik, R. 2007 [1986]. What is lost space? In M. Carmona & S. Tiesdell (eds), *Urban Design Reader*. Oxford: Architectural Press.

Unwin, S. 2000. *An Architecture Notebook: Wall*. Abingdon: Routledge.

Unwin, S. 2007. *Doorway*. Abingdon: Routledge.

Weisman, A. 2008. *The World Without Us*. London: Virgin Books.

Williams, R. 1973. *The Country and the City*. New York: Oxford University Press.

Williamson, J. 1986. *Consuming Passions: The Dynamics of Popular Culture*. London: Marion Boyars Publishers.

Wirth, L. 1984. A bibliography of the urban community. In R. E. Park & E. W. Burgess (eds), *The City: Suggestions for Investigation of Human Behaviour in the Urban Environment*. Chicago: University of Chicago Press (Midway Reprint).

Index